NOMADIC DREAMS:

TREASURED MOMENTS OF A CURIOUS ADVENTURER

Volume One
1987 - 1998

BY
SUSAN S. PHILLIPS

Copyright © 2020 by Susan S. Phillips

All rights reserved.

ISBN 978-1-62806-265-6   (print | paperback)

Library of Congress Control Number 2019920710

Published by Salt Water Media
29 Broad Street, Suite 104
Berlin, MD 21811
www.saltwatermedia.com

Cover: A young mountain gorilla high up in Rwanda's Virunga National Park looking in astonishment and awe at perhaps his first introduction to the tourists who have trekked many miles through dense vegetation and rough terrain to gaze upclose for one hour at this majestic and endangered primate. Photo credit to Blaine T. Phillips.

Dedication

To Blaine, who each day inspires me with his knowledge, makes me laugh with his subtle but constant sense of humor, and enables me to keep grounded in the real world.

TABLE OF CONTENTS

INTRODUCTION 7

1987
TANZANIA, KENYA, ZIMBABWE, VICTORIA FALLS, SOUTH AFRICA 11

1989
MOROCCO, KENYA, TANZANIA, RWANDA 59

1993
ECUADOR 109

1994
SOUTH AFRICA, ZIMBABWE, BOTSWANA 132

1995
UGANDA, TANZANIA, KENYA 180

1996
ARGENTINA AND CHILE 224

1997
RUSSIA 250

1998
RUSSIA 270

APPENDIX 282

responsibilities. It really enables us to open up our minds to what God gave us to utilize in a wonderfully beautiful and most productive way. Even driving back to camp at night in the dark to see the almost full moon, southern Cross, and Scorpio, to smell the different animal odors of Africa — some good — some putrid — with each curve of the road, to taste the hot African coffee before dawn warming hands on the cups and the body next to a roaring fire waiting for daylight to appear. To hear the hippo outside our tent at night munching on the dried grass occasionally calling in a territorial voice to a neighboring hippo or the laugh of a far off hyena looking to scavenge a kill. We are indeed lucky to be here. We leave tomorrow for Kwara camp on the delta.

A sample from one of the journals

Introduction

Where is the likeliest place to begin a journal that encompasses 30 plus years of one's life? I suppose for me it could be a few months before I married Blaine. He casually asked, one afternoon, if I would be able to join him on a quick trip to the Turks and Caicos, where lies a small insignificant island called Providenciales, which at that time no one we knew had ever heard of. I was living in St. Louis and thought this would be a great time to brush up on a little snorkeling and catch up on my reading. We flew from Miami to the Turks and Caicos International Airport, but had no continuing plan to get to Providenciales. We managed to wangle a ride on a small 4 seat plane that had no unoccupied seats, so we sat on the floor with our cooler full of food between us. We had been forewarned that the one grocery store in town was fairly useless, so we arrived with some necessities, including a bottle of vodka, and hoped we could catch fish to help sustain us.

We landed on a dirt runway on an almost desolate island, but from the air, appearing to have a very beautiful beach. Blaine had arranged for us to stay in an isolated house at the far end of the leeward side of the island. We somehow managed to rent an old wreck of a car, a Chevy, vintage 1950, to transport us from the very small village of Providenciales on the one dirt road traversing the island. Our house was truly at its far end, with nothing but birds, lizards, and an uninhabited beautiful white sandy beach which stretched to the horizon.

After coming back from a morning of snorkeling, I was over the top with excitement by telling Blaine I had been swimming quite close to a 5' white tipped shark. Until then, I think he was just figuratively dipping his toe in the water to see if I would enjoy his love of outdoor life, but the next trip we took to Providenciales we asked Blaine's children and my daughter to join us, and we announced our engagement.

Blaine and I married in 1982, lived in a darling rental house that belonged to Donnie and Susie Ross, and enjoyed the bucolic scenic 126 acres in the town of Chatham, PA, surrounded by horses and pastures. I knew this was a marriage made in heaven when Blaine's Christmas gift to me that 1st year were a Jack and a Jenny, miniature Sicilian donkeys. I know his 1st thoughts were that I was from Missouri, "the show me state", whose state animal is the donkey, but I absolutely loved both of them from the start, and had a very successful breeding stable for the next 18 years. I soon bought a few sheep to keep the donkey's company, and eventually learned to spin and dye the wool from my sheep, and turn the spun wool into sweaters, mattress pads, woolen hats, small fireplace rugs, and more.

Having lived all of my life in the city of St. Louis, I had always longed for a life in the country, and now I was finally living my dream.

In 1984 we bought two wonderful houses. One in Chadds Ford, PA, that accommodated the donkeys and sheep with 2 large pastures and a 3 stall barn. It was surrounded by woods, and a spring fed very swimmable and fishable pond. The 2nd house was in the area of Easton, Maryland, an easy 2 hour drive south of Chadds Ford. It was near historic Oxford, and its outstanding appeal was its location on the Tred Avon, one of the Chesapeake's most inviting and beautiful rivers. We have been commuting between these two houses for 34 years. Sometimes with a U-haul to bring down a litter of 12 yellow lab puppies, and once with a large box in the back of our station wagon so we could bottle feed our new born baby lambs.

The first few years just flew by. I obtained my certificate to tutor from the National Literacy Program, which has allowed me to mentor and tutor functioning illiterate adults and children, which I still enjoy today. I always spend quite a few days each month being a docent at the Brandywine River Museum, featuring the art of our Chadds Ford neighbor, Andrew Wyeth. I was also honored to be asked to join the

Board of the Chesapeake Bay Foundation. It was such a joy for me to feed my passion of helping to "Save the Bay", and by being one of the first docks on the Tred Avon to aquafarm oysters. Lastly, I would be remiss if I didn't mention becoming an official member of the National Jack-Ass Society.

Along the way, Blaine and I are blessed to have 6 children, who were all either teenagers or early 20's, when we met. Harriet, my daughter and the youngest of the 6, was taught to drive in Providenciales by Andrea, Blaine's older daughter, who was 20, and Harriet was 12. Blaine Jr. has had an illustrious career, but 30 years ago he lived with us for a time while awaiting his dream job, and thought he could make his first fortune by writing the definitive book on "how to have a useful and productive life on $1.00 a day." Since that time, Blaine Jr. has made his mark nationally in the land conservation world, including at home establishing a national park for Delaware, the only state without one. Riley, Blaine's younger daughter, has captivated the souls of all young children as a magical teacher. John, my older son, plays his magic with plants and cooking. And Louis, my middle child, thought he might make a decent life as a singer and skier in Aspen, Colorado; until realism set in and he went to law school. Both John and Louis are doing well in their respective careers, dabbling in commercial real estate and running the oldest privately owned thoroughbred race course in the United States. Andrea gave up giving driving lessons and received double degrees at the University of Virginia in landscape architecture and also in law. The youngest of all, Harriet, went to cooking school, opened a restaurant in St. Louis, wrote a book called *Marathon Mama*, and enjoyed keeping fit doing competitive ballroom dancing. We couldn't be more proud of all these children, who are now mothers and fathers, and have bestowed on us 14 "perfect" grandchildren whom we have so enjoyed over the years.

But back to the year 1987, with all 6 children either in college or working in the real world, Blaine suggests that we take a once in a lifetime trip to Africa. This has been a steadfast dream I have had since I went to the St. Louis Zoo as a very young child, and was fascinated by the colobus monkeys, with their black bodies and long bushy white tails. Blaine took over all of the planning of the trip, which included a lot of long distance calls to Ker & Downey, who had no representatives in the U.S. We asked our dear friends Jane and Tyke Miller, Sally and Bob Flinn, and Judy and Bill Luke to join our safari.

I had many sleepless nights awaiting our departure in January, 1987, and spent Christmas week before our departure with our children at our house, "Rackturn," in Easton. As we looked out our window on Christmas morning it was a bright sunny day, snow had covered the ground, and our beautiful Tred Avon was frozen. For the first time in memory the Chesapeake Bay froze solid from one side to the other. Pipes were freezing, schools were closed, normal activities were curtailed, a sense of emergency prevailed, during the middle of which we were embarking on our maiden African safari, warm summer days and cool nights in Kenya and Tanzania. A momentous time, especially for us!

What follows is an unforseen product of my habit as a part of each day to jot down the highlights of our daily experiences.

– 1987 –

Tanzania, Kenya, & South Africa

January 20
85° wonderful degrees

Blaine and I had departed on our trip a week earlier to explore Egypt and environs (Cairo, the Nile, pyramids, etc.) and flew down to Nairobi a day early. The Flinns, Lukes, and Millers arrived from frigid Amsterdam, where they ice skated on the frozen canals. Sally, Blaine and I immediately go shopping for some needed safari items (at Colpros for brimmed hats and lightweight tan hunting shirts, for example, and at African Heritage, for some useful handmade baskets, and a few select carvings, etc. – all at very good prices, and all after haggling – which was great fun!

We stay at the fabulous Norfolk Hotel, whose fame includes Teddy Roosevelt's departure from its front porch on his historic hunting safari with a native support staff numbering in excess of 100 men marching in file carrying needed supplies on their backs, including not only tents, guns, foods, equipment, but even numerous wooded cases of champagne and other comforts. Must have been quite a sight! We think that the Norfolk is still the best place to stay in Nairobi.

Our first afternoon in Nairobi we toured Karen Blixen's house in Karen, outside Nairobi – she being the principal depicted in the film "Out of Africa" – and from there to nearby Giraffe Manor, a classic manor house, sheltering on its grounds several translocated Rothchild giraffes who regularly poke their long necks through the house's large open windows seeking to be rewarded a Purina food pellet. "Betty

1987

Tea at Giraffe Manor:
Left to Right: Jane Miller, Tyke Miller, Dave Richards, Susan, Bob Flinn,
Blaine, Judy Luke (Not pictured: Bill Luke and Sally Flinn)

June" is the friendliest and displays her 18" tongue frequently. We each held a pellet in our lips to receive an unforgettable "Betty June" kiss, which was exciting to say the least. We next visited Sue Wood's bead factory, which was highly interesting. She and her husband, Sir John Woods of the Flying Doctors fame, thought that the native women in the area were being taken advantage of by their lazy husbands. The men played cards whilst the women ground the maize, cooked family meals, carried buckets of water on their heads to and from a community well, cared for the children and cleaned their huts or shelter, etc. So Sue visited a number of them, offered to pick them up in her mini bus and bring them to her house where she set them to work making necklaces and earrings out of clay. She paid them and was successful in organizing several at first, and now has hired over 60! They make beads out of clay, of their own designs, paint them, fire them, string them, and offer them for sale. At the house they sell for about half of their retail price – namely for 80 – 250 shillings (that is U.S. $4.50 to about $20). They are now sold world-wide, under the name "Kazuri".

After cocktails on the Norfolk terrace we had dinner at Tamarind Restaurant – said to be #1 in Nairobi. Specialty of the house is the gigantic Blue Mangrove Crab – more than twice the size of our Chesapeake crabs – a bit different taste – but delicious. Also very good is the smoked sailfish and the Mombasa oysters.

The next morning we took a minivan at 8:30 a.m. arranged by the Norfolk for a day excursion to Lake Naivasha, known for its beautiful birds. We see over 28 varieties of birds. Tyke excitedly claimed he saw a "Blue eared Starling," at which Blaine scoffed, asserting Tyke made it up, because everybody knows birds do not have ears. A bet ensued with Blaine forking over $5 to Tyke who produced a picture of this gorgeous bird in his bird guide. Went to Crescent Island where Blaine foolishly took 2 rolls of film of one close-up waterbuck. Nearby we see 5 hippos wallowing in shallow Lake Naivasha with birds all around them.

The lunch on Sundays at Lake Naivasha Hotel is quite an occasion for local residents – who were numerous – and for lack of a better description, colorful and interesting. The buffet lunch on the expansive lawn was excellent – highlighted on a hot day with icy cold Tusker beer. After lunch we visited nearby Myers Farm and a Masai village where we inspected a manyatta (Masai village) with its huts made by the women (not the men) out of cow dung and urine. The young men's contribution to the visit was a rather spectacular war dance. Touristy, but we liked it, being assured by Ker & Downey the rest of our trip would be in select, non-touristy locations.

Helen deButts who is working for Ian Douglas-Hamilton collecting more data for his acclaimed research of elephants was waiting for me at the Norfolk when we returned. She, her brother Budda, and his wife, Shelly, had just climbed Mt. Kenya – they are all very attractive 20 somethings.

Tomorrow we leave Nairobi and embark on our private safari.

Masai woman who built this hut from cow dung and urine

January 22
Arusha / Ngere Sero

Up at 7:00 a.m. for our charter flight out of Nairobi to Arusha. Two twin engine 6 seaters – Africair. BTP and I had considerable difficulty getting through customs at Killy (Kilimanjaro Airport) because we had South African visas included in our passports. After much argument Blaine had to pay a corrupt custom official $50 U.S. dollars in cash before we were allowed to enter Tanzania from Kenya. We are met outside of customs by our 2 intrepid white hunters from K&D and depart Killy in our Land Cruisers for the 1 hour drive through Arusha on to Ngere Sero – The "Leach Plantation" - turned lodge and arrived in time for lunch. Took 2 magnificent bird walks over lovely grounds – including trout ponds and streams. Saw an old fashioned bee hive made out of a hollow log hooked up in a limb of a tree – the bees hover inside and make honey – which the natives get by lowering the log. Dinner was excellent and our sleeping rooms were very comfortable.

January 23
Cross Country / Animal Viewing Enroute to Ngorongoro

Left early next morning in our 4 wheel drive open Land Cruiser vehicles enroute to the distant Ngrongoro Crater – considered the Eighth Wonder of the World – a deep circular depression in the earth – its verdant floor measuring 12 miles across and providing a spectacular haven for vast numbers of Africa's fascinating animals. To get there we traveled over difficult terrain, sometimes jostling over very rough, twisting, dirt roads, but mostly off-road over endless savannah, seeing at close range very large numbers of exotic animals and birds – hundreds of giraffes, thousands of zebras – and scads of birds and vultures – all new to us. Our Ker & Downey guides – Dave Richards and John Fletcher and John's native tracker – Sangau, had a full day identifying and explaining all the exciting and interesting creatures and other things we were encountering. The rest of their support staff had gone ahead of us in a large lorry carrying our duffels, tents, equipment, foods, beverages (even including ice!) in order to have camp set up when we arrived in mid-afternoon.

Mutt & Jeff

1987

The site selected was absolutely spectacular, right on the crater's very lip – overlooking an awesome vista far beyond and also down to the distant floor below scattered with pods of wildlife – especially including elephants. How did they ever manage to get down there? Or more difficult yet – how do they ever climb back up the crater's rocky wall?

Needless to say, cocktails and dinner around the campfire were memorable. Our first taste of the night sounds and smells of Africa.

Later that night – after everyone was sound asleep in our most comfortable tents, we were provided with a very different African experience. A violent storm awakened us with frightening noise and tornado level winds. Tables were turned over along with everything on them – some tents were collapsed – our metal tent poles were bent – the large bar with many wine and other beverage bottles were knocked over on the cook and injured him – The staff worked the rest of the night to put things back together again. John Fletcher decides he will never locate a campsite on the lip of the gorge again – He was

A violent storm almost sent us into the crater.

really afraid we were going to go over the precipice – tents and all!! Understandably the staff overslept our planned 5:30 a.m. wake up call due to the storm problem, which meant we got a late start the next morning embarking on the difficult descent to the crater floor.

January 24
Ngorongoro Crater / 60° Rain & Sun

Arrive in the crater late (10:30) but we see our first lions, elephants, and rhinos – also see Hartebeests, Thompson and Grant's gazelles, wildebeest, and zebra. At lunch we had a bird called a kite that swooped down and grabbed meat almost out of our hands. Dave and Blaine threw some salami up in the air and the kite repeatedly caught it in his claws. After lunch, more buffalo, waterbuck, jackals, and seven rhinos (including a baby born 12/24/85 – fittingly named "Noel"). There are only 10 left in the crater. On the way back to camp we came across a cheetah and her 2 month old cub. It still had white fur along

A herd of buffalo resting in the crater

the top of its body like a furry mane. A herd of 18 giraffe are standing by the side of the road. After we all went to bed, two huge herds of wildebeest stampeded behind our campsite. We could hear a leopard roaring and hyenas crying. Dave and John suspect there was a nearby kill during the night.

In the crater, our first lion looks like our dog who wants his belly scratched.

January 25
Olduvai & Serengeti

Up at 6:00 to "jambo", the local greeting for good morning, and on the road to Olduvai by 7:00. We see the herd of stampeding wildebeest and zebra that we heard last night. Also a great big family of baboons. Our first stop is the Leakey Museum where Mary Leakey found the skull of Homo Erectus which proved that man was in this area over 1.5 million years ago. We are told the name "Olduvai" comes from the spiny cactus-like plant in the gorge whose name is "oldupae" but when the Europeans asked the Masai for the name they thought the Masai said "Olduvai."

Blaine and I are with John Fletcher who has been a hunter and guide since the 50"s, and has a great respect for and knowledge of the larger animals. He's a wonderful storyteller about the "good old days", meaning before all the photographic safaris started. He was on location in the movie "Flame Trees of Thika" and was involved with the entire making of "Out of Africa." He tells us that lead actor, Robert Redford, was a real wimp, or as they say in Africa, a "wee-wee." He refused to sleep in the tents after a snake was found in one (not even near his tent) and thereafter insisted upon being helicoptered to a hotel in Nairobi every night after shooting on the filming location. As we are driving to our campsite in the Serengeti plains we stop at a place in the middle of this vast landscape which has a remarkable mound of very black, fine sand – dimensions about 30' high by 100' wide. The wind on the plains is constant and moves only in one direction and its pushing the top layer of sand up over the top of the mound making it move inches a year across the plain. An extraordinary phenomenon indeed.

John Fletcher

January 26
Ndutu / 80° Sunny

We are off bright and early after chai (tea), coffee, and a hot breakfast of porridge, eggs, ham, juice, toast. Our first sighting is a Wild Cat (about the size of our house cats) – and then a larger cat – a very

1987

Dave Richards

hungry male cheetah on the prowl. Next we come upon a zebra killed by hyenas. There are 8 – 10 standing around and 30 – 40 vultures and a marabou stork. After kibitzing for quite a while, and making sure that the hyenas are gone, Dave, our guide, decides he needs a closer photo and gets out of the land cruiser – crawling belly down until he is nearly on top of the kill. He shoos the remaining vultures away and picks up the zebra mane which is still on the skull and the skin is still soft. He guesses the kill was only 15 minutes before we arrived.

We drive on to the kopjes (pronounced "copies") which are huge formations of rock where lizard, speckled rock pigeon, lion, and an occasional snake hang out. It is quite an exceptional morning topped off by a zebra baby with its mother. We stop to photograph it because it is lying very close to the road. It is only a couple of hours old and struggles to get up to inspect us. Its mother runs away and it began to follow us - closely. He has imprinted on us and we fear he will continue to follow us. We high tail it out of the place so he can't catch us. After our 4:00 p.m. chai and later afternoon game run we came across a pride of lions very close to our campsite - 4 females, 3 cubs, 1 old male, 2 teenage males. They begin to roar in a cacophony of sound as we sit and study them 20 feet away. What a splendid day! Cocktails around the campfire – a few vodkas, dinner, and bed by 10 pm.

January 27
Ndutu

Wake up call – "jambo" at 6:00 a.m. Cold – need long pants, shirts, sweater, jacket. Dave is our guide and tells us that last night the lions

The baby zebra has imprinted on us.

circled our tents to mark that this is their territory. Dave is an Englishman, between 45 and 50, and holds the world record on number of birds sighted in a 24 hour period, about 290. He wrote the best safari birding guide in East Africa, and authored several books. He can hear any bird and know its name. He is an incredible guide as his eyes spot everything. He is also very patient and loves to explore. He has a wonderful story about each bird or animal to help us remember the name, i.e. a male ostrich has a penis that faces backward – or is retromingent – which means it sprays backward. That is true also for the lion and the rhino. The dik-dik, impala, tommies all have glands, either in their eye or their legs, that mark their territory. A female elephant has teats between her front legs. An Egyptian vulture is the only bird which uses a tool to get his food. It picks up a stone with its claws and bangs it on its prey because its bill is quite soft and unable to accomplish this. A wheatiar bird has a white rump (ass) which is what "wheatiar" means in Old English.

1987

January 29
Ndutu

Up and out early to find more animals. Our goals are the Simba kopjes to see lion, but on the way we spy some elephant in the distance, so we trek across country to find them. Dave is our guide and I am standing on the front seat spotting for dangerous aardvark holes as we speed across the plains. We see a bunch of wart hog and then a herd of cape buffalo – about 80 – they charge us full bore and come within 40 yards of our Land Cruiser and only then all turn at the same time and run away. Quite a scare! Off we go toward the elephant again. We spot them. There are over 100 – all ages, shapes, and sizes – one huge one, probably the matriarch, stands a foot over the others and has such smooth fat tusks they look as if they've been filed by an emory board. We are told by our guides that the elephants are spooked because they have been poached so much recently they really huddle together as a herd. They are truly an awesome sight. So powerful, so big, and yet so silent. The afternoon game run is quite exciting as we watch a huge

A truly awesome sight

herd of wildebeest (also known as gnu) go down to Lake Lagadja for a good drink. They are incredibly stupid. They have the whole sandy beach but dangerously they all swim en masse to a narrow spit of sand and huddle together as one to drink and cool off. Lions, hyenas, or wild dogs could have a field day!

Going across the plains in this season of the migration on the Serengeti is really an indescribable sight as it touches all your senses and is impossible to put into words. Mile upon mile of grazing wildebeest, zebra, gazelle, by the 1000's, and a scattering of wart hog, jackal, and hyena. Here and there herds of topi, kongoni (Swahili for Coves Hartebeest) or eland. So many species of birds with vibrant colors and song, and such peace. An occasional grunt of a gnu or bark of the zebra, twittering of the cisticula, or toot of the hornbill. Eagles, harriers, stork, vultures, kestrels, and kites all soaring overhead, keeping an "eagle eye" on all below. You can see forever as there is no smog or pollution and only a smattering of trees in the distance. All around are mountains rising out of the plains. Occasionally, we come across an indentation in the plain where packs of hyenas have dug out holes in the side of the dust bowl to make a den. A little further down the plain we seek the kopjes – a perfect home for resting lions and sleeping snakes, especially cobras. And then there is the occasional sadness, as we witnessed today. A male lion had been attacked – or gotten his foot caught in a snare. His hind leg was totally gone from the knee down and he lay helpless in the grass. He will be a meal for the hyenas tonight.

On our way by road to our Ndutu campsite I spy something small in size rolling on the road. We stop and watch this peculiar sight. It is a dung ball made by the scarab beetle. Usually 2 beetles work on a dung ball rolling it over and over until it gets to be the size of a golf ball, then they bury it which contain the beetles' eggs. The eggs hatch and little scarabs come out of the ground. There is a tern which flies all the way from across the Russian steppes to eat dung beetles. We

Dung Beetle and Dung Ball

have found this little ball so innovative and interesting that we have named our group the "Ding Bat Dung Beetle Society."

Back at camp I am intrigued by the ring necked doves whose call sounds like "poor father, work harder, poor father, work harder" – repeated endlessly with a British accent. The call is almost identical to the Masai war chant in their tribal dance. We come to learn that the dove calls are one of the compelling and everlasting sounds of East Africa.

January 29
Serengeti and Manyara / 85° and Sunny

Our last morning in the Serengeti we are leaving our Tanzanian Staff. Interestingly, Ker & Downey have operated in Tanzania only since December. We are just the 7th safari K&D have brought to Tanzania and this is the first time our camp staff (of 12) have worked with our guides. Julius is the head man and wonderful. The others are very green!!! We are the guinea pigs but they are learning. Our personal boy (We could never understand his name. He gave us a different one every time we asked) burned holes in my new African heritage shirt when he was ironing it with a wrought iron he warmed over hot coals, but then was too frightened of risking his new job to return it to me. It just disappeared. On another occasion, he could never get the water in the shower (a bucket hanging over our tent with a pull chain to lower the water out of the bucket) without spilling half of it on the ground.

Alas, time to go – "Kwaheri" ("good bye") to the Serengeti. We're on our way to Lake Manyara Lodge. Drive for two hours over the plains (no road) across very rough terrain. Driving past Ngorongoro Crater – through villages and huts made of red clay and sticks. Many Masai and cattle along the road. Arrive Manyara in time for lunch and a swim before our afternoon game run. The Manyara park is an underground water forest. Everything is very lush and green. Baboons, vervet monkeys, and lots of hippos are performing in the nearby water course. The lodge is terribly run down as Tanzania has just opened up again to tourism. No bourbon, no tonic, no breakfast meats, very iffy drinking water, filthy bathrooms, and leaky toilets. Fairly good impala stew dinner, but the same everyday for lunch and dinner. The Tanzanian wine – which we were told was dry and delicious - is worse than my words can describe. The view, however, is spectacular overlooking the large lake and the parkland below.

January 30
Manyara / overcast, humid, and hot

Men are off to the park again in the morning and the ladies leave with John Fletcher around 9:00 for a bit of local market shopping. The natives all want American $. I bought a beautiful carving of two giraffes for $5.00. Lots of bargaining - my bandana, belt, and a ball in return for hand painted batiks, spears, and spectacular wood carvings. Then off to the larger village open market at MBO-TWVE. Lots of bargaining again. The men show up with Dave Richards. While we were all bargaining a fight broke out and a large rock was thrown into our windshield and broke it badly on the driver's side. Sally and John, who witnessed most of the fight, saw an old man on the ground and

1987

Bargaining off my clothes at the village open market

some young native ruffians beating him up and kicking him. Amazingly, the rarely seen police happened to be there but ignored our windshield as well as the fighting. We all rushed back from our purchases, jumped in the cars fast and scampered. The girls drive back with John. We arrived in Ngere Sero in time for lunch.

January 31
Samburu / Tanzania

Up at 6:00 a.m. for our flight from Killy airport to Nairobi and then north on to Samburu. "Samburu" means butterfly in Swahili because the Samburu people dress so colorfully. Some of the Masai red, but also yellows, blues and oranges. The Samburus are tall and robust athletic looking. Perhaps because they have a more nutritous diet than the bland maize and goat milk of the nomadic Masai who are very tall with extremely long skinny legs. The 10 seater Cessna twin bounced us around and was extremely rough going over the Rift Valley – great view of Mt. Kenya in the air and then a hairy landing at Samburu airstrip with barely minimum visibility. On our drive to our campsite we saw a family of Ndovu (elephant). Samburu is similar to New Mexico – a lot of scub brush (called salt scrub) and funny tall skinny palms called "Duom" (pronounced "dumb"). It is terribly dry and dusty – we are no longer in red clay – but gray dust. There are no vultures or obvious predators which were so prevalent on the plains; therefore no skulls and bones which are so numerous on the savannahs. Many elephant, waterbuck, gerenuk, gazelle – the browsers versus the grazers. Lots of parrots, hornbills, bee eaters, weavers.

The staff in Kenya is truly first class. Francis is Dave's head man. Young, clean, always smiles, gentle, and kind. Michael is John's head man. Definitely Kikuyu (with the tell-tale receding hairline), short, 50ish, serious, dependable. Our personal man, Donald, does our laundry, cleans the tent, makes the bed, brings the shower water, chai and coffee in the morning, and water for the washstands. He is young, cute, smiley, reliable. Sangau was John's tracker for 15 years, and very experienced. One time, back when John hunted, Sangau was picked up by an elephant and had his shirt ripped off.

February 1
Samburu / 50° early, 85° later

The morning is spent winding our way down the river bed looking for Ndovu (elephant). Not much going on – some parrots, monkeys, crocs, and a gray heron. The afternoon is really hot – and Sally, Judy, and I go for a swim in a little pool of sparkling fresh spring water. Waterhogs and zebra are all around us. Wild night around the campfire. We all wear colorful Kikois and Kangas as it is so hot. Drink tons of wine – in fact all of it. Get the Miller's tape machine and dance around the fire. While we are all being rather raucous, Jane looks down at her feet and what is crawling over them but a huge scorpion – stretched out it measured at least 4". It is bad luck – so say the Kikuyus – to kill

1987

Wild night around the campfire!

Spot a family of elephants on our way back to camp.

a scorpion – so Dave picks it up in a glass and pitches it in the woods. Obviously, I shook out my slippers and shoes from then on. Well, we needed a few after-dinner Grand Marniers after that and then bed around 12:30!! Late!!

February 2
clear 50° a.m, 100° pm

Glorious day – crisp and clear. Our first animal is a mama cheetah and her two cubs. We stop at the Ewasho Nero river and watch some vervets frolicking in the trees. Dave is our guide today and we drive to Samburu game lodge. Attractive – lots of flowers, thatched cottages. Spot Ndovu on our way back to camp and we follow them to the river. Darling babies, teenagers, moms. Rolling in the mud. Hosing themselves with water. Scratching themselves on tree trunks. Back at camp we have a cold yummy salad lunch. Our afternoon run is so beautiful – herd of at least 60 beautiful impala and a few waterbuck – only a few feet away from the Land Cruiser.

On the way back to camp late afternoon we run into David Mead, guiding another safari, who tells us the awful news that since we saw her recently Helen de Butts has been charged by a rhino cow and very, very seriously injured. She is in the Nairobi hospital and lucky to be alive.

February 3
Mt. K.S.C. / 95° and sun

We arrive at Mt. Kenya Safari Club in time for c-tails and lunch – very swish place, made famous by Hollywood actor, Bill Holden. Flowers, elephant ivory, and trophy heads are everywhere. There is a heated pool and we share a cottage with the Flinns. A very large living room with a bar, a bedroom on either end, and huge bathrooms with sunken tubs. Took a long swim. Bill took a video of Sally, Judy and me doing a water ballet – utilizing a sunken window under the pool. Tyke discovers a beauty salon and we find him sitting in the beauty chair with a cape around his shoulders getting a cut from an African with a Bo-Derick hairdo.

Can't wait to go to the animal orphanage. I hold a chimp (which is wearing clothes and has become quite human), play with a bush baby which has very sticky fingers, feed the bongos, pet the baby ostrich, and the dik-diks.

Late afternoon, we take a bird walk through a fruit and vegetable orchard, down a horse path, and a very well-manicured golf course. The 5 course meal at dinner is delicious in the Members Dining Room (John is a charter member). There are fireplaces lit everywhere. One roaring in our cottage, one in the bar, one in the living room of the lodge. So charming, romantic.

FEBRUARY 4
MT. K.S.C. / ABEDERES

One mile bird walk at 7:00 a.m. We're all dragging a bit, due to the altitude which is 7,000 feet and directly on the Equator. And then off to the Abederes after a hearty breakfast. A quick photo stop at the Equator (which we crossed 3 times). Bought a few carvings and bracelets in Nanyuki just outside of the Safari Club.

The countryside is staggeringly beautiful. The ground is red clay like Albemarle County, VA. Lot of bush farm land, sheep, Charlais cattle, a few hartebeests, and tommies grazing. It always amazes me as you drive down the road to see wild animals – baboons, monkeys, zebras, gazelles happily grazing. Abederes National Park is at 6,500 feet in the salient (which means an outreach of forest.) It is jungle with many tall fig trees, lavender veronica flowering bushes, cape chestnuts, rivers, streams, bushbuck, cape buffalo, elephant, warthogs, mongoose, one spectacular male leopard (which we saw for 20 seconds) Colobus monkeys swinging in trees, Sykes monkeys 30 feet from our campsite.

1987

Colobus monkeys all around us.

Commodious tent with shower bucket hanging in the back

1987

The cook said a hyena came through our campsite the first night and stole his pots and pans which he later found in the bush. We have to lock up all our personal things in the tent at all times because the baboons and Sykes come and steal anything they can get their hands on (even the soap in the water container). This is such a refreshing change from the Serengeti or even Samburu. It is cool – but sunny. Crisp and breezy in the shade – arid, hot in the sun. Our Kenyan tents are commodious with the shower bucket hanging in the back of the tent and a long drop toilet back by the dressing area, and dual sinks.

February 5
40° morning, 80° afternoon

"Jambo" – chai, coffee at 6:00. In the Land Cruisers and gone by 6:30. No more than 40° - feels like ice. Run into a herd of cape buffalo in the road, bushbuck are drinking in the streams, warthogs are munching away at the grass. We see a huge hole in the side of the hill where the warthogs have dug in the clay for the natural salt. It is fairly deep and we can see the salt in the red clay. A leopard is standing in the middle of the road. In the salient everything is so lush that if you don't spot an animal along the road you can't find him because the bush is just too thick. We are driving with John. Sangau, his spotter, sits in the back hatch and sees everything (and I like to look at Sangau to observe what he is seeing.) He knocks on the roof when he spots something. This park has the highest elevation of any park in the world. And I feel as if I'm on top of the world.

Back to camp for a 10:30 late breakfast of eggs, sausage, bacon, toast, porridge, cold cereal, papaya, juices. Off again for a mid-morning drive – see frolicking Colobus monkeys and a very good view of a suni which resembles a dik-dik but is even smaller. The forest is beautiful – ever changing – my favorite place so far. Back at camp for lunch. There are baboons all over the campsite. John feeds one an avocado from his hand. The staff have made a pit of old fruit and the baboons go crazy trying to get enough to eat.

On our afternoon game drive Colobus monkeys are so close the leaves fall into our Land Cruiser as the monkeys climb the tree next to us. A very different experience from my memories of the Colobus monkeys in cages at the St. Louis Zoo where I first saw them as a young child. A little farther on are two teenage bull elephants fighting tusk-to-tusk. Then a baby warthog in a pit along the side of the road. No more than a few hours old and not bigger than a cereal box.

We drive to the top of the ridge 7,000' and can see forever – lush all around. The entire place – Africa – affects all your senses. The screaming and chattering of the baboons. You always hear the call of the dove ("poor father – work harder") there are shrikes, brubrus, cuckoos, hoopoes, barbets, weavers and cisticulas. The high pitched bleep of the tree frog in the pitchy dark of night. Visually, the light changes daily, hourly, you never see the same thing twice. Everything smells – from the sweet flowering trees to the elephant or cape buffalo

John feeding a baboon an avocado.

1987

dung. The things you feel are different from anything I've experienced in the past – dung beetle balls or dik-dik dung, to the black shifting sand of the Serengeti or the cool wet grass of the Abederes in early morning. And the smell of the coffee as you lay in your tent before light and then the taste of the coffee made from Kenya or Tanzania coffee beans, the warmed up cashews for c-tails, or the lemon drops that I brought from home and eat constantly to quench our thirst out on the drives – all are memories of Africa for me.

February 5
Abederes

Our campsite is located very close to Tree Tops (where visiting Princess Elizabeth went to sleep as a princess and woke up the next morning as the Queen of England because her father, King George, died during the night). We can see the elephants eating the salt every night under the spotlight at the resort. Our baboons also leave to go to Tree Tops and get some more freebies.

Now for a bit more of John and Dave trivia: – warthogs have two long teeth that protrude from their bottom lip, each of which is called a TUSH (not tusk). It is used a lot in jewelry – because it resembles ivory – but is calcium like our teeth. An old warthog is about 10 years old. Marabou stork have totally white legs – which aren't really white but are yellow legs covered over in their own dung (which bleaches white) and theoretically keeps them cooler. They have a large protruding sack under their heads which resembles a crop but which is actually an extended left nostril (never a right nostril).

February 6
Island Camp – Baringo

After a nice relaxed breakfast we leave the Abederes for Baringo. First stop is Thomson's Falls where the old Happy Valley Crowd (infamous "White Mischief") had a club. The falls are pretty and drop 230 feet. More curio shops – but we resist temptation. Bill dances with a few dancing natives who are dolled up in tribal outfits and war paint. Arrive from Lake Baringo four hours later. I mean it is really hot here!!

Coming from 7,000 feet down to sea level the temperature has gone from a cool 80° to a scorching 125° at least!! Take a long primitive boat over to Island Camp and walk up at least 100 stone steps (seems like 1,000) to our tent. Our permanent tent overlooks the lake – there are hundreds of varieties of birds. We take a nap, a cool swim (in a very attractive pool) and a bird walk – in late afternoon.

I walk through a native village on the island. It is the driest, most barren place I have ever been. A few bushes for the goats to nibble on, but rock and dried earth underfoot (not a blade of grass). A 10 year old boy named Samson adopted me and is my private guide and carries my bird book. There are huts in the village made of clay and then painted different flower and abstract designs with natural dyes of

Susan with Village Children

ochre and white. Children with dirty faces and bare crusty feet seem curious and want to follow us around the village. There are goats and children everywhere and total poverty. They eat only goat and tilapia fish (which they catch in the lake) and maize. We saw the butchery where they had just slaughtered two goats and drained the blood into a big pot.

Back on the terrace of Island Camp for cocktails. It has cooled off a lot due to a quick rain and is delightful. After a very good dinner we all go back to the terrace for coffee and liquors. We meet a dissipated womanizer named Allen who is rather entertaining after a few Grand Marniers, and who has part interest in Island Camp. He wears only a kikoi and monocle and speaks only French to Sally and me – which, after drinks, we speak perfectly at this hour of the night. Sally, Bob, John, Dave, Allen, and I stay up too late – but are having a real giggle.

February 7
Barringo / Hot / Back to Nairobi

7:30 comes way too quickly for a boat ride bird watch. We see thousands of shore birds. Lesser flamingos, ducks, geese, and a few hippos – one whom we ran over in the boat – he gave us quite a frightening jolt!! After a 9:00 breakfast we quickly pack and leave by boat to the Lake Baringo Club. What a contrast. Everything is well-watered, flowering bushes, green grass very well-manicured. Birds of startling variety are everywhere. A nice pool, but crowded – numerous bird watchers twitching everywhere – quite amazing – very English – very dowdy. After a nice duckling dinner we take our coffee out under the stars.

We are joined by a Nissan rally driver named Michael. He is presently 9th in the world. He is 39 years old and owns the Tarmarind Restaurant in Mombasa. During a rally the drivers go 230 K.P.H. There is a co-driver telling Michael every turn, every rock, and how fast he should be going. The rally around the Baringo Escarpment is 4,000 kilometers.

We sleep under Mombasa nets – which Blaine is crazy about. A mysterious person enters our room and I don't move a muscle – almost stop breathing. He is very quiet, looks around and then leaves. Happily nothing is out of place or taken. Scary!! Very scary!!!

February 8
Lake Baringo

7:00 a.m. bird walk to the Baringo Cliffs. Vereaux eagles, chats, hornbills, and hyrax scampering around the rocks. After a late breakfast we're off again. Make a quick detour through Lake Nakuru where there are thousands of greater flamingos. Then off to Lake Naivasha Hotel to stop off for lunch. Because it is Sunday, the grounds are jammed with picnic tables and hundreds of people. They serve a traditional hot curry and rice which we wash down with a cool Tusker beer.

The dress code for Nairobi is summer. Lots of bright skirts or safari pants and shirts during the day. Very informal at night. Men wear safari jackets or blazers with open shirts - no tie. Women wear light weight dresses - light or dark - doesn't matter, with a shawl for evening warmth.

Arrive Nairobi – Exhausted. Dinner party in the Ibis Room of the Norfolk at 8:00 p.m. John, Korinna (new g.m at K&D), Dave, Val (Dave's wife), and us. We enjoy a rowdy dinner with lots of toasts and Bill's ever present video machine recording everything from the piano player playing "Malaika" (our very favorite song) to us doing the Watusi. We close the place down at 11:00 still raring to go – but Sunday night and all the bars are closed. To bed with sweet dreams of wonderful memories of a spectacular safari. Kwaheri!!

The Flinns, Lukes, and Millers flew back home Monday morning, and we are off to the Kenyan coast!

1987

FEBRUARY 9

We arrive on the coast of Kenya, to a town called Lamu, after a 2 hour flight on Sunbird Airways (there is one plane in their fleet). Blaine and I are met by Islamic Swahilis who transport us, and our luggage, to the Peponi Hotel via a large dhow. The captain of the dhow controls the sail lines by twisting it around his big toe. He blows his shell horn to signal our arrival. The whole island of Lamu smells like some kind of strange sewage. The Peponi is 3 kilometers from town, but smells also. Everyone dresses very casually in kangas and kikois. The office of the hotel, where you check in, is the bar. Our room is very large, with a commodious bathroom, two beds encircled by one large Mombasa net, and a comfortable porch with lounge chairs overlooking the ocean. The water is crystal clear, and the white sandy beach goes on for miles, consisting of very few people.

FEBRUARY 10

Blaine and I take a public dhow from the Peponi to Lamu at 9:00 a.m. The dhow is filled with native Islamic women with buis-buis covering their faces. Everything smells. The town is fascinating. The dock is at the end of the town square. They are selling everything from bunches of bananas to bunches of miraa in the streets. (Miraa is a stimulant - legal - it is the stem of a plant you chew.) The main street is just wide enough for 2 or 3 people to pass each other without colliding. The old section is just about the same as in the 1700's.

We went through a Swahili house, which exemplified how much women were 3rd class citizens. The 1st floor was for the men and boys. The best bedrooms are for the boys and parents. The girls slept in a windowless room in the back. The kitchen was on the 2nd floor, so the women couldn't be seen when company came. But they could walk out on the roof to talk with neighbor women.

Blaine and I hired a Swaleh to take us around. Some of the side streets are only a couple of feet wide. We saw a dhow boatyard, and the old fashioned tools they use to drill holes for the pegs in the boat. Being in Lamu is like putting your five senses on steroids, awakening every superlative you can imagine to the extreme - both pungently sweet and repugnantly obnoxious, both eye-catchingly wondrous and shockingly depressing. We catch the noon dhow back to the Peponi and I take a long walk and swim. Late in the afternoon, Blaine and I take a private dhow. Omar, the captain, has a fishing line trailing the boat as he sails, moving the rudder with his back. Beautiful sunset as we sail on the Indian Ocean.

A cold vodka with ice tastes splendid before dinner, which we eat under the stars on an outdoor terrace. Early to bed under our Mombasa nets.

FEBRUARY 11

Hot. Town and Country magazine editor is staying at the Peponi, doing a feature on Lamu, Manda, and Kiwaihu for next January's or February's edition. They tried to chum up with Blaine, but he brushed

We took a private dhou for a sunset cruise.

them off abruptly, thinking they were with some travel agency. We learned just before leaving of their being with Town and Country - alas, too late. I take a dhow across to Manda, to do a bit of snorkeling. The water was too murky to be any good.

We're off again, via a 6 seater twin engine Sky Bird Airline to Mombasa, flying low along the coast is very scenic. Claire Young, our guide, takes us immediately to the Tamarind restaurant, which is both a conventional restaurant and a dhow. The dhow takes up to 60 people, but has less than 20. They had held the dhow for our arrival, immediately gave us the best table, served us exotic dinners, and struck up the music. Blaine and I met Ivan, the owner, who joins us for dinner. He also makes his own light airplanes, and is in partnership with Mike, the rally driver whom we had met in Baringo. There is a full moon, and a live band playing Maleika. A fresh lobster dinner, couch type seats with huge pillows, candle light, and the lights of Mombasa on the water, it sets a very romantic mood as we quietly sail down the river. Wow! We should be in a movie!

Claire met us and drove us to our hotel. We are staying at the Inter-Continental. It is very new, very gaudy, and horrible, but a great pool and a very nice beach.

FEBRUARY 12
MOMBASA / HOT, 100 DEGREES, AND SUNNY

Claire picks us up at 9:00 a.m. for a fascinating trip to old town. What a contrast to Lamu. The first thing you notice when arriving in the old section of Mombasa is an overwhelming smell of spices. Merchants hawking their wares in the streets: fruits, veggies, spices (like cinnamon and nutmeg), teas, kangas, carvings, sandals ($4.00 U.S.). Thousands of Muslims, Asians, Africans, Europeans - a real potpourri roaming the streets. Blaine buys some kikois in the market, and I buy some wonderful spices. We drive to the wood carver's workshop. This is where 60 or 70 wood carvers sit on the ground under thatched tents and carve masterpieces with a chisel, hammer, and ax. They start with a single block of wood (mahogany and ebony), and painstakingly carve each piece by hand. At this workshop you can buy the carvings wholesale - about half the price as in the shops. Lunch is at Le Pichet, a quaint seafood restaurant overlooking a beautiful small creek lined with palms. Great Mombasa oysters, crab, and lobster.

We go back to the hotel for a swim and early dinner. Our flight to Nairobi is easy and quick. We are met at the airport by Christine Leonard and her very British husband, Dave (who clicked his heels when introduced, and then gave a little twist to his Adolphe Menjou's moustache). We have a glorious cottage at the Norfolk. A huge suite: living room, bedroom, and large bathroom. It is our third stay at the Norfolk, and it seems like a perfect second home.

February 13
Nairobi

Another glorious day in Nairobi. I ring up Jennifer Hewitt, a friend who lives in Nairobi who asks Blaine and me for lunch at the Muthaiga Club (given unwanted publicity in "Out of Africa" - wouldn't that be fun!!), but we decline. I go visit Helen De Butts in Nairobi Hospital. What an ordeal she has gone through. Her 4th operation was last night. A cow rhino picked her up three times and threw her like a rag doll in the air. She has 8 pins in her femur where the cow gored her. Budda and Shelly (her brother and sister-in-law) were only a few feet away. Rob, the researcher studying rhino on this 90,000 acre farm, had to run over a mile to his vehicle to call on his CB for help. He luckily got the main farm house which called for a flying doctor from Nairobi. They then had to cut a track into Helen, who was deep in the bush, just to carry her to the car. Budda held her open wound together for over an hour. They strapped her onto the car, made it to the plane, and landed in Nairobi 5 hours later. She is a real trooper. Unbelievably, no infection set in, and the cow didn't hit a major artery (which would have left her dead in 15 minutes).

Went briefly to the National Museum, saw Ahmed the Elephant (whose tusks weighed 148 lbs each. Lunch again at the Norfolk (I had fried prawns again for the 4th time). Left on Air Zimbabwe for Harare, Zimbabwe (formerly Southern Rhodesia). Air Zimbabwe is 1st class! We have a delicious snack of fried chicken and prawn quiche. The stewardess sets up a bar in the front of the plane so you can get a drink (free) whenever you like. It is a three hour flight to Harare (formerly known as Salisbury). We stay at Monomatapa Hotel, and look out on a manicured park and 4 hotel swimming pools. We dined at Pinos Restaurant (so-so), native - we sat in a small room of 6 tables, 5 were black and us (one very definite communist calling everyone comrade). Harare is very European, with beautiful roads, very urban, and flame trees in bloom. This hotel is new and uptown.

February 14
Zimbabwe - Victoria Falls / Sun 90°+

The next day we leave on an early morning flight to Victoria Falls. Arriving with no glitches, we are met by our attractive Abercrombie and Kent guide, and driven to the village several miles away. The Victoria Falls Hotel is early 1900's chic, with 12' high ceilings, and the famous "I Presume" bar. We go to the Falls with our guide and a family from Australia. There are 3 main falls: Devil's Crater, a middle one, and Rainbow Falls (the most famous one) which tumbles millions of gallons of water down into a gorge hundreds of feet below. The falls are spectacular, stretching more than a mile wide. We walked for about 2 hours along the edge, getting totally drenched with the spray. The sun is bright, but it is as if we are in the middle of a huge rain storm. The Zambezi River flows from Zambia to Zimbabwe, and the

Falls constitute the border between the countries. At Rainbow Falls you can always see a rainbow, as the water drops precipitously into the gorge.

We had lunch on the terrace of the hotel, listening to a live African band. We then walked to Finn Allen's Curio Shop (which we had been told about by Claire Young). Blaine buys a trade bead necklace (it is Valentine's Day), which Finn's wife made (we learn later in Mala Mala that her necklaces are famous all over South Africa).

At 3:00 p.m. we take a small twin engine plane ride over the Falls. At one point our daredevil pilot dives and rolls only 130' above the Falls. The plane's windshield is drenched with the spray; very exciting, and very scary. You can easily see the gorge, and how the river has cut through the layers of basalt over the years. The plane then goes on a "strafing mission" meandering along the river, wingtips nearly touching the water (surely no more than 70' over the river). We see hippos bathing, and many herds of elephants browsing in the trees. Back to the hotel for a late afternoon swim to calm our nerves after such a hairy flight. We are then off to an African Dance Spectacular, the Shangaan and Mikishi Tribes are entertaining us.

FEBRUARY 15
SOUTH AFRICA - MALA MALA

The next morning we catch our first glimpse of South Africa. We gas up, fly for 45 minutes, and land on a grass strip at Mala Mala, where we are met in a Land Rover by Tony Williams, our personal ranger, and Jim Shaangun, our spotter and tracker. Mala Mala is an exceptionally attractive place. We have a wonderful thatched bandu (hut) with twin baths, 20' ceilings, air conditioning, and overlooking a grassy meadow.

We often get right in the middle of an entire herd of Cape buffalo, or track down a lion or leopard. The Land Rovers are open. The ranger has a loaded rifle on his dash, and a pistol on his hip. Jim sits on a perch at the rear and carries a sheathed knife. The animals are accustomed to the Rovers, so as long as we keep relatively still we can get within 3 feet of buffalo and even lion (if full and lazy), within 20' of white rhinos, and within 20' of huge bull elephant (2 the 1st day). We tracked a female leopard through the bush, knocking down 12'-15' trees with the front grill of the Rover, over rocks, through gullies and streams, up hills, through more bush - 20 minutes later we have cornered the leopard into a spot that we can photograph and view until she gets restless and moves on.

Back for breakfast by 9 a.m. Anything from fried eggplant to South African rarebit, eggs, bacon, fresh fruit, yogurts, and many different juices. Then we settle down for a nap, reading, swimming, bird or butterfly watching, or simply watching the world go by from our patio. We have cocktails before a 1:30 lunch, which you are made aware of by the sounds of a native woman blowing a kudu horn.

Tony and I take a safari walk after lunch. He with loaded rifle and pistol, me with bird book and binoculars. We see beautiful yellow spiders, birds, monkeys, waterbuck - but the most exciting was creeping up on a herd of Cape buffalo. I was sure they could hear the beating of my heart, even though I completely stopped breathing. What an awesome sight on foot. We hid behind an anthill so they couldn't smell us. We forded a stream, went through papyrus jungle grass, through bush, on a dirt track - all terribly exciting.

Back in time for tea, hot or iced, and fattening yummy cakes. At 4:30 we have another game run. We have great luck tracking down 4 of "the Big Five". A herd of buffalo, females and calves, about 75-100 of them. It is calving season. One cow is dilated and contracting. You can almost see the baby coming. Some of the calves are one or two days old, some only weeks. We are so close to this herd that if we had a baseball bat we could scratch their backs. The big bulls stay on the perimeter to protect the herd. What a feeling of oneness we get in our open Land Rover. There are two bull elephant chomping on some trees. Tony backs the Land Rover to within 20 feet of one of them. Blaine's telephoto was way too close. I can see the pulse on the bull's trunk. A female lion has just killed a wildebeest. She is an old granny (about 18 Tony guesses). She is panting and full, and we are so close we can see down her tonsils. She is blind in one eye, and is missing a few teeth.

We have a perfect setting for sundowners at sunset. A table is set up in front of the Rover and we have Smiles (a euphemism for vodka on the rocks) or anything else from beer to orange juice to tonic, and impala kabobs, meatballs, or warthog in hot sauce that Jim our tracker warms up. Jim stands guard while we are out of the Rover, enjoying our drinks, and watching a glorious sunset.

After drinks we turn on the spotlight and look for eyes in the dark. We run into 5 lions, 4 females and 1 male, on the track. A couple of rhinos are grazing not far off the road. Night jars (owls) jump up out of the road and fly in front of the Rover. White tailed mongoose are plentiful, and there are herds of impala everywhere. We get word on the CB from another Rover that a leopard is not far from us. Tony tears off. We cross a river, go through tall grass (at least 8 feet tall) and push it out of the way with the bow of the Rover. We plod through a dried river bed of sand, leaving 10" ruts. Jim is spotting with the light constantly. We find the leopard, but he won't stay still for us. We're off again, tearing down trees, bushes, anything in our way. Unfortunately we try to climb one bank that is too steep and get really stuck. Tony calls on the CB and another Rover comes and tows us out with chains. Blaine and Tony both hear the leopard growling just a few feet away.

Back to camp in defeat at 8:30 p.m. I change into a long skirt or caftan after a jiffy bath, and have cocktails either in the bar (which has three monkeys mounted on a perch speaking, seeing, and hearing "no evil"), or on the terrace watching the moon rise. Down by the pool under a marula tree, we can see an elephant getting sloshed on the marula fruit (the baboons also vie for this fermented fruit and have been seen drunk on it as well).

At Mala Mala they made the most wonderful jelly out of Marula, which is served with impala. One night we stopped on our way back to camp just to look at the moon coming up over the horizon - we are so lucky to have a full moon. Another night we stopped and looked at the millions of stars in the black sky. We learned where the Southern Cross is and how to find it. There is an Orion's Belt in the Southern Hemisphere, but no dipper that we could find.

Dinner is served in a boma. Each person has his own table, placed in a circle around a bonfire in the middle of lead wood. A 900 year old ebony tree is the roof over our heads. We are called to dinner by 6-8 native girls dressed in long red dresses and red kerchiefs around their heads. Three of them are playing drums, beating them with vigor. They are all singing, and at times one or two break into a stomping native dance, keeping rhythm with the beat of the drum. The youngest one gets so frenzied with the rapid beat of the drum that she slumps in a trance.

Dinner consists of a soup, fish course, wild game, salad, dessert, and coffee. The game is impala or warthog, served with marula jelly, and it is just delicious. Blaine and I try the South African champagne; which we find very mild, dry, and light. We are anxious to get a preview of the wine treats we will experience in Cape Town wine country. Dress at Mala Mala is both casual and elegant. Women get dressed up more than men. It is very hot during the day, sometimes reaching over 100°. The land cruisers are open, so there is no getting away from the sun; but we are only out til about 9 a.m. and then back again at 4 p.m. A hat is essential. For the evening run I might take a light jacket for after the sunsets. Men do not wear jackets to dinner., but women do wear long skirts or a nice, but simple, cool dress.

A cute expression the rangers in South Africa use for bird watchers is "twitchers". One might say, "Have you been twitching with your twitching irons?" (binoculars). On the last day's early morning drive we see a pack of 10 wild dogs. They take a lot of tracking. In searching for them we run into a cow rhino and her baby, and only stay long enough to say hello. Then we see some kudu, with their bent heads grazing in a carefree manner. There are 2 giraffe on the road, whom we wave to, and a ground hornbill who flies out of our path, a dwarf mongoose is sunning itself, impala herds are everywhere. We tear down acacias, tall grasses, go through river beds, and finally (we have lost all track of time) there are the dogs, spotted white, black, and brown with long white fox-like tails, and huge dark brown ears. They look quite docile in the bush. We heard that in Tanzania all the wild dogs had been killed there only shortly before we arrived. They sent the remains to the U.S. to perform autopsies to find out how they died (poison, a disease, aids - no one knows). We stop under a shady acacia tree and have a bush breakfast, all prepared over a wood fire, making it all the more delicious. When we return to camp we are all told by the staff there is a mix up, and we are to take a charter to Johannesburg that a couple has hired to bring them to Mala Mala. Lucky us. We say a fond farewell to David Raltray, the General Manager, and to our dear Tony and Jim.

February 19
Johannesburg

We arrive in Johannesburg after 50 minutes of smooth riding in an eight seater, luxurious, private plane. Marthy picks us up (white mercedes), and drives us straight to Pretoria, a dynamic, intellectually growing city. They have opera, ballet, and the Government House, architecturally, is outstanding. Marthy is a wonderful guide from Luxemburg, having lived in Johannesburg for 14 years. She is very bright and informative.

There are elections on May 6th which may change the history of South Africa. Many locals are pulling out of South Africa (including Bishop Desmond Tutu, who says he will leave if there is a war). There is no area for people to live in downtown Johannesburg (no apartments or condos), everyone is spread out in the suburbs. The wealth in the residential areas we saw was staggering. Every house is surrounded by a wall, either stucco or brick, recently built for protection with gardens and tennis courts in nearly every yard. Each house has a security guard. The situation is tenuous at best. They say the people of South Africa have not as yet felt the effects of U.S. sanctions.

The blacks are attending the universities, but in high school it is segregated. One of the major stumbling blocks being the language barrier. The tribal natives do not speak English. A lot of English speaking people don't speak Afrikaans. The Zulu and the Isosias, 2 large tribal groups, have totally different languages, and there are at least 10 more tribes who speak their own dialects. Tony, our safari guide from Mala Mala, told us that Natal, where he went to school, is integrated, and English is taught to all. But that is the hub of the Zulu tribe, and they are more educated.

Butheleze is prime chief of the Zulus, and everyone feels he is a dynamic leader. He wants to have a dual government with the whites in Natal. He is brilliant and reasonable, and his people really listen to him. It is impossible, because of their heritage, for the tribes to live with democracy the way we are pushing them to. The natives must first relate to their tribes, and in their tribes there is a hierarchy which works up to #1 chief. The lesser people in the tribe must follow the line of command up to the top chief. A young man must obey his father - who must obey his father - who must obey the chief. Each tribe has its own hierarchy and chief, and no one wants to give up his power. It is like having 15 presidents of the U.S.. No tribe has any desire to follow the white man's government. Many tribes still don't get along.

Marthy told us a week ago she was on a bus tour with a bunch of German lawyers, and stopped to witness a tribal ceremony. One tribe had killed a member of a neighboring tribe, and they had slaughtered a goat and were drinking the blood in a tribal ceremony celebrating the murder. Life means nothing to these natives.

Conversely, in Soweto, there are many millionaires. There are more Mercedes and BMWs there than you'll find in many European cities. Certainly Johannesburg is more uptown, cosmopolitan, clean, and successful than any place in East Africa. Marthy reminds us that South Africa is surrounded by communist countries - Zimbabwe, Swaziland, and Mozambique. If the A.N.C. wins the election, the country may succumb to war.

We have wonderful accommodations on the Blue Train leaving the afternoon of February 20 - destination Cape Town, South Africa. We have cocktails in the lounge, and meet Ross and Gail Flanery from New South Wales, Australia. Ross will be playing rugby in Cape Town against an apparently fiercely competitive team.

We have children all the same age. Ross and Gail ski Aspen almost every year. And by the evening's end we know we will be life long friends.

Fast forward a few years - Ross and Gail have come to visit us a number of times in Easton. Our children have stayed with them at their sizeable sheep station in New South Wales, and their children have spent many nights in the U.S. with our children. Who would have guessed this one night on the Blue Train would produce such a close and lasting friendship?

FEBRUARY 22
CAPE TOWN / SUN, 80°

Mr. Philip picks us up at 8:30 for a scenic drive along the water to

1987

Blue Train

Cape of Good Hope. You can see the ocean on three sides. The cape is in a national park. False Bay on one side, where Diaz, (a Portuguese), first discovered the cape. Then Vasco de Gama came 11 years later (who really became more famous for the discovery). There are thousands of black cormorants nesting in the cliffs next to the Cape. There are few animals in the park, but we did run into a family of baboons along the main road.

After viewing the Cape and its breathtaking scenery, we drove to lunch at a restaurant called Sea Forth, either in Simmons Town or Fish Hoer. So lovely to enjoy lobster and wine in a very atmospheric restaurant overlooking the ocean, swimmers, and the beach.

We drove back down to Cape Town via Constantia (where the "elite" live), and saw Groote Schuur Hospital (where Christian Bernard became famous). We drove through the neighborhood where coloreds live, which have very nice houses with gardens, clean, and well painted. The Malaysians live in equally nice houses where the

Blaine at Cape of Good Hope

1987

Lunch with Mr. Philip

price of real estate is quite high. Alex Philip pointed out the neighborhood in which he lives near the highway not unlike those of the coloreds, and in a residential area next to them.

FEBRUARY 23
A FEW SPRINKLES

We head out to the wine country after a nice leisurely breakfast in the room. We drive via the town of Stellanbosch, which has the Africa University, where 85% of these classes are taught in Afrikaans. Cape Town has the English speaking University. We go into a Dutch Reform Church. Stark white outside with a black thatched roof. Inside we find a beautiful pulpit carved out of stink wood, enveloped by greeny turquoise walls, and plain wood pews. This area is where the Boer influence is heaviest.

University girls live in separate buildings from the boys. From the windows of the girl's dorm a cord hangs, the boys pull the cord which rings a bell. The girls come to the window and the boys ask them out

Dutch Reform Church

on dates. On Sunday the boys wear a black suit, the girls wear long dresses, and gloves, and a hat to go to church. Everyone we see is very well dressed - girls in fashionable skirts.

The campus is immaculate. We take a short, picturesque drive on to Boschendal winery, where we have lunch. Once again a 5 course meal of curried soup, poached yellowtail snapper, pork roast, chicken, cold cuts, smoked mackerel, , veggies galore, delicious variety of desserts, cheese (all made on the property), coffee, and dry white wine. A very relaxing 2 hour lunch and a $7.00 bottle of Boschendal.

We stop at Lanzerac Hotel, where people stay who want to be out of Cape Town. A country inn, very close to Stellenbosch, with good food, a lovely swimming pool, and a pleasant country flavor. We drive on to Paarl, where there is a monument to the Afrikaans language. There are four pillars. From left to right the pillars represent the languages spoken to make Afrikaans. Flemish was the most used (so the tallest pillar), then German, then French Huguenots, and then in the middle of the steps, the smallest pillar represents the Malaysians.

1987

Walking up the steps you go through a tunnel, which takes you to the highest pillar, 186'. It represents the 4 years it took for the language, Afrikaans, to catch on in Parliament, 1914-1918. There is a small waterfall representing the fountain of youth. The last pillar on the right represents the Voortreckers struggle Northward. The three humps of differing sizes represent the various Zulu tribes and their influence in South Africa. The scenery everywhere we go is shockingly beautiful. You see no poverty in any of the country towns. Paarl is no exception. Beautiful white stucco houses with black thatched roofs on main street. The gardens and lawns are ultra well manicured. The roads are perfect (not a pothole to be found). Alex tells us so many important facts. One of the things I hear which surprises me the most is, the many people who speak Afrikaans (coloreds and whites) do not speak English. The blacks speak their own tribal language and not Afrikaans or English. Many English speaking people don't speak Afrikaans. The Muslims lead totally separate and segregated lives. They also have a different language. The Muslims even have their own beaches because of their religious belief that women should not be seen - so the women swim in their bui-buis.

The Malaysians also live in a separate community - which is their choice. We visit one of these neighborhoods on a steep hill with cobblestones. It is neat as a pin, and there are many very well to do who live here. There is only one poverty stricken area in Cape Town that we have glimpsed in 2 days of sightseeing. That is a shanty town just outside of Cape Town, where blacks have come to live in order to get work in the city. There have been riots and killings in this shanty town of maybe 100,000 people - among the people themselves. Many people from different tribes live here, and they just can't get along. The teenagers cause the most trouble because they are bored and uneducated.

From everything we have heard and seen, the majority of the people would really like to end Apartheid, which they admit has become an obsolete way of thinking. The problem has been the Dutch (Boer) right wingers who have a strong hold on the National Party. So much of South Africa is farmland - country versus city - and the farmers are all for the National Party because they personally have no Apartheid problem. They have coloreds working for them, who go to school, own their own houses, and make a good wage. This is true of the people who live in Stellenbosch, Boschendal, and Paarl. One tragedy is that South Africa, being surrounded by communist countries, really needs our backing and support; and we are cutting off aid to one of the only democratically run countries in Africa.

As we drive along enjoying this beautiful country scenery, "Wee-Wee" Philip tells us another bit of trivia which I found interesting. The word Transvaal means to cross the murky river or waters. (So you have a Northern Transvaal, Eastern Transvaal, etc.) He also says there are more Mercedes in South Africa than in Germany (do we really believe this?), and there are two kinds of Mercedes made in South Africa that are not even made in Germany. 85% of all gin is made near Cape Town (I might believe this, maybe - Gilbeys, Booth, Beefeaters). A lot of French cognacs are made in South Africa and sold inexpensively. Then they change the labels and send them to France and jack up the price. South Africa supplies electricity to 50% of southern Africa's entire population.

We have dinner at Van Douch Restaurant on our last night in Africa. It is in the Heergreeht Hotel, and very elegant. Blaine and I comment on the very attractive group of blacks sitting at the table next to us, and how the reporters in the United States never talk about the equal treatment of blacks in South Africa. The group turns out to be Archbishop Desmond Tutu and his entourage.

February 25
Brazil - Rio de Janiero / 85°

1987

We're off on a shopping spree first thing Tuesday morning to buy some elephant carvings (about 12 elephants that range from 2" to ¾") and found a Miriam Mekeba tape of Malaika. Blaine goes to the Mt. Nelson for a haircut, and I go to Tutu's Anglican Cathedral at the end of Government Avenue. It is a very old English stone church with beautiful stained glass windows. After church, I walk up Government Avenue to the South African National Gallery, with lots of contemporary, way out, African art.

I wear a comfortable skirt and blouse during the day, and a nice cocktail dress at night. The type you'd wear to the St. Louis Country Club on a Saturday night in summer. The lobby of Mt. Nelson is so retro at night, with a piano bar playing mellow tunes, and people sitting on comfy sofas and chairs talking very British.

Flight on South African Airways, the finest, so clean with wonderful flight attendants. There is a delicious 4 course meal with South African champagne and wine. The flight took 7 hours and 20 minutes, leaving Cape Town at 2 p.m. and arriving in Rio at 5 p.m. Rio time. We went through customs in a jiffy because a green light went on, which meant they didn't want to open our bags. We got a cab and went to the Park Hotel in Ipanema.

Our room faces the ocean. There is a nice pool and restaurant on the roof (23rd floor). We had soup sent to our room and slept through the night. We awakened at 5:30 a.m. to a beautiful sunrise. We took a long morning walk (8 a.m.) along Ipanema, and then took a cab to Copacabana Beach.

I have never seen such beautiful bodies - men and women. The tangas women wear, all strings, with three triangles, and they fit everyone amazingly well. The Brazilians are really a fun loving group of people. Always singing and laughing. Not a bit of serious work gets done. Blaine and I went to a tourist trap the night of the 26th called El Platforma. We watched a floor show of Watusi Dancers and South

1987

Beautiful sunbathers

It's Carnival time in Rio!

Americans dancing the Samba, all wearing very elaborate costumes.

The next day we went to H. Sterns Headquarters and took a tour of the gem factory, learning how they find, cut, polish, and design jewelry. Blaine bought Riley a tourmaline ring, Andrea a pair of Citrine earrings, and a necklace made of multicolored gemstones for me, gorgeous! We have a car and a guide named Amy, who is 25 and speaks halting English, to drive us up a windy mountain road to the top to see Christo, a huge stone sculpture of Christ. We then drove down along the ocean, where the surfers play, and then on to the cable car at Sugarloaf Mountain. We enjoyed a cocktail and watched the sun set over Rio, and then all the lights go on around the city. Such a fantastic place. Rugged hills, green lush foliage, white sandy beaches, clear blue water - no seaweed. Lots of condos, hotels, houses (not so pretty) and thousands of cars and tunnels. 16 million people live in the city.

We have an excellent dinner at El Pescador, where we hear Spanish guitar music and see Flamenco dancers. Amy picked us up after dinner and took us to Chicos, near our hotel in Ipanema. It is packed; very good Brazilian music, singer, piano, and bass. They measure the drinks in these restaurants and bars by putting a tape measure on the side of the bottle and then billing you for the amount you drink. They leave a bottle and ice at the table so you can serve yourself. Everyone is very gay as carnival starts tomorrow. When we get back to the hotel, the lobby is full of revelers. And now it is time to go home. Early non-stop flight from Rio to New York, and then a quick flight to Philly. Rainbow cab was waiting for us at the airport. And now, back to reality.

- 1989 -

Morocco, Kenya, Tanzania, & Rwanda

January 21
Chadd's Ford to Morocco

Left Pond House at 1:00 p.m. to drive to JFK Airport where we are to catch Royal Air Maroc to Casablanca at 7:30 p.m. John Winther, our house-sitter, is at the house to say goodbye and to stay with our sheep, donkeys, and dogs. Arrived NY -- no hitches -- good driver from Escort Limo -- arrive with 3 ½ hours to spare. RAM left on time -- we are in tourist class so I can stretch out and sleep. Good dinner but no vodka! Arrived Casablanca on the dot 7:10 a.m. and caught the next flight out to Agadir at 8:45.

January 22
Taroudant
75° Sunny, 45°- 50° at Night With a Full Moon

Arrived Agadir at 9:30 a.m. Large 727 jet with only 20 people on board and the only plane in the Agadir airport. Customs a breeze as I am speaking my best French. Brahim, our driver, with his Mercedes, is waiting for us. Easy 1 ½ hour drive to Taroudant on good roads. Gazelle D'or, our hotel, is very charming and we immediately order some vodka because our room has everything else but. They brought us a bottle of Stoly. It costs $112 (versus $9 in U.S.) Vodka is obviously not a major item in the life of the these Muslims. We have a very private bungalow with a big king size bed and fireplace in the corner. Very quiet, romantic, many birds, flowers, and glorious weather.

1989

Said, our valet, lays the fire and starts it every afternoon when the sun goes down. After a long afternoon nap, went to town with our driver Brahim and our guide — Moustapha. Moustapha showed us the different souks and helped us bargain. Went to Hassan Amis souk. Full of kaftans and beautiful rugs. After much discussion (all in French) and displaying of carpets, he brought out mint tea for us all to drink. It is a mixture of mint leaves, tea, and absynthe. One glass is pretty

Moustapha and Susan in Taroudant Agadir, Morocco

good - but plenty. Back to Gazelle D'or for dinner. Jacket and tie for BTP. Silk skirt and sweater for me. Even though this is a resort and we are south, people wear dark clothes because it is January and gets quite cold (45°) at night.

January 23

Brahim and Moustapha picked us up the next morning at 10:00 a.m. We drove out to the country and visited an orange plantation (3,000 trees) belonging to our guide's aunt and uncle. After diddle-dawdling around making polite conversation and eating oranges from the trees, we were asked in for mint tea. We went to the parlor where you sit on the floor on goat skins which are placed on beautiful Kilim rugs, surrounded by large pillows to rest your elbows or back. And of course, you take your shoes off before entering this room. No woman is allowed to be seen. Moustapha brought in the tea and the

Blaine and Brahim sitting on goat skins placed on beautiful Killan rugs

owner joined us. They both have on djillabas and the owner is barefoot. BTP is welcomed to look around the house and then the women came out to shake our hands but they cannot show their faces to local Muslims. The house is white stucco on the outside -- very plain -- but inside is a beautiful atrium with rooms all around with lovely tiled pillars in the middle. They had a t.v. but I'm not sure there were any plumbing facilities. We then drove to another village which would have been impossible to find without Moustapha. No sign. You turn off the main road and go for about 10 minutes on a dirt road along a windy path lined with olive trees and acacia thorned hedge fence. Then out of the blue you come across the village. All red stucco walls -- no cars -- not a car -- few people -- more children than adults. The women (through some kind of inner sanctum telepathy) come outside their doors to say hi to Moustapha. The children follow us down the street. It is very quiet as we walk along the narrow little streets. No men around except 1 or 2 old men who ask that we come in for mint tea. Blaine and I were going to throw up if we had anymore mint tea -- so thank God Moustapha said no.

1989

We went from the village to the main bazaar. I bought a stone sculpture of a mandolin player. Blaine bought a kaftan for me and a leather belt. Hassan wanted us desperately to buy a rug -- but we resisted. Some of the only contact these shopkeepers have with the outside world is bargaining their wares. It is a social thing to do and they almost beg you to bargain so they can talk with you. Bargaining lasts between 15 minutes for a little item to about 1 hour if you are buying more than one thing or something large. Took a look around Palais Salem. The only good hotel in town. It was built about 170 years ago for the pasha -- or mayor -- of Taroudant and is very lovely. Lots of water and plants inside the high outer walls of the Palais. Nice swimming pool and comfy looking bar where you sit on the floor surrounded by large pillows.

Lunch back at Gazelle D'or around the pool and then back to the room for a siesta. The afternoon takes us on a horseback ride across the wild countryside. I must be getting nuts in my old age -- I rode a white, Arabian stallion with an English saddle. Terrified! Just Blaine, the guide, and me. I trailed the two of them and, of course, my horse

White Arabian - a wild stallion ride through remote villages

would go galloping away just to try to catch up with them. There's nothing to hold onto on an English saddle -- I had my camera around my neck, my sunglasses kept falling off because I was sweating so much, my feet kept coming out of the stirrups and all the while we are galloping (not cantering) across the wild countryside ostensibly having a wonderful time. We went through three different villages in the middle of nowhere -- out of the blue. Red stucco walls, a few women who must have a few children, some donkeys. And then when we're not going through these very primitive villages, it is wild bush, some agriculture, lots of olive trees, and everywhere young shepherds and goatherds yelling bon jour and waving. Everyone is so friendly and seemingly so very content with their extremely simple farm life. Needless to say, no plumbing or electricity in any of these villages. Back to Gazelle D'or to bathe and change for dinner. This is definitely off-season. Only a handful of people. No Americans -- some English and Germans. Early to bed by the light and warmth of our fireplace, with sweet dreams of simple, happy, and gentle people.

January 24
Marrakech

Up early for a drive to Marrakech in our comfortable Mercedes. Nobody so far speaks any English so the old Française has really been getting a workout. Surprised myself how quickly the words come back to mind.

Six hour drive from Taroudant across the high Atlas mountain range. Sheer cliffs with a very long drop on one side -- rocky mountain slope on the other -- conducive to rock slides. Snow on upper reaches of mountains. Luckily we are driving on a sunny day and for the critical 1 or 2 hours never saw another moving vehicle on this extremely narrow twisty road. Snow and ice on sides of road, but road surface melted and clear. Villages tucked neatly away in the side of moun-

1989

tain. Red clay buildings blending so beautifully into the landscape. Shepherds and goatherds tending their flocks everywhere. Winding, twisting road going higher and higher over the Tis n Test pass. We were really looking forward to getting to the top of the famous Tiss n Test pass where we could stop for lunch and an aperitif. Finally, after this tortuous but beautiful drive we arrive and there's nothing to this Tiss n Test pass but an old van that has been set in concrete where the wheels should be. I asked in my best French for a toilette but they just laughed and said "mais no, madame." It is now about 3 hours into our safari and this is the first place to stop and stretch.

Finally, after a few more hours of this very scenic drive we came upon a village that has a delightful but touristy French restaurant, Sonlier que Ferme, that is accomodating tons of buses and European tourists who have driven from Marrakech to view the High Atlas. We arrive Marrakech at about 4:00 p.m.

Marrakech

Staying at Es Saadi, penthouse suite #510 overlooking swimming pool and city. Beautiful vase of fresh long stem roses. Terrific service -- not charming, but very Moroccan. We are really beat -- take a nap and then go to La Mamounia for cocktails. Very uptown bar. Black piano player playing a lot of American songs -- many Europeans. Had two vodkas each; $40. This vodka is just not a typical Moroccan drink. The lobby of La Mamounia is big, glitzy, not quite Miami, but looks like it would attract money. A casino is part of the hotel, but we never ventured into that. Blaine might have hit the slot machine jackpot, as he did last year in Atlantic City! In contrast, the Es Saadi bar is full of only Moroccans, and mostly men, and again, no charm at all. Get room service for dinner which is done to perfection with impeccable service. We are too tired for words.

1989

JANUARY 25

Up early to a beautiful day. Hire a guide from Es Saadi to take us through the medina and square. Visit mosque where the sultan is buried with lots of wives, children, and servants. Bargained for a few belts and kaftans. This bargaining is so foreign to us because they are always saying, "Ok, what is your final price?" and they always debate what you say is your final price which is agreeable to everyone and you are meanwhile three souks away and you have to walk back -- everyone all grins and thinking they got the best deal.

The square in Marrakech is world famous, pretty unbelievable, full of locals -- all men -- and has a full range of entertainment. These are storytellers, snake charmers, monkeys doing tricks, acrobats, musicians, people selling hot food that is cooked on charcoal in front of you, stalls selling oranges, nuts, dates, pastries (and flies) and 100's of men standing around waiting for this free entertainment — never women. The acts really get going at about 4:30 p.m. in the afternoon and go on everyday of the year until about 11:00 p.m. at night. Any

The Pharmacist

1989

women that are in the square to shop are Berber women who cover their faces with veils (or Bui Buis) only letting their eyes be seen.

Going to "Fantasia" for dinner. There are about 10 enormous Arabian desert tents and music from at least 8 different tribes. The entrance walk is flanked by armed horseman. Some Berbers, some wearing lots of bangles, some belly dancers, 2 men juggling rifles around like batons, men and women singing. Each different tribe comes to the tent

The Real Estate Agent

where we are seated on cusions on the floor with a large round table of ten people to entertain us all through dinner. Dinner is a five course meal starting with soup -- then a shoulder of lamb which you sort of tear apart with your fingers. Next is Couscous (which is seminole or finely ground wheat) which comes with vegetables, spices, and chicken, followed by huge bowls of fruit for dessert. The Moroccan wine is mediocre, made in Mekres, and called L'Oust elet. The red is a little better than the white and is more rose than red in color.

After dinner all the lights are turned out and the guests stand around a huge empty square which is just red clay. There are a few camels sauntering about and then in the dark out of the blue 10 Tauregs in white flowing robes and turbans come galloping on horseback towards you shouting and shooting off their rifles. This is terribly dramatic. But then you look toward the palace and there is a flood light shining on a man and a woman flying across the sky on a magic carpet. Quite an extravaganza. All terrific fun.

January 26

Next morning up early to do some sightseeing and leave Marrakech. Go over to La Mamounia gardens for a stroll then to Yves St. Laurents' gardens and bright blue house which he no longer owns. Drive by Katowbia Mosque, one of the oldest in the world (dating back to the 12th Century). There are three balls on top of varying sizes which is typical of all mosques, but two are brass and one on top is solid gold.

Once leaving the town of Marrakech it is immediately farmland again and small red clay villages. We arrive at a small town named Beni Mallel for lunch. The hotel is in the middle of nowhere, but has a lovely view overlooking the mountain, shepherds, and pastures. We are the only people in the restaurant and maybe in the hotel. Continuing our safari after a very nice lunch we run into a lot of rain. There are two very major auto accidents along the road which is surprising in that there are so few cars at all along the road. There are always many people walking along the road. People on donkeys with plastic covering to protect them from the rain or the very well off with pochos that cover them as well as their donkeys. The villages everywhere typify the personality and characteristics of the people. Very simple and clean on the outside hiding behind a dense wall -- just as the women hide behind their veils. Of course, no plumbing or electricity anywhere. Arrive in Kinifra almost at dark. Rain turned to sleet. Very cold. We have only hot weather clothes. After much searching and inspecting Hotel de France which is terrible -- we finally find a lovely hotel out of town which is part of the Slam Chain called Mouha ou Hammou Assayani. At the bar it is typically Moroccan, only men. Fairly decent dinner of Tagine de Kifra (meaning cooking pottery of special meatballs with fried egg). The electricity is only in the bedroom (and that only until 3:00 a.m.), in the bar and in the restaurant. The main lobby, and sitting area have no electricity and at 30° it is really frigid.

1989

January 27

Awaken to a clear, sunny, freezing cold day. Crisp. Clear, and lots of snow. Drive through the Cedar Forests near Azrou. At least 4" of snow. We are the only car going through the forest. It is pristine with huge cedar trees 100's of feet tall, no houses, and everything white with snow. After leaving the forest and getting back on the main road, all the children along the road are throwing snowballs. Arrive Ifrane for lunch. This is a resort town that is fairly empty now in the middle of winter. Lovely Swiss looking chalets which are rentable in the summer. Beautiful lake which is used for swimming and boating in summer. Stop at a typically Moroccan hotel for lunch which turns out to be a four course meal served with the ever present L'Oust elet. Bathrooms are Moroccan and take getting used to, meaning there is only a hole and a place for your 2 feet to stand on either side of the hole.

After a scenic drive through more villages and goatherds along the road, donkeys and camels carrying their loads, we arrive in Fez about 4:00 p.m. Mohammad, our guide, is there to greet us. We go to

Stop along the road near Azrou to throw snow balls

the very famous Moroccan Room at the Palais Jamais for dinner. We stick strictly to Moroccan and have pigeon pie or B'stilla. It is pigeon (bones and all) in puff pastry with powdered sugar and cinnamon on top. Also had Hirira -- a tomato based soup with lamb and chickpeas and deliciously spiced. All this eating done on very, very low sofas with hugely stuffed pillows in a room that looks like a palace with lots of Moroccan tiles in lovely reds and blues and deeply plushed Moroccan carpets. In the background is soft melodic Moroccan music and a belly dancer keeping marvelous time to the music with her bare feet and veiled body movements. There are only three tables of diners this evening which is Saturday night. Once again, we get the feeling that we are really in Morocco in the off season.

January 28
Fez

Mohammad picks us up at 9:30 a.m. for a tour of the Medina. No cars allowed inside the old town as the streets are only 3' to 6' wide. There are lots of donkeys like Calhoun, my miniature Sicilian donkey, with 300 pound loads. When two donkeys meet loaded down, it really causes an altercation because there is not enough room for the two to pass so one donkey has to turn around which is a huge feat with the load on his back. Cobblestone walks, a variety of peculiar smells, women in bui buis and men in gonerales or djellebas, men urinating in the street, children begging, everyone with something to sell. The tannery is especially odiferous and as antiquated as it was 100's of years ago. There is

A very overloaded donkey

a mixture of lime, pigeon droppings, and water to clean the hides. Men are standing in this with bare legs lifting the hides up and down like wash. There are 1,000's of horns in 6 foot piles. Some people are scraping wool off either sheep or goat hide. And on all the walls you see hanging hides drying in the sun.

We walk through a maze of streets dodging donkeys and people and come to the medersa or Koran school, then on to the old mosques which are also found in the medina. There are shoes outside the mosque doors and people inside meditating on beautiful carpets in lovely tiled rooms. Blaine hit the nail on the head when he says Jesus could be walking through medina this day and no one would bat an eye as the look is no different from 1,989 years ago. The tools used are still so primitive. The forger just has a hot oven, the knife sharpener has a wet wheel that he turns with his foot. The metal workers hammer their wares with quick ticks. There are soap makers, silversmiths, pottery makers, tool makers, shoemakers, dress makers, vegetable vendors, fruit vendors, meat and poultry vendors often you see 6-8 live chickens being carried by their feet through the streets. Mohammad takes us to a carpet souk where, of course, we have mint tea and look at 100's of rugs. Prices are very unreasonable ranging from $800-$1,000 for rugs about 6' - 9'. After our mint tea and many regrets we finally get out. Buy a few kaftans after much haggling and then we are led to another rug souk and have more mint tea. Luckily, Blaine and I both like one rug that is not too big. It is an antique Berber rug with the natural dyes of saffron, indigo, and henna. After much haggling, several cups of mint tea, and

After one too many mint teas, we bought the rug.

wrapped in huge rugs to ward off the chill, Blaine bargained them down to a mere $250. Walk about 4 miles -- about a 3 hour trek. Back to Palais Jamais for lunch around the pool and a nap in the sun by the pool. Go to a pottery factory in the afternoon. Young children sitting on the floor in bare feet painting tile and pottery.

Please! No more mint tea! -- Fez, Morocco

January 29-30

Leave Palais Jamais, at the ungodly hour of 5:00 a.m. for the drive to Casablanca. Coffee break at Meknes and arrive Casa airport with hours to kill before our 12:45 flight to Cairo. RAM again, arriving Cairo 7:30 p.m. and then have a five hour wait for Egyptian Air to Nairobi. Big mistake! We did not send our bags through to Nairobi from Casablanca -- so they took our passports and tickets and we could get no one who spoke English to retrieve our bags from luggage claim (which was off-limits to transients -- guarded by soldiers with automatic rifles) and get them ticketed to the Air Egypt flight. Blaine has all the gendarmes, RAM personnel, Air Egypt personnel, ticket agents all in an uproar -- but it all finally worked out and we spent our day at the Air Egypt lounge where we meet up with Tyke, Jane, and Missy Miller. Left Cairo at 12:30 a.m. -- arrived Nairobi 6:30 a.m. on the dot! We had been travelling for 26 straight hours.

NAIROBI, KENYA

Arrive Norfolk and have room #60. John Fletcher and Dave Richards have met us at the airport and everything has gone very smoothly. The Millers are on the same flight so we go in tandem to the hotel. Have a great lunch on our favorite terrace of the Norfolk with Laird and Peg Stabler (who arrived in Nairobi on a British American Airways flight from London just an hour or so after us). Cocktails with Mark Stanley-Price (African head of A.W.F.) on the terrace, for a fascinating update on poaching, etc., and dinner that night at the Tamarind with famous huge Mangrove crabs, not to be confused with the Tamarind Dhow we went to for dinner in Mombassa.

Courtyard at the Norfolk Hotel — Donnie, Blaine, and Susie Ross

January 31

Awaken to a beautiful sunny day with the sounds of African birds -- ring necked dove, fishers lovebirds, Ross' Turacos -- singing loudly from the birdcage at the Norfolk courtyard. Lunch on the Lord Delamere terrace with Donnie and Susie Ross who have just arrived, the Stablers, the Millers, and Helen de Butts, who uses a cane and has a limp but is in great spirits. (Helen was badly gored and broken up by a rhino during our last visit to Nairobi; has had numerous operations since).

Afternoon spent at Sue Woods' bead factory, which has grown to 80 working women and a large new building, but they are still making the famous Kazuri jewelry. Next stop Karen Blixen Museum and then to Daphane Sheldrick's orphanage. She now has three elephants, one only three months old and no taller than the top of my thigh, two rhinos (one is two years old Sam -- the other is the year old baby of the mother rhino we see later in the Mara) and two oryx. Dinner in Grill Room at the Norfolk. One of our favorite spots. Champagne and birthday cake as we are celebrating Jane's birthday. The piano player is the same -- we have him play all our favorites, including Malaika about 100 times. As usual, close up the bar with Jane, Susie, and me singing around the piano.

Kazuri Bead Factory Worker

Sam, a black rhino

1989

FEBRUARY 1
TANZANIA

Safari day! John and Dave have driven on to Tanzania and we catch Safariair with a very attractive woman pilot at the controls. Arrive -- no hitches at Killy Airport -- at Ngere Sero in time for lunch. Our first bird walk in the afternoon where we saw Colobus monkeys very clearly playing in the trees. Babies clinging to mothers, long white tails dangling, and a few exotic birds including silvery cheeked hornbill. Met Mike Leach and his wife who have really put this little jewel of a place together, especially the living room where we have after dinner coffee on wall benches with lots of pillows and a roaring fire and very mellow lighting, and a view through the open arch of majestic snow-capped Mt. Kilimanjaro.

FEBRUARY 2

Up and early for a long drive to the Ngorongoro Crater. Make a short stop in Arusha. Bought a wonderful (genuine) Moconde carving of a sitting giraffe made of one piece of ebony ($140).

Lunch at Gibbs Farm which is another little gem of a place and then on to the crater tent site which is dynamite. We are perched right on the edge of the crater overlooking the soda lake, the game, the birds, and the acacias. We have a lovely breeze and a golden sunset.

FEBRUARY 3

Up and gone by 6:30 a.m. to make the dicey trek to the bottom of the crater as early as possible. See seven rhinos (two with extremely long horns), elephant with very long tusks, hippo wallowing, lions nuzzling, scratching, yawning, and sleeping, tommies marking their territory -- wildebeest having babies, hartebeest, ostrich showing off, kites eating part of our lunch, vervets eating the plums from lunch, and, of course, the ubiquitous birds. We have the crater to ourselves because we are down so early -- what a difference an early morning start makes. We picnic on top of a hill overlooking a lot of the crater. I am sitting on a small rock about twenty feet from the land cruiser and everyone else. John says -- "Watch your sandwich, the kites are around." So I no sooner protect my sandwich with my hand than a large kite comes swooping down. Knocks me off the rock with a swoosh of his wings and grabs my sandwich in his claws. I am completely unstrung, undone, and terrified. Leaping to my feet, I burst into a fit of frightened tears. As if the crater isn't exciting enough without this.

So much fun in the crater -- so much to see. It's about 100 square miles so there is tremendous diversity in the wild life. We have seen a baby wildebeest only minutes old -- umbilical cord dangling. Black and wet with the placenta still coming out of the back of the mother. It has a hard time standing. It wobbles and falls and keeps searching for its mother's milk. And the rhino we see have huge horns -- and are grazing seemingly without a care in the world. Noel, the baby we saw two years ago, is still with her mother and growing nicely. And then at the end of our crater stay we see the vervets. Dave has saved a couple of plums from lunch. The monkeys go ape (so to speak) over our plums, climbing all over the land cruiser and even reaching in on the dashboard to grab one. There must be ten or twelve around us at one time. The most aggressive ones are the mothers who are carrying around their babies, hanging on to their mothers' bellies. After this intriguing picture taking foray we head back to camp up

Vervet monkey and baby looking for a handout

the treacherous wall (Susie holds her hands over her eyes and won't talk or look) and another glorious evening around the campfire and cocktails and exaggerated discussions about our spectacular day.

February 4

Leave at dawn for Olduvai. Have a very nice concise lecture by Peter (who speaks English with a Chinese accent). Then off to Ndutu and the Serengeti. Find a lovely picnic spot in the shade of a big acacia tree with giraffe eyeballing us from about ¼ mile away. Look at an exceptionally large female cheetah who is on a stalk, but no time to really follow her and we're off again to our Ndutu campsite. Run into the famous shifting black sand along the way. It looks identical to our view of it two years ago -- but has obviously moved a bit. Study the superb dung beetle who is tirelessly pushing his/her little dung ball across the plains. Stop at Naabi Hill to get our permit and then we're off to Lake Lagadja and our campsite. What a grand spot. Our tents overlook the soda lake and the territory of King Lion and his pride. We can hear him roar at night just below us. Early to bed after a magnificent dinner led by Sylvester and his staff.

February 5

Of course, we are up again at 5:50 a.m. and out on the plains by 6:30 a.m. just minutes from the tents. The migration is all around us. The panorama is unreal! In every direction for 360° you can see wildebeest, jackal, zebra, Thompson gazelle, Grants gazelle, hyena, and vultures. The vultures don't fly until about 9:00 a.m. and the sun has dried their sizable wing feathers. But we are looking for kills without the help of our feathered friends and find one within fifteen seconds. A hyena is running after a baby Tommie. The mother and father gazelle are frantic -- the chase is on. Back and forth darting and dodging but after only seven to ten seconds the hyena grabs the baby and liter-

Front Row: Susie Ross and Susan
Back Row: Tyke, Jane, Peg Stabler, Laird, Blaine, and Donnie Ross

ally chews and swallows every morsel of her in about three minutes. The bones, head, and body are all consumed by this one hyena. The mother and father run around frantically for a few more minutes and then go back to their group to graze and grieve. Another cycle of life and death has happened in the Serengeti.

Not many minutes go by as we drive cross country that we find another kill. This time it's a large, full-grown zebra. The kill is only minutes old and the vultures are tearing out the eyes and eating away at the stomach. There must be fifty or more birds hanging around for a nibble or two. Lappet faced vultures, two bataleur eagles, some Marabou stork. They are all jumping around and squabbling with each other, making raucous noises with wings flapping and throat calls. Donnie and Dave very bravely decide it's safe to leave their land cruiser and do the Serengeti crawl and get a good video and better audio of the kill. They get within ten feet of the action with the vultures literally ignoring them. Then with a frantic warning of an approaching hyena, they bound back to the land cruiser.

We are just getting over this zebra kill and enjoying the scenery when we come upon a third kill. This time a wildebeest. There is a hyena devouring the tasty insides of the wildebeest and vultures on the periphery hopping around, squawking, hissing, and eating everything the hyena leaves. Then we're off across the plains again. Tyke spies a premature wildebeest baby that is still breathing but has the placenta still around it. It's obviously very premature and perhaps the wildebeest kill we saw was the mother as both animals were found not far from each other. This baby gnu will be a tasty treat for some animal today.

Our late afternoon run takes us down to Lake Lagadja for a quick look for our lions that were here two years ago. We find three of them. One male and one female who are in a courting stage. We see him mount her after a few minutes of foreplay -- a few licks around the neck and then the copulating lasts for about one minute. They are oblivious of their very attentive audience. From our astute observations we feel they are on their third and final day of mating. We have seen him mount her three times, each time forty-five minutes apart. A male lion is retromingent -- but in copulation he directs his penis forward.

Back to camp for drinks and dinner after a superb #10 day. It's extraordinary to think of all that has happened here on the savannah between 5:30 a.m. this morning and 10:00 p.m. tonight. And the amazing thing is it happens day in and day out, year after year with no timeouts for Christmas or the 4th of July.

February 6
Serengeti

It looks like rain this morning so we decide to go to Seronera to search for chui (leopard). It takes about one hour from Naabi Hill to Seronera so we go as usual across country through the migration. The noises are really grand with wildebeest snorting and zebra braying. As fortune is on our side, we run into a pack of wild dogs. (Dave thinks they should be called Hunting Dogs) who are giving the wildebeests fits. Which is precisely how we found them as we looked through our binoculars at the gnus running helter skelter and then followed that disorderly conduct until we saw the dogs. There are seven dogs seemingly in peak condition. (Most of them had died out by some strange malady, probably rabies, when we were here last). There is a male leader and two of them are collared. They are compactly built but have the tell tail bushy tail and large white spots on dark spots and not such long legs as the ones we saw in South Africa. We followed behind them for over three kilometers (1.8 miles), at about 20 MPH. That's quite a delicate maneuver when you are dodging warthog holes and circumnavigating hyena dens, all of which are well camouflaged by long tufts of grass. Finally, after much discussion via CB with the other land cruiser, we all decide we are wasting time and that we are not going to witness a kill -- so we're off again and immediately run into a pair of cheetah (duma) just on the other side of Naabi. Then shortly after glassing the cheetah and their movements we come across a pair of lovable lions who we feel are about to mate -- but six mini-buses come up which is just too much competition to view this spectacle so we take off again. We eventually get to Seronera after much oohing and aahing over red bishops and yellow longclaws, baboons, and lizards, weavers' nests, and termite mounds, and try a path where we hope some leopard is resting in a tree. After going over and through some very rutty, muddy trails, we finally find a mother and two cubs frolicking in a tree. The mother looks trés fatigué, but the kids are having a ball climbing the tree, jumping all over mom, falling to the ground and climbing up again. We are very close and can get a real feeling for this little family of leopards.

A quick trip to Seronera Lodge before returning. It is built with enormous architectural imagination right out of the kopjes. While we're scouting out the place, Dave is watching the car. And three baboons jump down through the open hatch and play havoc inside the vehicle while Dave is sitting in the driver's seat. He is a bit unnerved by their nerve and the audacity of these little devils. They steal our very favorite biscuits and are sitting on top of the flagpole eating our food when we come out of the lodge. We are lucky -- Dave could have been badly bitten.

There has obviously been a huge storm in Ndutu while we've been gone and the roads are barely passable. It's a bit like hydroplaning to our campsite. There are a couple of feet of water where the road is supposed to be and like boating on the Chesapeake, we leave a huge wake as we wind our way down the path. At times the water is splashing so much that we feel we are in a tunnel of water. All the birds and animals have gone into hiding. Our tents are soaked. My two sweaters are wringing wet and hanging from the tent poles to dry. All of our clothes are damp and the beds and blankets a bit moist. I'm afraid our tents were set up in an arroyo and when it rained they were swamped. The shower room and loo are total puddles. Sylvester's crew has done their best to keep the tents livable under such adverse conditions. Ah well, it's all part of safari. The staff light a huge fire, and we all huddle together and get warm. How the cook has managed to get our dinner cooked with all the rain is a real believe it or not.

FEBRUARY 7

Wake up to a very cloudy day. We're a little nervous about the road conditions but decide to brave it and leave camp. The road is really bad news -- just about washed away. Well, you can't waste a minute on safari, so we continue albeit at a very slow pace. Eventually manage to get to the plains -- there are far fewer animals. The migration has really moved on, so we head on across country in search.

Wouldn't you know, we land kerplop in a huge warthog or aardvark hole right down to the left fender. The land cruiser is really perched at a precarious angle. We call John on the CB for help and after much jacking up and putting the spare tire under the belly of the car for support, and shoveling dirt behind that, and lots of free advice from all the men, John at last tows Dave out of the hole amid much black smoke and loud cheering. We decide after this episode and the lack of wildlife nearby to call it a morning and limp back to camp.

Catch up on some chores, repack the old duffel, air out some clothes, generally have a lazy day and then go out with Dave. Susie is the only brave soul who also wants to go out. We sight some fabulous birds, including the purple grenadier, spotted fly catcher, black and white cuckoo, scarlet chested sunbird, slurping frogs, two slinking hyena, and then the magnificent black maned lion. It is about 6:30 p.m. and time for him to wake up. Dave plays his hyena tape which hurries things along. Simba roars and then begins to walk around. He marks the shrubs with a retromingent squirt and then he does his flemming look which is curling the upper lip trying to pick up the female scent. He is alone, magnificently grand, and then roars again. Then he walks

A lone male lion in the Serengeti

1989

not ten feet from our land cruiser and lets out six of the loudest belly roars you have ever heard. What an awesome experience. Susie is still talking about it. Everything after that will most certainly be anti-climatic.

February 8
Kenya

Awaken at 5:30 a.m. (again) for a very early trip to Arusha and then a flight up to Kenya. We are really nervous after all the rains that the Ngorongoro pass will be impassable. We are off at 6:15 a.m. for our eight hour drive, and sure enough the roads are really bad. The rains have washed most of the topsoil away leaving spine jarring rocks and ruts that look like canyons that we have to navigate. We stop at 8:00 a.m. for a scrumptious fried egg breakfast and to stretch our legs, but when we open the boxes the staff has neglected to pack any coffee, any breakfast food, or any juice. We have instead rotten ham, smelly salami, hard boiled eggs, 1 avocado, a couple of tomatoes, and some bread. Groan -- but we won't see food again until we arrive in Arusha at about 2:30 p.m., so we grin and bear it. Oh well, it is a lovely sight on top of a hill overlooking the entire Ngorongoro Valley. Off again with stops at the Manyara village shops and MOT WA MBU (our favorite Masai village) where I bought several nice ebony carvings for $1.50 each. Finally reach Arusha and Ker & Downey Headquarters, at a coffee plantation on the outskirts after a mere eight hour, bone jarring, hair raising, ear deafening, all too miserable trip. Have a second incredible lunch of rotten ham, salami, spam, etc, etc, etc, during which we experience one of the worst thunderstorms and heaviest rains you can ever imagine.

Catch the charter flight at 5:00 p.m. with an excellent view of snow capped Mt. Kilimanjaro from the air. Arrive at Giraffe Manor outside Nairobi at 6:30 p.m. What a port in the storm after a thoroughly miserable day. The house is charming. Gothic stone with magnificent paneling in the large front hall, dining room, and den. We are lucky enough to get a very nice room overlooking the front lawn where giraffe frolic. Dinner is superb. Penny and Brian, who are running Giraffe Manor, treat us to an excellent meal with beautiful china, crystal, and candle light. Needless to say, we were really ready for this comfort and really appreciate it. I can't wait to get to bed so I can wake up to Buttercup -- a young giraffe and Betty June's baby.

FEBRUARY 9

One of the staff goes and rattles a few alfalfa chips and Buttercup follows him right to the breakfast room. She sticks her head in the window and we all feed her. She does indeed give me a big slurpy 18" long tongue kiss. I have never been so happy in my life! What a treat and how incredibly majestic and tall these very gentle giant animals are. After a leisurely morning, which we all needed, and a very long bath and hair wash in my 6 ½' long bathtub and a scrumptious cheese soufflé lunch, we're off to Lewa Downs. Arrive by charter flight and

A Kiss at Breakfast from Buttercup

a bumpy forty minute trip in time for the afternoon game run. See a couple of nice herds of elephants and stay out late enough to turn the spot light on and catch the bright red eyes of the bush baby. It is our first night with the Kenya staff and Kenya tents, and oh my, what a difference! Little things mean a lot. The weather here is a little bit of perfection. Quite warm up to the 90's in the heat of the day and 55ish at night. Blue cloudless days and star filled nights.

FEBRUARY 10

We awaken early for a trip to Samburu. It is about one hour away. Samburu topography is different from Lewa. More like New Mexico -- white clay, dry mud, and low sagebrush, acacia trees, and the unusual Duom Palm which is the only palm tree in the world with limbs that go out from a central trunk. We take a circuitous route to the Awasha Neru River where we see a few elephants at a distance and a few crocs fast asleep.

Just to digress a bit, every evening someone has given a lecture on an animal. I did the giraffe, Tyke the hyena, Laird the baboon. So when we see these animals, they are more meaningful to us. This is really true of the baboon, which is a real family minded animal and now much more fun to watch.

After lunch we come across a large bull elephant which is accomodating enough to pose in all directions for about twenty minutes. He even gives us a huge trumpet and a fake charge. He is probably listening for the infrasounds of the female in estrus who could be miles away. Then further down the river we come across a big herd of thirty elephants who all cross in front and behind our land cruiser seemingly oblivious to our presence. It is interesting to look at the tusks of these elephants and tell if they are left or right handed (which you can tell by the tusk which is used the most).

Asleep fairly close to the land cruiser is a 3' monitor lizard, and not far away some gerenuk who stand on their hind legs and nimbly eat the leaves from acacias. They are like lovely ballerinas on toe shoes as they sort of pirouette around the trees. The Grevy zebra is also native to this area and we see many of them as well as Burchell. One difference of these two zebra is that the Grevy male leaves when the female has her baby, leaving only the female Grevy to protect the young. The stallions then return after the baby is a couple of months old. The Burchell, on the other hand, stay together as a family unit. Another interesting bit of trivia is the red and white barbets (which we are seeing a lot of in Samburu) build their nest inside a termite mound. They just dig out a little dirt and sit -- pretty lazy I'd say! The Donaldson Smith sparrow weaver is only found here in Samburu and is fairly dull compared to the vibrantly colored golden breasted starling and the golden pipit that we see here. We get back to our tents at Lewa about 6:00 in time for cocktails and tales of all we've seen.

FEBRUARY 11

6:00 a.m. wake up call. At night it has been so cold Kamani, our tent boy, has put "hotties" in the bed to keep our feet warm. This morning begins with a horseback ride across the countryside. Susie and I aren't too thrilled with the idea -- but we definitely don't want to be left behind -- so we go. It is such a beautiful ride. We ride through a group of about forty giraffe -- maybe more. They barely bat an eye as we saunter past. There are young, teenage, and adult male and female reticulated in every color possible, from light tan to rich coffee. We are sometimes as close as twenty feet to theses quiet wonders. Riding across the plain full of aardvark and warthog holes we also see gerenuk and a herd of eland which really look enormous close up. One of the thrills of being on horseback is the quietness of the countryside, and the added perspectives you experience through your senses. The sights and smells are so much more acute out here on a horse. By 9:00

1989

Riding among the wild giraffe

a.m. we are told to dismount in the middle of nowhere and are told to walk down a path through the woods where, lo and behold, there is a beautiful shady glade and a surprise breakfast awaits us. Bacon, eggs, sausage, hot tomatoes, hot cereal, juice, the best Kenyan coffee I've ever had. There is a little bubbling brook beside some mammoth fig trees with sunlight filtering through creating a very serene and relaxed mood. After breakfast, we go to the Craigs' house where we meet Dehlia who gives us a guided tour around the house and guest quarters. They really have a pad and a half! 45,000 acres of self-sustaining ground.

Very close to camp along the river we come across a herd of elephants. The rest of the group want to return to camp so, Dave, Blaine, and I are alone for some terrific photography. There are well over seventy, maybe 100 elephants. So quiet. We are so close. There are some very young totos (babies), one which can barely reach its mother's knee. She can be no more than one week old. It is such fun seeing their little trunks wavering around in the breeze picking up all the new smells and tastes. We see a couple of nursing totos and some teenagers tussling with wrapped trunks. We see big bulls pushing down huge limbs from trees and a trumpet or two emanate from some of the old ones. We see them nuzzling each other and rubbing themselves on the trunks of trees like a hoochy-coochy dancer. We see at least five with only one tusk and a few with none. We see them splash in the water and grab huge mouthfuls of greens with their trunks. Their trunks are both sensitive and gentle as well as rough and strong. They are increasingly interesting to watch. They are all distinctly different in personality which makes the elephant so fascinating to study. They are incredibly silent as they march past us at a very steady but unhurried pace. This has indeed been a memorable experience.

February 12 - 14

After a quick one hour birdwalk at 6:45 a.m. we have a substantial breakfast and we're gone. 4 ½ hour drive to Nakuru with an intermediate stop at Thompson's Falls where they are selling so many soapstone pieces of sculpture that it's mind boggling. The Nakuru Lodge is actually a very pleasant surprise. Our room (#64) is high up on a hill overlooking the lake. Everything is very lush and green. The bouganvilla is in full bloom and beautiful contrasting colors of deep pink, lavender, and purple. Our afternoon game run is interesting in that it is so different from the usual game park we have seen so far where everything is fairly spread out over many thousands of acres. Here, everything seems fairly compact. We see so many waterbuck just standing by the side of the road it almost seems unhealthy (of course, their musky smell, which is very strong, contributes to this feeling). The best part of the park besides the huge Euphorbia forest are the flamingos. There must be easily 2-3 million of them. Lesser, greater, and in profusion. The pink colors contrast to the gray soda lake and the blue sky is dynamite. Not something easily described.

There is only one male lion in the park which we saw -- but he is apparently quite ferocious (understandably, since he has no female to comfort him) so we didn't get too close or stay too long. On the drive back to the lodge we ran into strings of newly hatched flies. It is the weirdest phenomenon -- but they look like clusters of waterfalls. We drive through patches of hundreds of these strings of fake waterfalls in the forest.

FEBRUARY 14

Up early for our eight hour drive to the Mara. The word "mara" means "spotted" in Swahili. When you look down from a plane, the land is indeed spotted with acacias, so the Masai named it appropriately. Arrive at Keekorok Lodge in time for lunch and a spur of the moment downpour. Buy some very nice jewelry in the back of Vicky's store. It is Valentine's Day so everyone gets a little something. After a hugely bumpy ride due to ruts caused by the rains, we finally arrive at camp at 5:30. We have been traveling for about twelve hours. Our campsite is very near a river where hippos frolic to and fro. We have two Masai men who walk around our tents all night protecting us from the wild animals. We hear a pride of lions not far away - roaring mightily..

FEBRUARY 15

Awaken bright and early with the Southern Cross still very clear in the sky. We have now been on safari for two weeks and have yet to be up after sunrise. The Rosses, Phillipses, and Dave Richards are off to Risinga (an island in Lake Victoria a half a dozen miles from Uganda) for a fishing expedition. The charter plane leaves from Governor's Camp. There has been so much rain we allow one hour and fifteen minutes to get to a place thirty-five minutes away. After fifteen minutes of very rough travel we turn around and head back to camp because the places we could normally cross the river are way too deep for our land cruisers. Finally, we find an opening and really crash, burn, charge, forge, push, slide, and shove our way across the plains. Susie is down on the floor with her arms over her head. What a hair raising experience and it's only 8:30 a.m. Our charter flight takes about forty minutes. We fly very low over lovely agricultural land. This is the natural habitat of the Rothschild giraffe and because of the newly farmed agriculture they have been trans-located. Many Rothschilds have been moved to Giraffe Manor, including Betty June.

When we arrived on our island we are greeted by David, our guide, and get on a very nice 19' boat with canopy and two 60 horsepower outboard motors. There are three rods. Donnie, Blaine, and I take them. I am in the middle and holding my rod in my codpiece in front of me. Donnie and Blaine are acting very nonchalant and leave their rods in their holders. I feel a tug after only ten or fifteen minutes. I have a real whopper on the line. It pulls like hell and then runs with

A 50lb Nile Perch in Lake Victoria

the boat. Then the fish gives a huge leap and jumps out of the water trying to throw the hook. I manage to hold on to him and land him after about fifteen minutes of exhausting work. It's a handsome Nile perch weighing in at fifty pounds and is quite extraordinary to look at. His eye is a huge orange marble that glares brightly in the sunlight. Since they are nocturnal it is very unusual for such a big fish to take the bait at 10:30 a.m. We all have a go with all three of us catching at least one -- except Donnie, who doesn't have as much luck and ends up with a seven pounder. After fishing we get the three perch we have kept and feed the guts (blown up like a balloon) to the fish eagles. They come swooping down not twenty yards from the boat and grab the fresh innards in their talons. The African kites are swooping as well. What a sight!

The island of Risinga and the neighboring islands are inhabited by the Luo tribe. They grow maize on the side of the hill and catch tilapia. Lake Victoria is 26,000 square miles and the water is very fresh and clean. The Nile perch was introduced to the area in the 50's and the record caught is over 500 pounds (but that was netted). The locals don't like the Nile perch because it is foreign to them. They prefer tilapia, but when there was a drought a few years ago and all their crops failed the only thing that kept them from dying was eating Nile perch. On our way back to the pagoda for lunch I am tempted by the beautiful water and jump overboard and swim to shore. The water is so refreshing, smells good, and feels great. After an enjoyable lunch of fresh fish and champagne we have an easy flight back to Governor's Camp.

Before long we are on our afternoon game run. Within fifteen minutes we run into an incredible sight. A mother cheetah has been separated from her two cubs by a female lion. We are almost on top of them and see the cheetah run the lion off. The lion turns and runs back after the cheetah and then she turns in anger and runs back at the lion. Unbelievably the lion gives in and slinks away. This has to be

View of Lake Victoria from the air

a rare occurrence. The cheetah is really perturbed and keeps giving these plaintive moans and sighs. She knows where she has left her cubs and dares not go back. Then over the hill comes twelve more lions. Several at a very quick clip. We are terrified that they will find her cubs. The poor cheetah mom started with five cubs on December 1 and couldn't have settled in at a worse place. Right in the heart of fourteen or fifteen lion territory. She has lost three in the last two weeks. The lions, at least tonight, haven't found the other two. The pride all tustle together on the hill. The males do some flanking -- meaning they push their way between two females and nuzzle. There is a huge male lion on top of the hill looking down on his domain and his children. Then a group of about five lions go at a dead run after the mama cheetah. At least she is fast and outpaces the lions. We stay with the lions until dark, hoping we can ward off the cub killing for another day. (We hear through the Africa grapevine two days later that the cheetah cubs are still alive -- Thank God!). Back to camp for dinner. We now have heard lectures from Susie on the gerenuk and

1989

Blaine on the cheetah. A couple of interesting facts about the cheetah. It is the fastest animal in the world -- clocked at 70 MPH for a short sprint. It does not have retractable claws. It is residential if the food is abundant, but will migrate if not. Cheetah moms care for cubs alone -- no help from the male. She will leave them alone for hours to hunt -- it is not an innate ability for the cubs to hunt. The mother has to teach them this skill.

FEBRUARY 16

Up before sunrise. 5:30 a.m. our boy brings coffee and tea to spur us out of bed. The Ross's, Dave, and Phillips are going to have breakfast out in the wild. The rest of the group will try their luck at fishing. We hope leaving camp so early we will see a kill. There is certainly an abundant supply of cheetah, lion, and leopard to perform for us -- but no luck. So many wonderful sights and sounds. The magical sunrise silhouetting the acacia trees, the sharp sounds of the early birds and the ring necked dove, the sweet smells of flowering acacias. We arrive at a bend in the river where thirty or more wallowing hippos greet us with loud snorting yawns. We have arrived at our breakfast spot where out of the blue Dave presents us with scrambled eggs, bacon, bread, and coffee. We are always on the lookout for cats -- but there is so much more that is interesting. If you're not looking at an antelope or a bird, you're focused on the variety of trees and flowers, or mesmerized by the giraffe, warthog, or zebra. We have seen about fifteen species of antelope, over 250 different birds, three kinds of giraffe. You're learning something new every day and every minute. In this part of the Mara there are hundreds of Topi. It seems as if every mom has a new born calf. The name Topi comes from the Swahili word MTopi which means mud, because of their two toned bodies, the bottom half looks like they have been sitting in mud, the top half a rusty red They also invariably stand on a mound very regal and still as a statue. Driving along after breakfast we come across a nice herd of elephants. The Mara elephant are very relaxed and spread out. A wonderful sign that the poaching is under control here. So many tiny babies -- some just weeks old. A mother elephant is missing part of her trunk (perhaps severed by a poacher's wire snare) and has a baby who really protects her from some of the larger elephants who are not accepting this handicapped elephant. The baby flares out his ears and lifts his very small trunk and trumpets with all his might. The baby is only about knee high -- but oh so brave! The mother compensates by using her foot to help catch the grass in her trunk -- sort of like using chopsticks. She is definitely an outcast and the herd will not accept her or her baby and they move on. We see some of the little totos suckle. The teats are in the front part of the mother -- between her two front feet and the logistics of getting the little trunk out of the way and getting under the mom is a fascinating sight to behold. Return to camp for lunch and a rest.

The weather has been ideal. Cool, crisp mornings and then scorching, sunny mid-afternoons. On our late afternoon game run we see two very well fed male cheetah. Dave plays his hyena tape and they react long enough to get some great pictures. I really don't approve of this tape playing. It's like crying wolf and unfair to the animals. However, it does result in some dynamic pictures. The moon is so bright it lights up the plains. We see two impala males clashing horns. They disturb the entire herd and they all start snorting and pronking (a sort of leap in the air) around in a frenzy. The sounds are fantastic with all the clashing and snorting. Another full, exciting, and action packed day.

FEBRUARY 17

Up at 4:30 a.m. I can't believe I'm doing this, but I'm terribly excited! Going on my first balloon ride. We leave camp at 5:00 a.m. in total darkness. See the Southern Cross and Big Dipper in the sky. With Sangau as our spotter and John driving, we wend our way to Little Governor's Camp.

The tracks and trails are still quite soggy and full of ruts, so it's pretty tough going. See the eyes of so many animals. Lots of tommies and impala. See some hare, night jars, and a spring hare - which resembles a miniature kangaroo. They jump on their hind legs and have a strong tail similar to the kangaroo which give them balance. A lion is silently walking across the Governor's airstrip. With Sangau's great eyes guiding our way we arrive at the camp by 5:45 a.m. and are greeted by a hugely loud trumpet from a very angry, charging bull elephant not fifty yards from us. We can't see him in the dark -- but from the sounds of him I don't want him getting any closer.

We have to wait for the boatman to come take us across the river. He can't get to the boat because the elephant is between him and the boat. He arrives at last, gets in the boat, and there is a huge splash of water. Sounds like a pistol shot. It's a very angry, very huge crocodile that has been shot previously so it is not at all happy with this trespasser. It is only about thirty yards across the river, and the only way everything gets to Little Governor's Camp. From cases of soda and beer, food, people.

We get to our balloon in plenty of time to see all the action. There are burners going in all five balloons that are for the public and there is one solo balloon. That is handled by a man who sits in a frame that looks like a wheelchair and pulls levers to get himself up and down. There are nine passengers in our balloon, and Mark, our pilot. A couple from Dusseldorf, the ex-queen of Italy who was deposed when Mussolini came to power, her granddaughter, Tyke, Laird, Donnie, Blaine, and me. It is a little scary taking off. We have to get a lot of height quickly because there is a forest and we must clear the very tall trees. We look like we're not going to make it. The wind is very strong for 7:00 a.m. but we just do make it, only barely clipping one tree.

We see an elephant silently walking in the forest below us and vultures in the tops of trees parallel to us. Topi and zebra scattered along the plain and a lone male lion sauntering down the road below. We see a galloping hippo, who is moving with amazing speed for such a huge blubber of fat. The wind is so strong we must be going 25 MPH.

It is a little scary taking off.

The trip only takes fifty minutes instead of the usual 1 ½ hours.

We have to crouch way down on the landing. Our backs leaning against the cushioned basket. We have a hell of landing lasting almost five minutes. We are coming in so fast we can't stop. The basket skids on its side, hits a few termite mounds with enormous force almost turning us upside down, goes aloft again, and then skids some more. We are all pretty shaken by the time we finally stop. Mark says he has seldom had such a rough, bumpy landing.

I have a lovely chat with the ex-queen after we all do the pretzel to dislodge ourselves from the balloon. She is 82 years old and says it was a bit rough on her back as she broke it in a plane crash 18 months

1989

ago! Quite an unbelievable gal.

One balloon has really had some trouble. It hit a tree on the way up which really spun the thing around like a top, which we saw from the air. Then the air currents took them away from us to Tanzania. Needless to say, they are very late in joining our breakfast group.

It is now 8:30 a.m. and the first bottle of champagne is about to pop open. It is an Australian champagne called Meisenberg, and delicious. Our group of nine is supposed to be sharing two bottles, but the five of us quickly purloin two more bottles. We all drink a toast to Queenie who then leaves and we snitch a bottle from the very tardy group who have landed in Tanzania. We are all getting totally smashed as we have now consumed three bottles of champagne, had nothing to eat, and it is 9:00 a.m. Well, the Tanzanian group still hasn't arrived so we (Donnie) take their second bottle of champagne, which brings our total to four bottles for the five of us. Ah, breakfast! French toast, bacon, hot coffee, and juice prepared in the middle of the plains (cooked on the balloon burners) with Topi running all around and those awful kites swooping down grabbing scraps of food. They are

Blaine, Tyke, and Laird — just need one more bottle.

more brazen than our worst seagulls.

The ride back to camp is tedious and long. Little Governor's is quite attractive with twenty or thirty permanent tents placed in the shade of acacia trees overlooking a lovely pond with reeds, weavers, malachite kingfishers, and just beyond, an elephant grazing in the grass. Get back to camp and crash. Had never before in my life had a hangover before noon. Sleep soundly for a couple of hours.

Afternoon tea at 4:30 p.m. and then our last game run. Laird is feeling punk -- probably too much champagne and sun. Jane, Tyke, and I go with Dave -- I hoped Blaine would join us but he opts for Peggy, Susie, and Donnie. Dave finds two sleeping cheetah. He plays the hyena tape of which I so disapprove and it awakens them. They look all around for hyena and spot an impala mother and baby about ½ a mile away. They are the two male cheetah we saw lying around yesterday with full bellies. It is even more interesting to notice their maneuvers since Blaine's lecture. They sit now, very alertly, and look all around them. There is a topi between the cheetah and the impala. We see them stalk across the long grass and assume they are after the topi. They are almost hidden as they crouch down in their determined stride. They pick up speed and are now at a low trot. They are halfway to the impala. The topi give warning and the impala begin to move away. The cheetah picks up speed but the impala are now seemingly safe and over the hill with the rest of the herd. All of a sudden, out of nowhere, two jackal cut off the impalas' getaway. The mother is now frantic and runs full tilt back down the hill straight for the cheetah. The cheetah now break into their full 70 MPH dash and cut off the baby from its mom. Within two seconds they have run it down. One of the cheetah was the definite leader and obviously the dominant one. We have now driven our land cruiser to within feet of the kill and see how ferociously and savagely they tear into the impala. We are so close we can hear the crunching of the bones and see the blood oozing

1989

Sibling cheetahs grooming each other after the kill

all over their faces. They gulp down the meat at a furious pace always alert for another encroaching animal. Every few seconds they look up and search the plains, always wary. They leave nothing for the jackals who were so instrumental in the kill. They devour the entire carcass in about twenty minutes and then lick each other's faces clean like pussy cats and settle down with full bellies for a long nap. Such is the way of the African plain. Survival depending solely on what you are able to kill and always watchful not to be killed.

Masai Man

Tonight being our last night, we are having sundowners on the plains under the light of the moon and a myriad of stars. We catch a glimpse of a beautiful African sunset. Donnie entertains us with a couple of Rastus and Mandy stories with the gestures and accents only he can do. Peg reads a poem she has written about night sounds. We are all so happy and mellow and sad as our safari is coming to an end. We stay on the hill overlooking the plains until almost 9:00. No one wants the moment to end. Back to camp for dinner. Our Masai guards are waiting for us by the fire. To see them standing there in the glow of the fire with their colorful red kikois, pangas, spears, and wooden clubs is an awesome but necessary sight.

FEBRUARY 18

Awaken quite late. The sun is up! It's 6:30 a.m. and another glorious day. Have a leisurely breakfast and then depart from Governor's Camp airstrip at 9:00 a.m. An easy charter flight back to Wilson airport in Nairobi. We all do some frantic shopping and then have a final dinner in the Ibis Room at the Norfolk. Delicious grilled prawns. Our favorite piano player is there playing Malaika for us and my favorite song Le Plaisir d'Amour. A last farewell and hug to Dave and Val. John is taking us to the airport tomorrow for our flight to Kigali. The Stablers and Rosses are flying back home.

Baby Mountain Gorilla

Visiting Mountain Gorillas in Rwanda
(From Blaine's Notes)

Objective: To observe at close range (under 20') the almost extinct mountain gorillas (less than 380 left) in their natural habitat.

Place: On the slopes of the Virunga Volcanoes in Rwanda, a beautifully verdant, heavily cultivated, densely populated country in the very center of Africa - west of Tanzania, south of Uganda, and east of Zaire.

Language: Almost exclusively French. Very few people speak English, although the Director of the Mountain Gorilla Project, Craig Sholley, and several of his staff are Americans. The guides who lead you to the gorillas, however, speak no English.

How To Get There: Commercial air service, on a non-daily basis, is available to Kigali - the capital. Air Kenya flies from Nairobi every two or three days; Air Ethiopia runs flights from Addis Ababa, etc.

The gorillas are located in the Park National des Volcans, a mountainous area three hours or so distant from Kigali by car.

Travel within Rwanda from Kigali is by car, and is best handled through an established travel service which will provide an English speaking driver and a 4-wheel drive vehicle. While the principal highway, built by the Chinese, is splendid, you will need the latter to negotiate the twenty or so mile stretch of very rough roads leading from the last town to the gorilla headquarters on the slopes of the volcanoes.

Rwanda Travel Service (RTS) is your best bet. They are highly organized and most efficient - not necessarily African traits. They provide modern vehicles and capable drivers who speak a fair amount of English. They are the oldest and most experienced travel service in Rwanda, and because it is state owned, RTS has a clear inside track. Power-house travel organizations like Abercrombie and Kent (A&K)

for example, have good vehicles and capable drivers also, and certainly are dependable in other parts of Africa, but we saw two different A&K tourist groups turned away because of Parc reservation difficulties. We were told by the locals that was not an infrequent experience for non-Rwandan travel companies, especially for A&K which is trying to buck RTS's early monopoly over the gorilla tourist business. Not surprisingly, RTS's clients do not seem to encounter similar reservation difficulties.

Where To Stay: Kigali has one or more satisfactory hotels (Diplomate, for example) and is close to the only commercial airport, but is not a very picturesque setting and is three hours or so distant from the gorillas.

Ginsenyi, a smaller town on Lake Kivu is prettier and a more interesting place, and has a most comfortable hotel (Meridian). While five hours or so distant from Kigali, many travelers elect to stay in Ginsenyi even though it requires a two hour drive each way to visit the gorillas. The drive through the mountains, and past literally thousands of colorfully dressed natives walking alongside the roads (before dawn!) is very interesting.

Ruhengeri is the closest town to the gorillas - being only twenty or so miles from the headquarters, but the town is not much and the hotel is bare bones adequate and only for the hardy.

For campers, limited facilities are available at Parc headquarters.

Costs: RTC charges approximately $2,500 for a 3 day/3 night stint for a couple, including vehicle, driver, a good room and meals in the best hotels, and Parc reservations for 2 days.

RTS charges approximately $900 for a 3 day/3 night stint for a single person, which includes a room and meals at decent hotels, Parc reservations for only 1 day, and a self driven Suzuki.

Obviously, prices change with itinerary and quality of accomodations. The $2,500 cited is par for a couple, traveling first class. The

$900 cost cited for a single person is on the economy side. If a person is willing to travel with a backpack and sleep out, the cost, of course, would be considerably less.

Length of Stay: Most people reserve two successive days with the gorillas, in case they should fail to meet up with them on the first try. Craig Sholley, Director of Mountain Gorilla Project, says that such failures are unlikely and have not happened half a dozen times since the public visitation of the gorillas commenced, but Rwanda is too far to go to risk success on a single effort. Take out insurance by signing up for a second day. You can always sit out the second day if the first is successful, but the chances are that you will be so excited with your first visit that you will be the first one out of the blocks for the second day.

Because flights to and from Rwanda are not on a daily basis, to get two days with the gorillas might require spending three, or possibly even part of a fourth day, in the country. Charters are available from Kenya which would eliminate such problems, but are expensive unless shared with others.

Volume of Other Tourists: Although it is beautiful country and its people are highly interesting, the gorillas are just about the only tourist attraction in Rwanda. A new park boasting a heavy concentration of beautiful Colobus monkeys is beginning to receive modest attention, but it is quite distant from the Virungas. The only tourists you are likely to encounter will be there to see the gorillas. They will not exceed twenty-four on any given day, because there only four groups of gorillas which may be visited, and strict rules limit the number visiting any one of these groups to six, excluding two guides. (Your visit with the gorillas is limited to one hour). You pretty much have the country and its people to yourself.

Required Physical Condition: In order to protect the gorillas, who have a close kinship with man, each person who visits them must not have any contagious disease or illness. Last year a gorilla died from measles, apparently contracted from humans. If you have a bad cold, you will not be permitted on the trek to visit the gorillas. The guides are charged to be strict with this, but if the English speaking staffers are not around to make sure, they are somewhat lax about it. Respect for highly endangered, almost extinct species, should cause everyone to observe the rule voluntarily and scrupulously.

You should be healthy and in good physical shape for your own protection as well. Trekking after gorillas, which commences at about 8,000 feet, requires considerable exertion in ascending and descending dense jungle over whatever routes the gorilla happened to choose the preceding night. You start off at 7:00 a.m. and, once finding their sign, you follow their meandering course through dense vegetation until you catch up with them. At times - usually in the bamboo - walking is easy and delightful, but in many places the footing is muddy and dangerous, over obstacles and under vines, through almost impenetrable vegetation, with seemingly endless ascents intermixed with equally exertive downhills. Even if the morning is chilly, most people break out in serious sweat within the first half hour, and soon get to puffing like a Baldwin locomotive. There is no guarantee, like in a zoo, that the gorillas will be obliging and be near the Parc perimeter. Some launch points require an hour's walk just to reach the Parc boundary, and finding the gorillas within an hour after entering the jungle of the Parc would call for celebration. Two hours, three hours, or even more, are not uncommon., and don't forget that you have to walk back out - although that can be accomplished over a more direct and less difficult route. You will find it advisable to get in shape for the treks by climbing and descending stairs, or similar exercise, long before leaving the United States.

Weather Prospects: Rwanda's big crop is bananas, and they grow best in a warm, tropical-like, damp climate. Rain, at some point during the trek, if not during all of it, is more likely than not, although it is entirely possible to encounter sunny days. Chances are it will be a bit chilly when you first get up, and also when you arrive at the upper elevations from which the treks commence, but the exertion, if not the thermometer, will warm you up. Little clothing is needed for warmth; perspiration is a great problem.

Travel Clothing: You will not see a coat and tie or fancy dress anywhere in Rwanda. You will see lots of sports shirts, safari clothing, skirts and/or pants. Very informal and casual and comfortable.

Trek Clothing: Full length pants, long sleeved shirts, gloves, fairly rugged hiking shoes, and a brimmed hat are extremely important. Gaiters to protect your legs, or leggings of some sort are highly desirable. A lightweight rain-suit completes the list.

You will need the rain-suit because it nearly always rains. Even if it does not rain, rain-pants worn over your regular pants afford increased protection, and should be worn in any event, unless you wear gaiters.

Nettles are the principal reason you will need so much more armor plate. In case you don't know, nettles are from stinging plants that sometimes grow taller than a person. They have little hairs that can impale you even through clothing. The stings are instantaneous, in micro-dot form, and will probably last for the rest of the day, although on a diminishing basis. The sting starts off with a sensation not unlike when your lab partner in grade school accidently sprayed your arm with an acid solution. People react to the stings differently. Some experience quite a bit of difficulty with them, but they are distinctly unpleasant to almost everyone - except the guides who seem impervious to them.

Also, there are ants which bite like the very dickens. Watch for them on the ground, and try to jump over them or adroitly dance through them. It is uncanny how they latch onto you. Even with your socks pulled over your pants, they will crawl up your leg and bite you half an hour later. They really are fierce little devils.

Therefore, full length trousers, tucked into the tops of your socks, are necessary to ward off the nettles and ants. Gaiters over the pants and socks work best, but rain-suit pants over your regular pants are OK, although perhaps a bit too warm.

Decent footwear is desirable, but not critical. Because it rains a lot, and because much of the terrain is very muddy, water-proofs are preferred. It is sometimes very slippery, so vibram or other gripper soles work best. Ankle height is ample. Heavy mountain climbing boots are not necessary.

Shirts - especially the sleeves, should be densely woven and fairly substantial, in order to provide protection to your arms in warding off vines and nettles. Gloves made of light leather or vinyl (not cotton or wool) afford the most protection against the nettles, and those with gauntlets or wristlets are preferred because they protect your wrists - one of the most vulnerable spots. A brimmed hat will protect your forehead and ears when ducking under the vines and nettles - as you frequently must.

What Do You See? The quest is to find and then observe a "group" of gorillas. There are four accessible groups, each called a different name or by a number for research purposes, (i.e. Suza Group, Group #13, etc.) ranging in size from twenty to fifty members each. The leader of each group is usually a "silverback", a dominant male having silver colored hair on his back, weighing over four hundred pounds. The members of the group travel together as a family, spending a typical day slowly ambling from one good tasting vegetation spot to another, and sleeping at night where their daytime travels happen to end. The guides try to find where the gorillas bedded down for the night, and then follow the vegetation they have mashed down while feeding until catching up with them.

That's when it gets exciting. The guides utter low grunts to signal the gorillas of their approach. Everyone else, absolutely quiet and stooped over so their heads are no higher than the gorillas, very slowly walk toward the group - to within about twenty feet. More often than not, that is when the silverback charges the observers, screaming loudly, teeth bared, and moving like a bullet. The guides have warned that it is just a bluff - don't panic - don't run - keep your head down - don't look him in the eye - appear submissive. It is a very tense, scary moment. The guide's escort carries a rifle, but it is old, wired together, and probably won't fire - no comfort there. But at the very last instance the gentle giant haults his charge, turns on his heel, and moves away with less threatening grunts.

Mountain Gorilla

Then for the next sixty minutes (which pass quicker than a wink) you watch the group feed and scratch and lounge and cavort and swing from vines and play - mamas, babies, old silverback - it is spellbinding. After the silverback's initial test, the gorillas seem totally unconcerned with the presence of humans, and go about their business as if visitors are members of their group. While the guides like to keep a distance of fifteen feet, they cannot control what the gorillas do, and the gorillas can - and often times do - approach literally within touching distance. While observing the Suza Group Susan and I, crouched almost side by side, had the silverback brush right between us. It's scary when it happens, but you simply must steel yourself to stay down, stay motionless, look down, and stay quiet. If one of the babies become curious and starts to approach the visitors, the guides will quickly order everyone to retreat for fear mama will come to the rescue. For most of your visit, however, the gorillas appear so contented, so peaceful, so innocent, so harmless you have to suppress the temptation to speak to them, or pat them, or somehow assure them you come as friends.

Is It Worth It? Once you see the gorillas, you will immediately forget all about the nettles, the ants, your huffing and puffing to get up the mountain, how much the trip costs, etc.

Seeing these awesome, wonderful creatures at close range - in the wild - with nothing between you and them to protect you should they become alarmed and dangerous - having them settle down and accept your presence on their turf - on some sort of kinship basis - is one heck of an experience - one that will remain with you for a very long time - one that you will have a very good feeling about. You will agree that it was well worth it. And then some!

Craig Sholley, the Director, took us up for our first visit. It exceeded any experience we have ever had in Africa. And being guided by Craig was very special. Our visit the next day, also very special, was led by the Parc's official veterinarian, which became sensational (and rarely seen) when two different groups unintentionally encountered

Craig Sholley

each other resulting in a fearful confrontation. Very exciting! And considered by the guides as very dangerous who hurriedly moved us back out of harm's way. Craig, who had been unable to join us the second day, was very disappointed he had missed the event, never having witnessed such a happening in his extensive experience with gorillas.

We will never forget our two gorilla treks in the Virungas!!

- 1993 -

Ecuador

April 7
Chadds Ford / Quito, Ecuador

Left Pond House for 1:00 p.m. flight via American Air for Miami, and then on to Quito. No hitches - but arrived Quito in a rain storm at 8:00 p.m. and flying around the Andes Mountains in the dark is a bit scary. The altitude is 9,280 feet, and leaves one a bit short of breath. My heart seems to be beating two times as fast as normal.

We flew with our tour group, who all look like the typical Nature Conservancy types. As yet, haven't introduced myself to anyone.

Awaken to foggy, foggy day. Went to fitness club in the hotel for a quick aerobic class that was going on at 8-8:30. Hotel Oro Verde very clean, servants very nice, no English - which is OK with me as I have been practicing my Español.

Our airplane to Tarapoa

1993

We arrive at the Air Force Base for our airplane trip to Tarapoa and lo and behold the plane we are supposed to take isn't going to come - so we have to take a C130 cargo plane - one of those camouflaged big things that have no windows - we are leaving 1 ½ hours late and we are not going to Tarapoa but to Lago Agrio. I told Florencia, our tour guide, that I couldn't fly in a plane without windows, so I sat in front with the pilots who let me walk around and look out the windows. I have meneire's disease, so if I can't see the horizon line, my inner ear goes haywire and I lose my balance. I'm sure they would have offered me a chance to fly the plane if I'd given them any inclination.

Well - from here we have a two hour bus ride on the worst roads you have ever laid your eyes on - I thought our potholes were bad - this was sheer mudslides as it has been pouring buckets for two days. We finally got to where the speed boats are docked along the Aguarico River. These fiberglass type boats seat three across on a bench with a wooden plank for a back rest - but there are twelve of us, and they just seat nine plus one in front - Blaine, of course, jumped in the boat immediately and I was left on shore with one other couple. Pancho,

Two-Hour bus ride to where the road ends

our naturalist guide, told me I could sit in front with him. We got on our way at 3:30 - we as yet have not had lunch, but Pancho hands out lunch boxes which have a wonderful variety of sandwiches, bananas, cakes, juice - I am wedged between Pancho and the Indian driver of the boat, with the two barrels of gas on the floor in front of me, and the five gallon cans of gas are at my feet. I can't see over the bow of the boat as the seat is set too low - and we remain like this for three hours - the weather is warm, but very humid and cloudy.

The Amazon

We arrive at the Hotel, which is a Boatel, which is our new destination since being so delayed from the start. It is dark as we arrive. The river is very flooded and the current is very swift - we have been dodging tree limbs and other debris while coming down the Aguarico. Now the Boatel is a welcome sight. They have great ice and Absolut, which is making for a glorious cocktail hour on the third deck, overlooking the great river. Our cabin is on the third deck and very scrunchy. Bunk beds and a couple of pegs to hang clothes, but a very adequate private bath and shower.

Breakfast at 6:30, after a 6:00 a.m. wake-up call. We're on our way by 7:00 a.m. as we have a long haul to get to Imuyu by dusk. This time there are only six people per speed boat - so Blaine and I have a seat to ourselves - Luxury! The day is sunny with a few billowy clouds. Our first stop is an observation tower 45 minutes from the boatel - of course our boat driver had no idea he was supposed to stop, so about ½ hour after we had passed the tower area, we asked in our best Spanish, *where was the 2nd boat?* (2 naturalists were in the second speed boat and none on ours). We ended going up river for an extra ½ hour to get to this tower.

Pancho, the naturalist I was sitting with in the boat yesterday, was taking a nature walk with a Columbian naturalist and two other South

Americans. I tagged along with them. We saw tamarin monkeys, cicadas and their daubs which they call home, wasp nests, monkey ladder vines (liana), many varieties of birds (wood-creepers, puffbacks). There was a flower whose yellow pestal is used to dilate the pupil of the eye. We saw bees with no mandibles or stingers, but they dig into your hair and part the hair strands as they dig deep. They often do this with animals. Pancho had about fifty in his hair, and I could see them working and parting his hair as they dug. We saw a tiny poisonous frog that was brown with bright yellow stripes, and a termite mound that had been knocked down and the insides used by natives. The inside is toxic to ants and insects, so if you burn part of it, it will keep varmints away. We saw bromeliads, flowers, nests, epiphites.

Bees that don't sting

We returned to the boat for the next exciting adventure down the Aguarico River to Sacha Pacha. This camp is set up in the Cuyabeno wildlife reserve. There are thatched huts with bunk beds - but like a motel - one room after another under one roof. The bar and eating area is also thatched and overlooks the Aguarico River, where it takes a sharp turn toward Peru. The scenery is lucious and green. The water is called a whitewater river, but it in fact looks like the muddy Mississippi. Orchids and bromeliads grow from almost all the trees - there is every shade of green imaginable. We arrive at the Imuyu Lake having gone from the Aguarico River to the narrower Lagarta River. The Lagarta River - at the border of Ecuador and Peru - is a blackwater river - the sediment and pH factor are totally different from the white water. We see lots of pink dolphins swimming and blowing. At one spot, Norby, our naturalist guide, says we can swim with them. I had worn my bathing suit so I couldn't wait to jump in. There was one mother and baby who came within about twenty feet of me. Not afraid at all. Blaine asked the guide if there was anything I should be worried about in the water, the guide said only the piranha, but she should be OK, but the electric eels are something else!!!

We get out of the speedboats and transfer to an 8-man dugout canoe. This trip takes us right across the lake to Imuyu Camp. We see a gorgeous sunset, hear howler monkeys, and see macaws and parrots fly by. Imuyu camp is very new - in fact, they are still building a lot of it. We are in a corner room, there are three in a row, and it is set up on a boardwalk about five feet over the water, but the boardwalk has no railings. This is the beginning of the rainy season and already it is very flooded. There is no electricity except one single fluorescent bulb in the living room area that has two hammocks and a couple of wicker, dilapidated love seats. Up in a tower there is a great overlook of the lake, of course there is no ice - but they do offer wine or beer, both are quite warm. I bought a bottle of Chilean white wine, a sauvignon semillon that could be delicious if it were a bit cooler.

Imuyu Camp
Unfinished Resort in the Amazon

The bathroom situation is also quite primitive. There are four toilets all in a row, but you can't put your toilet paper in the toilet, and they leave a little yellow plastic container to put your used toilet paper in. There are four sinks in front of the four toilets. The water looks a little copper color coming out but there is a bottle of purified water for you to use for teeth brushing. There are four showers all together, but just dribbles of cold water.

After taking an antivert for my meneire's disease, to stop me wobbling, I slept pretty well and only got up once in the middle of the night - had to put on shoes and a robe to walk to the bathroom - boardwalks with no rails and five feet over water, and on the way back to the room I got lost and ended up in the kitchen. Finally, after a few wrong turns, I ended up back in our room. After a beautiful starry night, woke up to clouds and heavy humidity. Went on a bird/monkey/nature boat ride right after 7:00 a.m. breakfast. We took two dugouts and went up a feeder river to Imuyu Lake. This was a narrow, blackwater river where at times we had jungle vines and aerial roots in our canoes. Saw probably sixty varieties of birds, some special ones were the red capped cardinal, yellow faced vulture (only found in the Amazon), trojans, and flycatchers. We also saw a large monk saki monkey - quite large, long bushy tail, about the size of a medium baboon. Norby, the naturalist, is very knowledgeable and has told us about what the monkeys and birds eat. We also saw the pygmy marmoset - the smallest monkey in the Amazon (or world). They mate for life and usually have twins.

Returned to camp in time for lunch, and we haven't been back ten minutes when a huge cloud burst opened from the skies - but we were under our thatched roof by ten. There is a bird indigenous to this area of the Amazon called a hoatzin which is in size like a guinea fowl. It is a very primitive bird and has been here since the beginning of time.

After lunch I took a swim in the lake. Norby rowed me out to a floating dock and I swam in the blackwater for about fifteen or twenty minutes. Back in time for a 3:30 canoe trip around the lake. Again many fascinating varieties of birds. The sounds here in the rainforest are even more exciting than Africa, enhanced by the joy of absolutely no artificial noises for many hundreds of miles from us. There are so many frog sounds as well as birds, as well as monkeys. The ugliest sounds are the macaws and parrots who just squawk. But the little wrens and hoatzins have a lovely sound.

The fluorescent light that I'm writing this by is run by solar power. Since we returned this afternoon, they have started putting a guard rail up on the boardwalk, and there is some more thatching being completed, but they have a long way to go. Dinner is pretty good under the circumstances, with either Tang or lemonade to drink (warm). It rains all during the night, which is a lovely sound on the thatching mixed with the peeping of the frogs. I had to go to the bathroom - of course - in the night so had to put on shoes and rain suit. As I got to the bathroom I saw this black glob hopping around - as I got a little closer I saw, to my amazement, it was a huge black bird, luckily there were still some of the workmen sitting up and I asked them to come with me, but in my unnerved state I didn't know the word for bird or bathroom so they were a little hesitant. Finally, one man came and captured the bird in a stall and brought it out to me - very proudly. It was a greater ani, and I'm sure he's just as happy to be free as I am that he's gone. Another trip to the bathroom with my flashlight; I almost went into a stall with a giant spider, literally, the size of a large tarantula - the rainforest is still full of mysteries!

April 11
Imuyu Camp at Imuyu Lake and River

I was really wobbly with a slight meniere's attack in the middle of the night after so much boating and looking through my binoculars as we moved. I couldn't go on the morning boat ride but went back to bed after breakfast and slept until 10:30. Blaine stayed back at camp with me and we took a canoe out ourselves and went up the Imuyu River by ourselves. It was the best part of the whole trip so far. It was so quiet, so much life going on around us. Two scarlet and blue macaws sitting, pruning themselves on a branch, herons and hoatzins, black capped donnacobias, jacanas (which look like kingfishers) which we saw catch a dragonfly and sit and bang his bill on branch to kill the fly and then eat it. Jacanas are quite shy, and when they fly away they turn from brown to a pale yellow.

This morning was truly special. The butterflies all flitted around us. The especially beautiful blue morpho butterfly which is huge - his wings are probably 3" long and the long nosed bat which is perfectly camouflaged until we scared it up and it flies. We have to leave this magic place after lunch. It will take us two days to get back to civilization. This is truly one gem of the Amazon - if you don't mind roughing it a bit. From the huge Kapok trees with their umbrella canopies down to the tiniest ant, there is nature as it has been since the beginning of time.

We leave our blackwater lake by the 25' dugout canoes with eight of us, single file, and a cheque Indian in the bow and stern paddling with small tear shaped paddles. After crossing the lake, we get into our long speed boats which held about eighteen of us and our luggage. The boats are about 40' long but only 5' wide - so pretty tippy. We get back to the whitewater Aguarico River, having left the Lagarta (blackwater) behind. Arrive at Sacha Pacha (which means Jungle World) in time for an icy cold beer (5:00). Our hut here is similar to Imuyu, but smaller in that there are bunk beds and the room is 6' x 6' - so we have about 3' to 4' to move once you get out of bed. There are six pegs to hang your clothes and they give you a towel and soap (same as Imuyu). There is no ice, but the beer is so cold, it is just wonderful. It is made in Columbia. Blaine and I sit outside and have cocktails overlooking the Aguarico. The sunset glows a dusky orange, and there is no place on earth I'd rather be. We travel again tomorrow on our second leg of the trip to Quito, so go to bed early (BTP is in bed at

Dugout Canoes

8:00 - I read by flashlight until 9:30). In the middle of the night I heard a loud crash - sounded like a tree had fallen outside our door. I find out later the man in the room next to us fell out of his upper bunk - luckily when he crashed to the floor he didn't break any bones. He ended up sleeping outside on a cushioned bench at the end of our rooms!!

April 12
Sacha Pacha / Hotel / Quito / Rain - 80°

Wake up call is at 5:45. It's dark - it's rainy but it's warm. We must be on our way by 6:45 as we have a long trek ahead of us. I am writing this in one of the speed boats taking us on the Aguarico from Sacha Pacha. This leg of the trip is two hours. We were given blue ponchos as it is pouring rain and there are no sides on the boat. We are three abreast with a board for a back rest. The scenery is magnificent. Kapok and fig trees majestically reaching for the sky with the lower ciczopra (trees whose leaves resemble sheffelera) reaching into the river. These are interspersed with palm trees, banana bushes, birds of paradise, flowers and passion flowers giving a bright redness to the green background. In the river are islands of shorter bushes, logs and sticks floating everywhere due to all the rain. At times we go over them and create havoc to the motor. Little villages - some large, some just single thatched huts, dot the coastline. The huts are all up about six feet on stilts as there will be over fifteen feet of rainfall before the rainy season ends. Pancho says the time to come here is January when the river is clear and low. You see herons and cayman lining the banks - but it is also much hotter.

After two hours we reached the Hotel Orehlana where we had a quick potty stop and then back for three more hours in our speed boat. The rain is still coming down in torrents. Everyone in the boat - there are nine of us, all asleep, but me, we will be in Tarapoa soon. Wrong! We first have to go to Chiritza where we will then get the bus for Tarapoa. There are so many sticks - so much debris floating down the river I wonder how our motors are going to hold out. I have now finished reading my book "Remains of the Day" - what a GREAT book - so well written - really enjoyed it.

We finally arrive in Chiritza. Pancho did give us a sandwich on the boat at 10:30 - so we are not completely starving. The bus is here! A miracle. We get on it for our 45 minute trip to Tarapoa - such a sight along the road. Pigs everywhere - cows munching grass, children coming home from school - it's 1:30. Laundry hanging on lines at every house. We've decided, 1) they put the wash outside when it rains to wash it and 2) they leave it on the lines because there is no closet space much less anywhere else inside the huts to put these clothes. God knows how many people must be living in these houses.

Arrive in Tarapoa and our air plane is there! Miracle! It is a very comfortable turbo prop that was the Governor of Ohio's as it still has his plaque on the wall and the seal of Ohio on another wall. Arrive in Quito at 3:00. Florenzia is there to meet us. Our bags are there; we get to the Hotel Oro Verde with no problems. Blaine and I have dinner at an old hacienda called El Meson de la Pradera. Had a delicious dinner of mussels and oven grilled shrimp. The local beer is called Club - but when you get it on draft it is called Chub. Bed tonight in a real bed and running water and T.V. is a real luxury.

April 13
Hosteria La Cienega, Cotopaxi / Cool

Awaken feeling relaxed and ready for another safari. Blaine and I have rented a car and driver, Joseph, to take us south along the Pan American highway to Hosteria La Cienega. The scenery is fascinating along the way. Lots of sculpture in and around Quito. Lots of modern - some you can't decipher - some humorous (about six giant, brightly colored eggs with a huge hummingbird, wings spread flying over them - or perhaps trying to sit on them.) Many large statues of military men. There are military bases everywhere. It is mandatory for every boy who turns 18 years old. There are few road signs, lots of roundabouts. Quito is set all around mountains - Cotapaxi is 19,000' and full of snow. We drive on the Pan Am, going 100K's. Our destination, La Cienega, is an old hacienda built in 1580. It is a very charming white stone building, which is 6' thick with a long allé of 400 year old eucalyptus trees.

Blaine and I go on a great horseback ride, only to rival the one in Morocco a few years ago. Our "hombre" who accompanied us was Alberto, who rode a bicycle and carried a switch which he kept using on my horse - at which point my horse would lurch into a gallup - unexpectedly. We went through lots of little villages - people standing on the road to greet us. Everyone wears a hat and the men tip their hat in greeting. Went by the local bull ring and saw some local restaurants and churches. Pigs, cows, all along the road. Dogs run out from every little casa barking at our horses. Came back just before a big cloud

1993

Our "hombre" on a bicycle leading the way

burst. Did lots of galloping and we're really stiff when we dismount. Our room is the master suite (room #7) with lots of windows overlooking both the allé and the flower garden. After a few vodkas, and a lovely dinner, we are off to bed.

José picks us up at 8:30 and we take off for the Saquisele Indian market. We park next to the alfalfa and walk around looking at pigs, cows, calves, donkeys for sale, sheep, goats, horses - what a scene! Only a handful of Americans and 1000's of Indians. José opens the trunk so I can get fresh film - he locks the keys in the trunk. With that we have at least twenty helpers all trying to jack open the windows - others use their keys for our trunk - nothing works. We finally managed to get back into the car by borrowing a stiff wire from the toilet bowl brush man. He didn't want to leave his wire, and was fairly frantic for it back, so I bought seven toilet bowl brush cleaners made out of horsehair to pacify him. They'll make great Christmas presents for the family!

The market is truly a jungle of bodies. All the streets are jammed with shawls, weavings, alpaca sweaters (costing about $15). There are special cotopaxi paintings made of sheep hide stretched and then acrylic paints - very bright. I bought two ($12 each). The people are colorfully dressed. Black skirts for women and bright shawls with felt hats to top it off. This is the province of Cotopaxi and the volcano, which is now snow peaked, is the highest active volcano in the world. Have a leisurely drive back to Quito, looking at the fields of lava boulders and bull farms (estancias) along the way. Stop at Mited del Mundo monument which is on the equator and depicts the life of different Indians in Ecuador. Went to Mare Nostrum for an excellent dinner - espresso and Grand Marnier.

April 15
Peguche, Ibarra, Cotacachi / Hotel La Mirage / 80°

Awaken early to get on our tour bus. Our first stop is Quayasamia Museum. As we drive the West and East Andes are on both sides of the road. We see chalk mines along the road, pigs, cows tied up to graze. We are in the plateau part of the highlands and drop from 9,200' that is Quito to 6,000' - we can see the valley below. Everything in multi-colors of green. Squares of fertile land delineated by rows of eucalyptus bushes or pampas grass. Little villages dot the landscape along the hillsides. Have lunch along the lake at Puertolago Restaurant, and then to Peguche, a weaving town. We stop at one of the weaver's houses where they demonstrated spinning and weaving. The spinning wheel is unique, and since I spin my own wool from my sheep, I tried to do it - very clumsy. Then we went to the wood carving center of Ibarra, a quaint town with cobbled streets situated around a square with a church at one end.

We arrive at La Mirage at 5:30. Blaine and I have a great room (104) which has a sitting room and a fireplace. There are hummingbirds and vermillion fly catchers, frogs croaking, macaws and parrots in a cage screeching. A roaring fire in our bedroom fireplace after dinner takes the chill out of the room and makes for excellent sleeping.

1993

Breakfast outdoors after a two hour bird watch. I awoke at 5:00 with the first call of the rooster. What a fabulous oasis this place is. The Otavalo market is a scene like nothing in the world. Literally thousands of Indians with cinnamon skin and straight aquiline noses, men with long, black braids, wool ponchos, fedoras, women with dark blue wrap skirts cinched in with brightly woven belts, and crisp white blouses embroidered in bright colors, and around their necks many strands of gold necklaces, dark headdress worn like a turban.

Spinning in Peguche

Bargaining is a must and they will be offended if you don't do it. It represents a social outing for them. At the market the Otavalans meet their relatives and share the gossip of the week. They will all get drunk on the money they make from selling their wares at the market by drinking a liquor made of corn called Chinche. Stop in Calderon where the bread dough X-mas ornaments are made ($1 for 8).

My early morning walk in Old Town Quito includes a visit to San Francisco Square where the liberty monument is around cobbled streets - the President's Palace, the Mayor's offices, many churches in the Baroque style with

Making ready-made clothes on a sewing machine

1993

The Market

gold ceilings and walls, paintings the size of murals, and sculptures of Madonna and child and Jesus - everywhere. Churches are packed - standing room only. Services every hour. The Jesuit cathedral was built in the 1500's - made of stone - carved. Went to the top of the city where a monument of the Virgin Mary made out of aluminum was built just fifteen years ago - the panorama view of the city is fabulous. Quito is twenty-five miles long - but its width is determined by the Pichincha Volcano and therefore oddly shaped.

April 18
Quito / Hotel Oro Verde / Cloudy - 70's

Lunch and dinner at Hotel Oro Verde. Blaine went off this morning to Cotopaxi National Park - I couldn't face another day on the bus so have opted to stay at the hotel. Take a two hour walking tour, 12th of Octobre Street, and then down a long hill which looks like San Francisco which is Colon Ave. Have found so many inconsistencies in Quito. It is a very cosmopolitan, sophisticated city and yet no man wears a coat or tie to even the finest restaurants, and I am overdressed in a skirt and blouse. Also, it is called the Eldorado, or country of gold, but you can only find silver in the market places. Nobody speaks English - even at Oro Verde, a very first class hotel.

We have lunch at the fitness club - ham sandwich and Sprite for $2.50, and we have a leisurely afternoon. Dinner is at La Pergola Restaurant in hotel.

1993

Galapagos

April 19
Galapagos

Up at 5:30 for our 8:30 flight on TAME (Equator Air) for the Galapagos. Landed on Baltra Island where we were transported by the panga, or the zodiac, to the Isabella II. Florenzia has arranged for us to have the Captains bedroom (#21) because of my seasick problem. The cabin has a spacious double bed and enough closet space to stay for a month. We are on the main deck, next to the dining room and bar. All the other cabins are upstairs one deck from us. Our first venture out from the boat this afternoon was to North Seymour Island. We can hardly get off the pangas for fear of stepping on the sea lions. We have to walk over a few rocky boulders to get to the path. There are swallow tail gulls that have a bright orange eye ring and are the only nocturnal gull. Blue footed boobies are all beginning to mate and we see quite a few foot stamping and skytailing by both the male and female. We see two pair of boobies actually mating. The male frigate bird is desperately seeking a female partner and has his gular sac in

Resting Frigate Bird

balloon size red display. The sea lions' pups are all searching out the mother's tiny nipple to suck some of her rich milk. The animals and birds show absolutely no fear towards any of us.

APRIL 20
HOOD ISLAND

We see a glorious sunset and are back on the boat in time for dinner at the Captain's (Carlos Montaya's) table. I am really wobbly even though we haven't even lifted the anchor yet - take an antivert and sleep as if I've been clubbed over the head by a bat. Awaken in a drugged state for breakfast at 7:30. We take the pangas to Hood Island, which is basically a nice walk on a sandy beach. We traveled 76 nautical miles from South Seymour to here. There are hood mockingbirds which come and sit on your arm, lava lizards, the female with a bright red chest, sea lion pups who have been left to fend for themselves today while their moms are packing in some tasty fish at sea. There are lots of green sea turtle nests which are big holes dug in the sand looking like craters and the eggs are in these craters. There are three kinds of finches, the little ground, large, and cactus warbler. We see the Galapagos hawk. A few of us go over to Turtle Island for a snorkel - the water is like crystal - you can see down 45' to the bottom. Lots of coral starfish, damselfish, the beautiful Moorish idol. Very little coral is left - the parrot fish, as well as climate change, has done away with most of it.

Before arriving on Hood, we took a panga ride around Gardner

Island where the sea lions followed us, daring them to leap right in the boat. We saw lots of yellow crowned night heron.

To get to Hood, we crossed Gardner Bay. The afternoon took us to the other side of Hood to Punta Suarez. We saw tons of masked and blue footed boobies, waved albatross, marine iguana - most of these we the people literally had to move off the path to avoid stepping on them. Sea lions lay stretched on the sandy beaches or on the black lava rocks, perfectly camouflaged. We walk to a very high cliff from which the waved albatross starts its flight. We look down to the aquamarine water and see a large blow hole geyser. The days are packed full of such animal and bird wonder, I can't even describe. The colors of the blue booby, the songs of the yellow warbler, the gentleness of the lovable sea lions, the sky pointing and blue body courting dance of the boobies are a wonder to behold.

April 21

Cool mornings, hot, 90° in afternoon

Thursday morning is a rather glorious day in the Galapagos. We first go around the inlets of Gardner and Watson off Floreanna Island. See a blue grotto and many sea lions performing their ballet style acrobatics in the water. Go to Devil's Crown for a fabulous snorkel after a mile walk on Punta Cormorant. The water is crystal clear, and the iridescent colors on the king angelfish and rainbow wrasses is spectacular. After lunch, we go in search of the small Galapagos penguin. This is the farthest north these penguins go, and we find two of them basking on a lava rock. We had to go out of the bay to find them and the tide is low so most of us in one panga got out and pushed the panga over the sandy bottom. After that we went to Post Office Bay, which has had a continual post office for 100's of years. You just put an addressed postcard in the post office barrel, and then, if someone comes to Galapagos who lives near that address, they take the letter or postcard and hand delivers it. I took a postcard that is to go to Arnold, Maryland.

April 22

This morning we're off to the Darwin Research Station. We stayed in the port last night so it was very calm - but I still felt the sway of the boat. The town in Santa Cruz is the worst trash you've ever seen. Lazy looking Ecuadorians looking to make a fast buck off of rich tourists. The research station is well done and interesting. They have taken many tortoise eggs from the various islands where the species is getting endangered and raise them until they are old enough to survive being eaten by the frigate bird, the feral pigs or wild cats, goats or dogs. We saw lonesome George, who could be 150 years old and was the last remaining tortoise on Pinta Island. They have brought in a sex therapist to help George - there are two females in with him and he seems a bit bewildered. Took a very rickety bus up to "Narwhal" in the highlands for lunch. It is very dry, even though the dry season is just beginning and the wet season has just ended. Take a long walk through the Scalesia Forest, which is endemic to this area with trees festooned with lichens and deep volcanic lava pits.

Lonesome George is not lonesome today.

April 23

Return to the boat exhausted at 6:00 - have 76 nautical miles to travel tonight, crossing the equator at about 3:30 a.m. Awaken to fog and mist. The garua has come to the Galapagos. It is here early morning and late afternoon, coming from south to north. Take a splendid walk on Darwin Bay, seeing many pairings of great frigates and red footed boobies. The male frigate has his gular sac all puffed up and gives a cry similar to the cry of the loon as the female flies over. As many as six to seven males will be sitting in a clump, and stretch out their

Red Footed Booby

feathery wings, shaking them up and down in excitement, and calling loudly to each female as she flies overhead. When she decides whom she wants, she lands, and they do this necking and cooing for awhile. We are very up close and personal with three mating red footed boobies which have very unusual markings. Bright red feet, blue bill, brown body (only 5% have a white body). Climb up a steep lava bank to look over a cliff. Three black tipped sharks are circling in the sandy water below. Snorkel along the cliffs of Darwin's Bay - the garua is still with us - so not very sunny, and water feels freezing. Many very large snappers and parrot fish, as well as two white tipped shark - about 6' in length - gliding by me close enough to touch - quite exciting as they swim only a few feet away. A terrific afternoon on Tower Island.

Blue Footed Booby

The great frigates are all courting, and the boobies have new born chicks. They are little white fluff balls - usually two, and then one is done away with - usually the younger - called siblicide.

APRIL 24

Take a fairly tough walk on the lava fissures, in some places dropping a couple hundred feet. Saw a short eared owl that had just captured a storm petrel. The beautiful cordia and prickly pear yellow flowers are in bloom and in such contrast to the black basalt.

Tonight we go 126 nautical miles and dock in Tajus Cove off Isabela. Our morning walk takes us up a steep lava hill on Isabela, to the top of one of the craters. We see little wildlife on the way up. A few lava lizards and the ever present ground finches. The view from the top is spectacular. You can see most of the rest of Isabela, as well as Fernandina next door. There is a huge crater lake that has a salinity level of 8% (the norm being 3%) which was probably caused by a tidal wave. Only a few briny shrimp can live in this salty water - no fish. The basalt lava rock is different on every island we go to, some of it is ropy lava flows, others are channel flows. Patsy, our naturalist, has explained the history of the eruptions, and how they came to erupt. There are six volcanoes on Isabela - it and Fernandina being the youngest islands.

Marine iguana with mottled scaly skin.

In the afternoon our panga drops us at Fernandina, which has trillions of iguanas. They have already made their nests, so we stick to single file on the path, as their nests are in the sand. These are marine iguanas, which eat the seaweed along the tidal pools. They have a natural habit of snorting the salt out of their nostrils - or desalinating. You see clumps of iguanas desalinating - which looks like the venom of a spitting cobra. They are molting constantly, so you see these mottled iguana with scaly skin and great long spiny white crests which resembles the prehistoric more than the present. The iguana are perfectly camouflaged on the black molten basalt. There are many tidal pools, and the sea lions and pups are cavorting in and out of the shallow water. Some pups are just teeny - three weeks at most, others whom we snorkeled with are more like four months to a year. The mothers nurse for at least one year, but go off to feed in the water, leaving their babies on the rocks for up to four days.

Every night we meet for cocktails in the bar at 6:30, and then a briefing at 7:30 about the next day's activities. Dinner at 8:00. The boat is run like a Swiss watch - everything is done on the minute. The boat is clean as a whistle and our room is spotless. Our bed is turned down at night, and we are in it by 9:30.

April 25
James, Bartolome Islands
Crystal Clear, Blue Sky, Full Moon, 85-90°

Tonight we traveled 73 nautical miles to James Island and the neighboring Bartolome. Walked along the tidal pools this a.m. looking at various sea urchins and tropical fish. The lava rock we walk on is very bumpy, and at times has big blow holes that shoot water out of their depths. One of these is called Darwin's toilet, where the water swishes around with the waves - comes to the top of the lava rocks and then flushes all the way down about 25'. There are three sea lions frolicking in Darwin's toilet. Again, there are marine iguanas on which we have to keep a watchful eye so we don't step on their tails. Brightly colored red, orange, blue, and yellow sally lightfoot crabs, which are really a contrast to the black lava. There are no inhabitants on James Island, but there are 90,000 goats, which are a real threat to the scalesia trees and other vegetation. The feral pigs have already killed off all the giant tortoises.

It is a hot day, and I'm looking forward to our snorkel. We snorkel from the beach, and there are lots of sea lions ready to play with us. One comes right at me like a torpedo an we almost touch nose to goggles. I am swimming along a rocky ledge that is filled with gigantic brown

Under water sea lion approaches with a kiss

sea urchins, some pencil spine, and the lethal black spiny sea urchins. A white tipped shark gracefully passes by me, its white tip shining so brightly in the sunshine. There are some two foot parrot fish, and the elusive cabrillo, which quickly dart behind a rock when it sees you. There are a few green sea urchins, which are the only natural ones, and the brown sea urchins seem to have taken over all the rocks and is going to destroy the balance of vegetation if not controlled soon.

In the afternoon we take a fantastically beautiful hike up to a lookout point on Bartolome. The landscape looks like the moon. There are spatter cones, which have deep craters. Everything is brown lava rock. The plants growing very close to the rock are all gray in color and look dead, but actually are flowering. This island was only formed 100 years ago - breaking away from James as we can see from this spot 350 feet above sea level, just where they used to be attached, so we can see the flow of water between the two.

We take a late afternoon swim and snorkel around pinnacle rock, and again have a totally different underwater view as you can see fissures and the rest of the volcanic island mass under the water. Our farewell cocktail and dinner hour brings out lots of excitement as well as sorrow at leaving this spectacular archipelago.

- 1994 -

South Africa & Botswana

August 28

Left Chadds Ford Pond House at 1:30. John Haley, driver. On arriving at S.A.A. ticket counter, they asked if they could upgrade us to Business Class. The plane left 2 ½ hours late - rain and radar problems at J.F.K. kept us on the runway. Eighteen hours later - but a very smooth and delightful trip - we arrived in Johannesburg at 7:00 p.m., August 29th.

South Africa
August 30-31
Johannesburg / sunny, 50's morning, 60ish afternoon

Slept on and off all day of the 30th, getting over our jet lag. Ate at hotel and did some in house shopping. Hired a car and driver, Simone Battani, to take us sightseeing on the 31st. After much discussion about our interests we left the Sandton Sun at 11:00 a.m. and went to the snake farm 45 minutes from town. The zoo also houses hyena, chimps, the endangered grey-bald vulture, Marshall eagle, pit vipers, mambas, and many more reptiles and animals. It was worth seeing - but animals are in ghastly cages.

The countryside is definitely in its winter stage, dry, dead, brown, and leafless. The topography is very hilly but the roads are excellent. Drive by many black children in uniforms going to and from schools, but no towns or houses visible from the road. There are nine main tribes in South Africa, all speaking different languages, having different traditions. There is hope of having a government where each tribe can still run its own group of people, but also work within a central government. Johannesburg and environs have about eight million people. Soweto alone may have as many as five million. South Africa is almost totally self sufficient. They have more minerals than any other country. They make BMW's and Mercedes cars; they are able to give energy to 50% of the rest of Africa. Johannesburg is not near any large body of water. This is one of its few drawbacks. We went over a dam that hadn't had enough water in its lake to open the gates in over four years.

There are only six million whites in all of S.A. - these including both English and Afrikaners. There are 900,000 coloreds (meaning the product of a white married either to a black or an Indian), one million Indians and thirty-three million blacks. Johannesburg is only one hundred years old and has been rebuilt five times, tearing down all of the old historic buildings to make way for the new. The diamond building owned by Oppenheimer/deBeers is a contemporary building downtown (directly across the street from the Witch Doctor's Emporium) made of tinted glass and has fifty-eight facets or sides as does a true diamond.

Our lunch spot was a charming honeymoon resort called Mt. Grace. It is very secluded in the Magalies hills with lovely thatched cottages, spring daffodils, and a cozy fire warming the living room. After lunch we made a quick stop downtown to visit the witch doctor. The smell in his shop is asphyxiating as there are all sorts of dead animals, skins, baboon teeth, roots and bark, horns and bones, herbs and spices, and God knows what else. Incredible things are hanging down from the rafters so you are constantly alert not to bump into zebra tails, leopard skins, ostrich feathers, and other unnameable objects.

Meet Lindsey and Adam Klein for dinner, who are Jo'burg residents. Lindsey is Tommy Fook's niece. They took us to an Italian

1994

restaurant. You have to use a buzzer to be let in the front door and a guard is standing watch outside with a gun. There are bars on all the windows. Adam tells us that a lot of people in Sandton are starting to carry guns - men as well as women. There are senseless murders everyday. The elections in April are already a done deal apparently, with Nelson Mandela's ANC party winning with they say almost 53% of the vote - even though there are twenty-six other parties. There are only a handful of people in the restaurant - but whether that's normal for a Tuesday night or due to the uncomfortable situation in Johannesburg, we'll never know.

September 1
Ngala - sunny 50-80

Arrive Ngala via Skukuza airport, and then change to a small single engine Cessna to Ngala airstrip. Ngala, a private reserve, is about 36,000 acres. The fence between Kruger Park and Ngala was removed three months ago allowing the animals free range through both parks. This gives the animals over four million acres of land to roam around. Our rondavel (# 19) is a spacious, new, total bathroom conveniences cottage with a thatched roof making it cool and dark. Unfortunately, there are real windows and doors keeping out the animal sounds I love to hear. We arrive in time for an elegant buffet lunch, a leisurely swim in the pool, some fattening cakes at afternoon 3:30 tea, and a very full belly on our afternoon game drive.

Start out in our open land rover at 4:00. The air is still quite warm. It is the first day of spring. Our first encounter is with a huge, old crocodile which is lying beside a pan (a pond of evaporated water) with his mouth wide open. He is aestivating which is the reverse of hibernating in a warm climate. It is a somewhat dormant state and we could approach this old croc within a few feet. He is amazingly prehistoric, about thirteen feet long, and seemed totally unconcerned about us.

Kevin is our guide, young, cute, and very knowledgeable. Remson is our tracker. We drive deeper into the bush, knocking down any little bush that gets in our way. It is quite dry and hot. Very little grass left thanks to the grazers and elephants, and no green leaves yet on the trees as we're coming out of S.A. winter. It does look very autumnal though with brownish red and orange leaves left on the mopani trees. These leaves are shaped like a butterfly's wings.

We are seeing an abundant number of wonderful birds. The yellow billed hornbill, grongo, Burchell's starling, red billed buffalo weaver, wattled starling, and long tailed shrike. Many impala are grazing, a few gray duiker, giraffe, and a very beautiful leopard who is on a hunt. We trailed him for about ½ an hour as he was stalking his prey. We are knocking down small acacia bushes and insignificant trees as we drive through the bush on his track. He is very healthy looking as he silently meanders across the low land veldt.

After this strenuous tracking we take a break for sundowners at 5:30. The sun is just about gone. Night comes so quickly in the bush. We have our cocktails and hot sausage hors d'oeuvres served by Remson and then back with our spotlight to check out the nighttime activities of the animals. We are really lucky! We are very close and get a good view of the rare African wild cat (red ears through the light is very pronounced), two spotted genets, and a serval. Kevin hears on the CB that some lions are sneaking up on a herd of Cape Buffalo so we pursue the pursuers. Arrive at the airstrip where four lions are resting. They apparently spooked the buffalo who ran off so the lions will have to recoup their strength and try again. The statistics are that lions succeed about one in every five or six attempts. But once they make a kill, if it is substantial enough, they are content for three or four days. Back at camp in time for a delicious dinner at 8:00 and then walked back to out thatched cottage with a night guard and sleep.

September 2
Ngala / Full moon, sunny

Awaken to a brisk knock on the door at 5:30. It is really cold this morning, long shirt sleeves and sweater weather. After a quick cup of coffee we're off at 6:05. Blaine is sitting in the rear of the land rover which is raised up much higher than the first seat, and he really feels the chill, wrapping a wool lap robe about him. My fleece jacket, lightweight gloves, and bandanna (to keep my ears warm) really are necessary this morning. We immediately come across a herd of about fifty buffalo. A few calves are in the group. Two full bellied and sleepy lionesses are resting on the bank of a dam. A family of baboons are scampering up and down a jackleberry tree, talking freely to one another; and myriads of brightly colored birds are darting from tree to tree, catching insects out of the sky.

Our coffee and juice break at 8:00 smells and tastes especially delicious being out in the veldt watching the sun rising higher in the sky, warming up our bodies with every passing minute. Dyke, our Shangaan guide, takes us for a walk after breakfast and tells us the tribal stories his grandfather, who was a doctor, told to him. Among other things he showed us the toothbrush bush, which when a branch is torn off and the outer bark is peeled back, forms bristles that look exactly like our store bought toothbrushes, We see grasses that smell like turpentine and are inedible, trees whose bark is poisonous when eaten, and milk from the leaves of a tree the bushmen used to poison their arrows.

We get back to camp just in time for a 1:00 lunch and an afternoon swim. After wearing my heaviest three layers of clothing this morning, I can't believe I can jump into this freezing cold pool - but it is very refreshing. Still getting used to the time change and jet lag. I fall sound asleep in the lounge chair by the pool and only awaken when the tea gong rings and we are soon off on our afternoon game drive.

Magnificent Old Rhino

Our first sighting is a very large male kudu with a curved rack that must exceed 35". Burchell's zebra are grazing nearby and Kevin tells us their stripes regulate heat - white keeping them cool and the black warming them. They also keep the grasses in the stomach a long time which is why zebras always look so fat. They are just bloated and when they run they expel the air which is why you always hear zebra farting as they run. In S. A. the wildebeest males are solitary creatures and territorial, so unlike the herds that we've seen in the Serengeti. We find a magnificent old rhino - maybe the biggest and oldest in this entire region of Kruger - with two very large horns. He is perhaps 45 years old and lucky to be alive. A bull elephant gives us a couple of very impressive fake charges, fanning out his ears and throwing his trunk to and fro. We're not quite as frightened as he'd like us to be. At dusk we spot a lovely male cheetah whom we track through the bush. He sprays and marks, often lifting his tail straight up in the air and leaving his scent on many trees and bushes. He is definitely in hot pursuit of some sweet young thing. We find a hyena den - it is now almost dark - and three young cubs come wandering out to examine us. They are extremely curious and very brave as mom is out on a hunt and they have been left to their own devices. They are about three months old and get close enough to nibble on Kevin's boots and the mudflaps of our rover. They sniff around our feet and decide we are not a predator. It's a shame the adult hyenas keep none of the charm the babies have.

Hyena cubs left with no chaparone are very daring.

Back at camp for dinner we are treated to a private dinner in the safari suite with champagne, candle light, and Sam, our servant, waiting on us. Hugh Marshall, the manager of Ngala, is a friend of Adam Klein (also a director of Ngala) and since we told him it is our anniversary, he arranged this lovely surprise for us. As we sip our champagne beneath the light of a full moon, we are sitting on the balcony of the suite overlooking a little stream reflecting the glow of the moon's beam. In the darkness we hear the cacophony of the high decibeled pitch from the tree frogs and melodious notes of the night birds, and know that we'd not ever want to be anywhere else in the world.

September 3
Ngala - Londolozi / 90° at noon, dry/sun

Out in the bush again at 6:00. It's a quiet, beautiful morning. Nothing much is stirring. We return from our drive early so we can pack, eat, and leave. Hugh points out a Scops owl that has made his home in a tree next to our Cottage #19. He has been there each day. We take our final farewell to our friendly Scops and Ngala.

Our flight to Londolozi is only twenty minutes and we fly right over Mala Mala which shares a river border with Londolozi. We are in Cottage #2 which is very spacious, brighter by lots, and roomier than Ngala with an outdoor shower in the boulders and a balcony overlooking a great spanse of trees and rocks where baboons and animals frolic throughout the day. In fact, we have to leave our sliding doors shut and leave nothing outside the shower area because the baboons, curious as they are, will make themselves right at home in your home. There are only three cottages on either side of the dining lounge, which is also set up high, overlooking the trees and rocks.

The pool is in the center with a cascading waterfall over the rocks. You are constantly feeling like there is some great animal or bird just about to appear from each angle, every bush, behind every rock, coming down from every tree. The sounds are all around us. I have the pool to myself - it must be too cold for everyone else - like ice - but the air is so hot. The skink are sunbathing next to me and the black headed oriole is calling from a nearby tree, and the buffalo are traipsing across the rocks to drink in the river below, and the baboons are just sitting on the rocks looking at me looking at them.

Our afternoon game run is led by Bruce, our ranger, and Kruger, our tracker. We are in a rover with six others, All S.A. except Mark, who is a top AIDS doctor from San Francisco who is in S.A. to speak in Johannesburg at the different hospitals and clinics. We are the only three Americans here at Londolozi. Our camp, which is called Bush

Camp, holds sixteen people. We head down to a pool or pan where close to 250 Cape buffalo are taking a drink in the hot afternoon sun. They are all shapes and sizes. Some males with huge boss, some infected with orange lice or insects. All are snorting and sniffing. We take a long run to the end of the reserve to check out a mother cheetah and her three cubs. It is dusk when we get there. She won't be hunting anymore today as they are diurnal animals. Her three babies are about eight months old and almost as big as she is. Since cheetah have to teach their children to hunt, these three will be on their own very soon. The mother will just up and leave them any day now, with no warning, and they will have to fend for themselves.

On our way back to camp, with spotlights, we spy a lioness chomping on a dead zebra. There are two lionesses who have already had enough and are asleep with full bellies. The third has this feast all to herself. We get ten to fifteen feet of her - she is used to our vehicle and seems undisturbed.

We stop for sundowners way into the night in total darkness and look up at trillions of stars. The moon is coming up very late so we can easily see the Southern Cross - the two pointers and other constellations, like Scorpio, with ease. Back at camp we have dinner in a

Lioness enjoying a small zebra for dinner

boma around a nice hot fire with impala kabobs for hors d'oeuvres and a lovely Niederberg white S.A. wine to sip with our scrumptious dinner. In our king sized bed our first night at Londolozi, I replayed our first day at this gorgeous game reserve: the red duikers we saw parting the low grass in low pounces; warthogs snuffling the earth with their fierce, ugly faces, a giraffe floating into a run that scattered the tick-seeking oxpeckers from its back, the birds' beaks splitting in alarm as their dinner table cantered away. And then nothing but sweet dreams.

September 4
Londolozi, 5:30 a.m. - 7° Celsius.

The sun is rising, we've had a knock-knock and it's 5:30 - all too soon. We're on our early morning game drive and immediately see three very alert lionesses, one of whom has three cubs. They are still quite small, about three or four months old. It is so cool that they're sauntering at a pretty good clip. The cubs jump over each other, run in spurts, and then lie down weary from the exertion. As we look at these super predators, I am reminded of John Varty's explanation of them. "They are neutral, neither cruel nor kind, fair nor unfair. We should not judge them by our own human emotions but they should rather be seen as how they are: supreme predators superbly adapted by millions of years of evolution to hunt and kill in order to survive."

We leave the lionesses and frolicking cubs after being totally entertained and see a low flying eagle owl flying through a dry river bed. It is an intriguing sight and we follow it to a tree that already has a Wahlberg eagle. The Wahlberg must have a nest nearby for she starts screeching loud noises in a fury. The owl holds her ground - they are both about thirty feet up in the tree and facing each other. The Wahlberg can stand it no longer and flies at the owl. The owl could not be more stubborn and refuses to move. Another Wahlberg comes out of nowhere and dive bombs the owl. The owl and both birds fly off in a frenzy to another tree and start the fracas all over again. Now it is time to move off in search of elephant.

Directly above from the sandy river bed we find a mother elephant and her very young baby. We guess the baby to be about three or four months old. She is very protective of her toto and trumpets us loudly, flares her ears, and charges us. We are quick to retreat but stay at a safe distance to watch as she and her baby eat. Mom breaks off huge branches from mopani trees and baby chews on the little limbs. Baby elephants start getting their first molars at about six months, so she's probably teething. Throughout a lifetime elephant will go through six sets of teeth, top, and bottom. The front teeth grinding down to nothing and then the five remaining ones, top and bottom, move forward. After all six sets have finally ground down the elephant will die of starvation. This happens at about 65 years. These strong teeth enable an elephant to chew branches and bark, as well as leaves and grass. Whereas the trunk is used for smelling, lifting, and inhaling water. The tusks are used for digging in the ground for minerals as well as support in knocking over trees. The dung of an elephant is a very good indication of what he has eaten as he will only digest about 40% of what he eats, which is about 100 pounds a day of food for a grown elephant, and 50 gallons of water. The rest of this food, or 60%, is put out as waste or dung which is great for other animals and birds who will then eat what the elephant discards. It is also helpful to the landscape, as elephants travel great distances and will drop seeds which will germinate in the ground at the most unlikely places. This mother elephant is very right tusked as it has been worn down a lot more than her left one. When they cull the elephants at Kruger Park, they kill off whole herds, sometimes up to 300 elephants. The two to eight year olds get transplanted to other parks, but anything under two, which is when they are weaned, is too stressful to the baby to keep alive. Elephants, being such social animals, are seen at times to go back to an elephant cemetery where bones are, and croon and sway and move bones around, and seem genuinely moved by death. After watching mother and child bash in a few trees, we move on to see what other excitement may lay ahead.

Very soon we spot a cheetah and her three cubs. The three youngsters are quite a bit younger than the ones we followed last night, and they, like the lion cubs, are having a great morning frolicking to and fro, running, jumping at and on each other, pouncing at scrub rabbits, scurrying up termite mounds, and around in circles. All this brings on a great thirst and they stop at a watering hole to slurp up the water with their agile tongues. Their thirst quenched, it's play time all over again. We follow the foursome for quite awhile. Mother cheetah is surprisingly relaxed around us. She understands that the vehicle is no threat even though it is open and we are perfectly visible to her. Cheetah are incredibly fast. They don't stalk an animal but run at it full bore. They will suffocate an animal by grabbing its neck after pouncing on it first with their dew claws. They often sit on top of a termite mound to look over the veldt, or plain, for their prey. The time has flown and we must leave mother and cubs alone to go back to camp for breakfast.

It is almost 9:30 and so much has happened already in the bush - and it happens every day of every year, with no time outs for Christmas or the Fourth of July. Breakfast is scrumptious with lots of choices of eggs, chili, tomato, sausage, bacon, toast, fresh fruit, cereals, hot oatmeal or cold bran flakes and granola, many juices, mango, orange, pineapple, coffee.

After sampling all of this, it is time for a walk to view the hippos. Our tracker, a Zulu named Finewell, takes our group through the bush. Our new friends from South Africa join our walk. What delightful people they all are. Antoinette and Chris Smith live in Pretoria. He is an ENT surgeon. Margaret works in the AIDS Department of a major pharmaceutical company in Johannesburg. Mark Conant is director of an AIDS clinic in San Francisco and world famous. Tino and Lyn are from Sandton, and he owns pharmaceutical factories which make natural vitamins.

It is 95° and not a cloud in the sky. Our walk takes us down to the river where we come head to head with a bull buffalo - who runs away. We are in a grove of date nut palms, which the natives use to make very potent liquor. Finewell explains the different tracks to us. He shows us the buffalo thorn tree which the Zulus place on graves because it has two thorns, one going up and one down, telling you where the soul is going. We see a tree from which the natives can make blue ink, the lead wood tree that is good for toothpaste, the toothbrush tree, the toilet paper bush, etc. We see a gigantic hippo actually swimming down the river. Their skins are three inches thick, but very sensitive to the sun. We see them emerge from their swim in the shady banks of the river. There are two enormous crocs swimming and many more lying on the rocks. We get back to camp just in time for another delicious meal and an afternoon swim.

The afternoon game drive is fairly uneventful - but informative in a way we really hadn't focused on. We drove over to Timbeli Lodge because we had heard a leopard was tracking a duiker. Along the road on the right was the fence of a homeland - bordering Londolozi. It went on for many hundreds of miles. Bruce said that John Varty, the owner of Londolozi, asked the chief of the homeland if he would remove the fence in exchange for some of the profits from the private game reserve, This would be a very tidy sum of money for the Zulu homeland and Varty stipulated the money must go to a better education for the children and better hospital facilities for the sick. The chief turned Varty's offer down flat, saying if he (the chief) couldn't pocket the profits himself he wasn't interested in removing the fence.

This to me describes the tribal issue in a nutshell. If one chief of one homeland won't compromise or give up any of his power, what in the world is all of South Africa, with its many different tribes, many languages, different customs, and many chiefs going to do about unifying this country.

By the time we arrive at Timbeli, the leopard has killed the duiker and we see him with the duiker in his mouth bound up a tree and hook the body up over the crotch of the tree so it will not fall. We leave the leopard to his prey as he seems very nervous with us around and it is so dark we have to now shine a spotlight on him. I'm sure he is thinking life is hard enough out here in the bush, so why won't these ogling people leave me in peace.

Camp feels mighty good after the sun goes down. There is zero humidity here - the nights are cold and refreshing and sitting in the cozy boma around a campfire under the light of the moon and stars is just a little bit of heaven.

September 6
Londolozi-Phinda

Another drive of the low veldt with Bruce and with Kruger sitting shotgun in the rear. Another exciting morning viewing 75 Cape buffalo all lounging around, chewing their cuds with cold steam air coming out of their nostrils and a foggy mist on their wet backs. The sun has just emerged, and to see these animals that look like brown boulders in the early morning light actually come to life is an extremely thrilling way to start the day. Buffaloes are ruminants (a four part digestive system) and 100% of their food is put to use in their bodies. Just beyond the lazy buffaloes is a single male elephant who seemed very relaxed until we drive by and then he not only charged our vehicle and trumpeted loudly, but even after we hightailed it out of there, he ran after us and gave us quite a thrill.

1994

Just over the hill we are fortunate enough to come across a very large white rhino and her young baby. The baby is between three and six months old and still suckling, We can see the mother rhinos swollen teats hanging very full as she walks close to us. The baby has just the first signs of a horn and if anything like mother, it will be huge. The horn is, like the elephant, genetically grown - so like mother, usually, like child. But unlike the elephant, whose tusk is made of ivory, the rhino's horn is made of keratin, like our fingernails. The wonders of Africa!

And as if this wasn't enough of a perfect day, we now see what has become of our very familiar cheetah and her three cubs. They are the three month old ones we followed for such a long time yesterday. She once again is extremely calm having us trailing her. She sits on top of a huge termite mound and the babies scamper to and fro as typical kittens do. Then, mother cat is off like a rocket! Within five seconds she has pounced on a small gray duiker and we can see her now with its neck in her mouth suffocating it. This is the cheetah way of killing. It takes her a few minutes for the duiker to stop breathing and then she gives out quite a few very sharp, quick yelps calling her three cubs. When they get to her, she lets them sniff and tug at the duiker, experimenting with how to tackle this delectable piece of meat. The mother cheetah always teaches her babies how to kill. Two of the cubs are definitely dominant. The third is submissive and almost afraid to take part in this duiker tug of war. After about ten minutes of this nonsense, mom finally gets into the act and starts the daily meal. She takes her fill quickly and efficiently, and then goes and lies down while the young ones finish the carcass. We leave them with fat little bellies, happy with the knowledge that they have made it through one more day in the wild. We have to leave this unusual wonderland right after breakfast, but it will be at the top of the list for a return visit.

Fly out of Londolozi airstrip in a twin Cessna with Warren as pilot. A cold front coming into Phinda makes for a very rough last ten minutes of flight. Carl, our ranger, meets us on the Phinda airstrip, which is about ½ an hour from camp. Phinda Lodge is set up on the crest of a hill overlooking the most incredible acacia woodland. Our first afternoon we go out on a boat they have called "Zulubelle", and mozy down the Mzinene River. Even though it is a misty, cold, cloudy afternoon, we see surprisingly many birds and crocodiles. Malachite kingfishers flit from one reed to another. Giant and pied kingfishers vie for fish. The goliath heron stands majestically on the shore as still as a stick. The greenback and gray herons squawk at each other, spur-wing geese and white faced ducks fly by in huge flocks. Hadida ibis are silhouetted against the gray sky saying "HADIDA HADIDA" as they pass by the Zulubelle. It is quite dark when we disembark and we wrap up in woolen blankets on the way back to the lodge.

September 7
Phinda / cloudy, cool, splatters of rain

Wake up call at 5:30 already finds me awake. I think I am truly catching on to this early morning schedule. Phinda, north of Durbin, and close to the Indian Ocean, is very different in topography and weather from Ngala or Londolozi. The shower and tap water are very salty. The pans have all dried up and there have been no good rains for two summers now. There used to be lots of hippos, but they have all walked to the rivers or died from lack of water.

We have been put in the honeymoon suite #12 called "Lookout," which has a lengthy deck overlooking the Lambobo hills. The acreage of Phinda is about 36,000 acres. It was a hunting lodge until two years ago, so all the predator animals have been killed and they have imported two sets of lions from Kruger (Timbivati, near Londo) and Namibia. Two cheetah from Namibia are very large males wearing collars. They also have imported about twenty-two white rhino, but we saw none. The white rhino is different from the black rhino in looks because it has a very wide mouth - the wide translates to white in African dialects. The wide mouthed rhino is not as endangered as the black. There are fifty-eight elephants brought from a culling operation in Kruger, and all these were bartered for in exchange for the local nyala which are everywhere in Phinda - but nowhere else in Africa. We saw no elephants but lots of spoor. Carl is a very good ranger - an ex-hunter and has been in Phinda since it opened two years ago. Jeremiah, the Zulu tracker, has lived in this area all of his life. We have a bush breakfast in a dry river bed with sounds of the purple lourie and spoor of elephant. Fresh fruit and yogurt, eggs, bacon and sausage, muffins, juice, and hot coffee make for scrumptiously good smells. Carl cooks with propane in a kind of wok. It's amazing how efficient his one pan can cook all these great dishes.

After breakfast we look around for the sparse game at Phinda. At present, the game preserve is cutting new roads to improve game viewing and to improve grass growing. There are so many acacias, Euphorbias, monkey orange trees, and plain scrub that there is just

Breakfast in the Bush

no room for any grass to grow as the scrub depletes the soil of all nutrients. There are also lots of Ilala palms which have little round fruits with hard brown casings. They make brandy from the fruit which is very intoxicating. Any poachers found in Phinda are put to work, instead of punished. One poacher got so good at making bricks that he now has a full fledged brick business with brick making machines. Another man converts felled trees into such wonderful charcoal he can't make it fast enough to keep up with demand. We see lots of splendid birds at Phinda. The scarlet chested sunbird, red collared Barbet, fish eagle, chin spotted scrub robin, but we see very little game. There are plenty of nyala, which is a huge treat, plenty of impala, a few wildebeest, zebra, and giraffe; but only the very minimum of cheetah, elephant, and rhino. We did stalk a couple of female lions tonight. It was very dark, no moon, so we had to spot the two lioness sisters with car lights and then quickly turn them off. We sat in total darkness for forty-five minutes with only the sounds of Africa to keep us company. There was a shadow just a few feet from the car. It was one of the lionesses. She walked to the back of our vehicle, marking our Land Cruiser as her territory, and then circled back again, getting used to our scent. If we had put our arm straight out she could easily have bitten it off. These are open vehicles with no doors or roofs, so we are basically eyeball to protruding lion tongue within our arms length. We didn't dare move an inch or she could have been provoked into leaping on us for a very quick dinner. We heard impala and gnu snorting warning calls to others. We switched on the spot for a few seconds and caught the lions running after the impala in our light. We quickly turned off the blinding light as impala are daytime animals and it would be an unfair advantage to the lion, whose eyes are nocturnal, for us to blind the impala. The impala and wildebeest scatter, they snort, the lions run after them, but not fast enough. It looked like a sure kill to us, but the statistics show that the success rate of lion

1994

Nyala — a rare species in Africa

Giraffe move both left legs and then both right legs.

kills is about one in five or six, so this was one of the unlucky ones for the lion.

After all this time spotting and tracking, I have learned the difference between servals, civets, and genets. I know the sounds of the crested barbet and the Senegal coucal. I can tell the tracks of lion, leopard, and cheetah, the age of a baobab tree and its uses, the leaves of a marula and of a mopani tree, the medicinal uses of many roots, barks, and leaves. I know the gestation period of many animals and the success rate of their young, and just what their habits are. It is a wonderful feeling to become comfortable and knowledgeable in the bush.

September 8
Phinda / Sun, hot, light breeze

A breathtaking sunrise greets us at 6:00 a.m. The nyala run hither and thither and through the camp eating the bushes. Beautiful sunbirds are darting around a waterfall which is under the swimming pool. Carl takes us up to the north rim of the property for a fantastic bush breakfast. The game viewing is tough because everything is so overgrown - but we manage to see the ever present nyala and impala, a few warthog, red and gray duiker, and suni, one very large male lion, two lionesses, and two cubs behind lots of scrub.

We get back to camp in time to pack up and have Warren fly us to Richard's Bay. Every plane arrives and leaves on the appointed dot. Everything works like a Swiss watch in South Africa. We take Com-Air to Johannesburg (a 1 ½ hour flight) which is a spanking new 767 jet with all of about twelve people on board. We order up a delightful dinner from room service once we arrive back at the Sandton Sun Hotel. Tomorrow, 5:00 a.m. will be coming very quickly.

1994

BOTSWANA
SEPTEMBER 9
JEDIBE CAMP / SUNNY 85°

Arrive back at Jan Smutts Airport in the dark, even though our plane isn't due to leave until 8:30. After checking in, I leave Blaine to go to the coffee shop and get rolls, coffee, and juice. Blaine goes through customs and sits by the gate. Little did we know when we checked in that our passports had been switched. Blaine's customs official just stamped his (mine) without ever looking at his picture. When it was my turn, one hour later, I couldn't get through with his passport and I didn't know where to find him. The customs official assured me he could never have gotten through on my passport, so I look all over the airport for Blaine. It is getting very close to departure time and I am getting a bit frantic. Knowing Blaine's propensity for sitting at the gate, I plead with the security guard to let me look for him. Most reluctantly, they take me by the hand (almost in handcuffs) and ask if I can point him out. Of course, he's sitting there at the gate reading the newspaper with no clue as to what's happening. After much ado (and the firing of Blaine's customs official on the spot) everything gets straightened out.

Our flight on Air Botswana is supposed to be nonstop to Maun but in flight the pilot announced we'd have to go to Gabaronne first to pick up some passengers. We all had to get off, walk almost half a mile to the terminal, go through customs, claim our bags which they took off the plane, check them back on the plane, then return to the same plane only to learn that our reserved seats were taken by the local Gaboronnies and we just luckily got two seats two rows from the last row in the plane. We finally arrive in Maun late. After claiming our bags, we got a ten seater Cessna with BTP as co-pilot. Jedibe Camp is our first stop in Botswana.

After landing on a bumpy, dirt strip we proceed onto the island by speedboat that made its way through the channels hidden by papyrus and phragmites. It is a charming camp and we are back in tented bush life again which I love. Our tent (#3) is spacious and set in the shade of a big fig tree. We can hear the birds and vervet monkeys all around us. Our group consists of Dorothy, who is blind, but has traveled all over the world, including two previous safaris; Suzanne, Dorothy's companion and a clinical psychologist back in Kentucky; Barbara Nicholson, who is a burned out, high powered executive who has left the Big Apple for Santa Fe, New Mexico; and John and Lyla Turner, retired from the construction business and homemaker respectively, and are from Ranchero Santa Fe, CA. After a big lunch and Olson's beer, we take a little snooze and unwind from our travels. It is windy and cool, sunny and wonderful. All the bathroom facilities - toilet, sink, and shower, are outside with just a boma around them for privacy. How wonderful to sit on the john and look up at the stars or at a monkey in a nearby tree. What fun to take a shower with birds, frogs, and lizards all watching attentively as if I am the entertainment.

At 4:00, after the heat of the sun has receded, we meet for tea and then hop onto the party barge, which is quite high and overlooks all of the delta. We amble up the river in search of fish eagles, and find a pair of nesting ones with a couple of fledglings. The name of our Botswana guides are BK, Trust, And Water I (there is a Water II, also). Water I spears some already cut up tiger fish with a papyrus reed and throws it to the fish eagles who soar down from their perch high in a tree to swoop it up with their talons. Good photo op - let's hope one of the many pictures we have taken will show the beauty of this bird.

Have a chilled glass of wine as Blaine sips his vodka and tonic and wonder if there is any more beautiful place on earth than watching the sunset on the Okavango River. The shadows from the papyrus reeds on the clear water and silhouettes of the trees against the sky is an awesome sight. Back at camp for a magnificent candlelight dinner announced by one of the cooks who describes with great relish the meal she has prepared.

Gliding through the reeds in a mokoro

September 10
Jedibe / 60° & sunny at mid-morning

At 6:00 we are greeted by the words "knock - knock" and coffee set outside our tent flap. What a glorious and civilized way to begin the day! The sun creeps above the horizon at about 6:30 and Blaine and I are off with Trust in a dugout canoe - which is called a mokoro. There is all of three inches between the sides of the canoe and the river - or in the worst possible scenario - the hippo or croc and us. At times the water splashes over the bow, and Blaine, who is in the bow, is constantly being bombarded with cobwebs as we make our way through the narrow channels, and we both are swatted by papyrus as Trust poles smoothly through the water.

The mokoro is made from large sausage, fig, mopani, or marula trees, and at times the channel we glide through is no wider than the mokoro. Trust paddles with a long, forked stick, about twelve feet long. He stands at the rear of the canoe and poles along the bottom of the sandy delta. The current is incredibly strong, but this morning we are going downstream. In narrow places in the delta, the papyrus and phragmites picks up silt and mud, often changing the channels from year to year. While some are closed by silt, others are opened by new grooves made by the swift current.

At about 8:30 we stop at an island filled with great white egrets and red lechwes in a field of grass. Lechwes are really water antelope and can run faster in the water than on land. On our walk we also see the different llala and date palms, acacia, and fig trees. The bird life so far has been extremely disappointing. But I don't know if it's because there are so few birds - or if our guide hasn't taken us to a birding area.

Back in our mokoro after a refreshing container of apple juice, we head back up river - which is really tough poling for Trust. All our weight in the canoe, as well as a strong current, makes for slow going. We see weavers and bee eaters, bulbuls, kingfishers, Hadida ibis, and

We get up 100s of whistling ducks as we glide by.

a small painted reed frog camouflaged nicely on a piece of papyrus reed, three otters, dragonflies, a variety of water bugs, but no crocs - thank heaven.

We arrived back at camp around 11:00, in time for a huge brunch, and then I go out with Alistair, and a few other hardy souls, for a swim in the river. We have to go by motor boat out a little ways, and Alistair revs the motor a few times up and down where we will be swimming, to scare away any crocs. He parks the boat and we all jump in. Icy Cold! I try to swim upstream with all my might and get nowhere. The current is so swift. The water is only about five feet deep, but crystal clear, so you can see the bottom.

We return to camp for a little bird viewing from my lawn chair. I see the most spectacular birds like crested barbet, firefinches, fiscal shrikes, and babblers all within a few feet of my chair and all making the most exotic African sounds.

I take a walk to a small village behind island camp. There are about twenty rondavels with thatched roofs and papyrus reed bomas. Amazingly I am told about 200 people live in this village, but I do not see a person. I can hear women talking and babies crying. The smell is rancid. There are carcasses and bones lying around. The Rondavels are set on dirt and sand. There is no grass, not a tree in the village. The chief has about twelve head of cattle which he always lets graze at Jedibe island camp, which really angers the staff at island camp. Water II and I walk back to island camp together. He tells me what "Water" means in Swana, but it is so unpronounceable to tourists - that he adopted the name Water, and since there are two Waters in his village, he is Water II.

Trust is head poler of all mokoros. He is so proud because he can read and write. He wants to come to the U.S. to live. He wants to get off the island. Our late afternoon is spent on the mokoro with Trust, poling through unbelievably small channels. Not many birds, but the

Fish Eagle fishing with us

scenery is breathtaking. It is so silent poling through the papyrus, with only the sounds of frogs and birds, the smells of marsh and grasses. The sight of sunlight filtering through the papyrus fans touching the water, it ripples through the water, and is icy cold, clean, and fresh. No plastic trash bags or plastic bottles to pollute this waterway. We stopped on an island in the middle of the delta, which you never believe in a million years could be found, and had our vodkas on a log, under a mangosteen tree filled with thousands of buzzing bees who are sucking the nectar out of the sweet smelling flowers of the tree. The yum yum tree is also in blossom and smells just like vibernum.

Back at camp for another cocktail around the bonfire and then dinner by candlelight. Rosa (a Botswanan), announced what we shall have for dinner, and then after dinner she says, "now close your eyes and open your ears," and then she sings two songs in Seswana, and we clap, and she claps, and then we praise her dinner. Tomorrow we go on an all day excursion. Penny and Alistair (the managers) tell us not to forget to bring our cossies (bathing costume as they say in S.A.) and plimsills (sneakers).

1994

SEPTEMBER 11

Awaken to brown fire finches and swamp boubous calling outside our tent. After a substantial breakfast, the Turners, Barbara, BTP, and I take off for a fishing outing. Go up the Boro River, which is where our camp is located, and then to the junction of the Okavango River. We stop to view the back of a very shy sititunga, and hear great slapping noises of the barbel catfish and tigerfish slapping their tails in the shallow reeds. The noise is amazing -- like a parade of soldiers coming. It is the beginning of the catfish run and we have hit it! Not fifty feet from us are two fishing eagles looking for their prey.

We start to cast our rods with what looks like a silver spoon. Blaine catches a sizeable - about three pounds - tigerfish fairly fast. The racket of the splashing is unbelievable. You can see the fish fairly leaping out of the water. The river is beautiful, clean, papyrus reeds lining the shores in various colors of green and brown. It is just beginning spring, so trees are still leafless. The thorn knob acacia has a fragrant white bloom, but everything on the ground is brown dirt, sand, or grass. The last rain was four months ago. We catch many tigerfish, most exciting!!

We have lunch under a huge mangosteen tree on Duba Island. We take a walk with BK, our guide, looking for the Pells fishing owl. There are signs of droppings, baboon, vervet monkeys, lots of hippo tracks, but no Pells. Alistair, Blaine, and I fish again after lunch. The tigerfish are really hitting. Blaine and Alistair catch at least four more each, with many strikes. I bring in one, and have a couple of strikes. There are three immature and two mature fish eagles fishing with us. They swoop so low we could catch them with a net. At times, it looks like they are going after the Rapella lure. They whistle, and keep whipping their heads way back as if angry with us for taking their fish.

A hospital boat with ten people on board turned over two days ago. A helicopter, and the only two boats in the Okavango, and the police boat all go by searching for three bodies still not found. They happen by just as we catch our fish and ask if they may keep them. Tigerfish are very bony, with teeth that look like shark's, but with beautiful orange stripes on either side. Back at camp at 6:00, in time for cocktails (Nederberg champange) enjoyed under the stars by a roaring fire.

September 12
Jedibe / Hot, Sunny

Water I takes us for a morning walk on Baboon Island. There is one baboon on the island whom we see. Look for sititunga - no luck. Lots of little bee eaters, watched a pearl spotted owl for a long time. Learned the medicinal uses of many trees, their roots and leaves. From Mila plant, Water told us about the white part of the stem used to improve ear aches. The root is used for stomach medicine. The stem itself is used to make fish nets. We saw the woman tree, whose bark is used to dye the basket reeds black. We saw the milk from the milk pod bush that the bushman used to poison their arrows. We saw the tree whose leaves are crunched up and fed to their dogs to make the dogs more mean for about four hours to hunt wild animals. Water showed us how to make a Francolin snare out of the leaf of a plant. Water I is a classic and always starts his stories "long ago, when I was a little boy," and ends the story saying, "you can't use most of the plants for snares or drugs or you will go straight to jaily."

Water I takes us to his tribe on the way back to camp. I want to buy some baskets. The village, called Jau, has about 300 people. They live in round huts made of almost concrete thickness. The women put on the thatching for the roof. I barter for the baskets, giving up my belt and handkerchief, but have some beautiful baskets. The men fought over the belt. The eldest one getting it and the second oldest getting the hanky - the women got nothing. The women are pretty, with very white teeth and wearing bright clothes, no underwear, and one woman is breastfeeding her year old child with one breast exposed as we talk with her. The school the children go to is five hours away by mokoro, their only means of transportation. There are way too many little children in the village, and such poverty.

September 13
Mombo / 50° early, 105° at 3:00 sun

Awaken with tea and coffee at the door at 6:00 with the sound of a drum beating. Off by 6:30. See an outstanding pack of wild dog. There are thirteen pups in this pack and twenty adults. There is one dominant female (alpha) who may reproduce. The beta females will join a different pack. In the Moremi Game Reserve there is the largest concentration of wild dog in the world. The adult dogs will go hunt in a pack, leaving a couple of sentries at home tending the pups. It is an ordeal that takes a couple of hours, as the pups seem to want to always go along on the hunt. After the hunting dogs kill, they then bring back the eaten kill and regurgitate it for the pups as well as the sentries. The puppies we see are 2 ½ months old and look like something you'd take home to grandchildren for a Christmas present. They are pulling and tugging on impala horn and the entrails that the mother alpha dog has brought home. They growl and bite each other beginning their show of dominance one over another.

Wild Dogs are on a hunt.

On coming back to the camp we see a very nervous male cheetah who wants no part of us. After breakfast, Botha takes us on a nature walk. He's no better on the walk than on the trail. The only informative thing he mentioned is that you get cream of tartar from the seeds of the boabab tree. The one we sit under to cool off is about three thousand years old. The afternoon game drive proves disastrous. We think we're going to the hippo pool with a check for lion along the way. Nothing but tsetse flies. But man do we run into the flies. We all looked like were doing the hootchy-cootchy dance trying to swipe at them. They are swarming all over us as we try to look for lion - back and forth across the grass, in and out of the acacias, swatting flies constantly. And it is hot, too hot, to put on a lot of protective clothing. By 5:30, Botha finally gets to the hippo pool - by which time all hippos have left. He says this would be a nice place for sundowners. We say "bag that - let's get out of here." Blaine goes to bed without dinner. What a disaster! Hear marvelous sounds all night. Lions roaring, a pack of hyena howling (we find out later, there was a kill at 1:30 in front of one of the tents), impala galloping between our cottage and Barbara's tent. Quite a commotion. It almost makes up for the tsetse fly game drive.

September 14
Mombo, Chobe / Beautiful

After morning coffee I go on a game drive with Joseph, who is a wonderful teacher. Dorothy and Suzanne have opted to sleep in. We come immediately on three lionesses. They aren't asleep, but they also aren't very lively. They walk around our vehicle, sniff a few trees, stretch, meander, and then kerplop - their morning siesta. We then start off for the hippo pool and get a call that Blaine's car, Botha has broken down. Rob, a ranger, picks up Barb and Blaine and brings them to our car. Finally get to the hippo pool. They are snorting and farting and lunging at each other. We get out for morning tea and Joseph regales us for about a half hour on how he was clawed and mauled by a lion. His gestures and voice and motions are so wonderful he could be on the stage. On leaving the hippo pool we get very stuck in a bog and have to call for Rob to pull us out. At least we are stuck in the shade with jacana, black ibis (the ones who fish with their wings spread open), open billed stork, Meyer's parrots, green pigeons, and many more wonderful birds flying all around us.

September 14
Chobe, Chobe Game Lodge / hot, more humid

Neil, our pilot, flew us in a single engine plane to Chobe from Mombo Airstrip. The flight was easy, taking one hour and twenty minutes flying at 9,500 feet. Chobe Game Lodge is a charming yellow stucco building with bougainvillea in abundance. On our trip from the airport we saw elephant crossing the road right in front of us! Roan, sable, and red lechwe antelope grazing along the road.

The cruisers hold about eight people and are open with roll bars for gripping and standing. Have sundowners with a herd of very relaxed elephant - about forty plus. Lots of ages including a suckling baby, a first for me. You can really see the damage the elephant have done to the park. There is a lot of talk about culling the parks because the land cannot sustain the damage the elephants are doing. They estimate there are about fifty thousand in Chobe Park. Elephants eat 100 hundred pounds of food a day and drink up to fifty gallons of water. September and August are the two best months for game viewing as it hasn't rained in four months, and the animals have to go to the Chobe River to drink, so you're guaranteed excellent viewing everyday. The grass is completely gone and the elephants get their three hundred pounds from leaves and bark. There are big craters in the sandy dirt where the elephant paw for salt mineral.

In the road back to camp at high speed we are looking for a lion before we go in at dark when I ask about a bird that I see. Harris slams on the brakes and says, "Senegal coucal." I am thrilled as it is a new bird for me. Harris tries to start the car - no luck. This is the third time today we are stuck in a vehicle. After about a twenty minute wait, and glares from non-birders, we got picked up in a second vehicle and head home in the dark. Our little group of seven all dine together. We have been in each other's company now for seven days and really enjoy each other. Dorothy still and will forever amaze me. She walks with great vigor and always knows to whom she's speaking and turns to look at you. Her mind is so keen and memory invincible. She always has a quick laugh and a happy frame of mind. She is so well informed and well traveled, I can't think of anywhere she says she and Suzanne haven't been. From Bali to Mefiornos down to Chile and up to Alaska. They have been on three African safaris. She jumps in and out of vehicles with alacrity (at 65 and totally blind.)

Awaken with a knock on room 405 at 5:15 a.m. My gosh, it is sure dark outside, with a new moon and Venus shining in the sky. I look out of my balcony overlooking the Chobe River and hear the sloshing of elephants crossing. Leave with Harris at 6:00. Within minutes we're smack in the middle of a herd of three hundred to four hundred cape buffalo. We are sitting on the dirt road and they stampede across creating clouds of dust. They are all sizes and shapes, young and old, male and female, big boss and small boss. After much oohing and ahhing, we continue through the park hearing there are lion close by. Come upon six lion, four males, two females, chomping on an elephant baby that was killed in the night. The lion are not thirty yards from the car and we get great photos. The crunching of bone and red blood on the face make the kill very realistic. The lion will be satisfied for a few days.

Back for breakfast at 9:00, and then we're off on a small, eight seater boat up the Chobe River. Stanley is our captain, and magic about spotting birds. The rufous bellied heron, stone char, and white fronted plover among some to add to my list. Stanley takes us to an island filled with literally hundreds of buffalo. We get within a few yards of them as they graze away on very plentiful grass. A month from now you'd never see the buffalo here as there will be plenty of food on the mainland as the rains come and the grass returns. Just across the river from the island, a herd of between twelve and fifteen bull elephant decide to cool off with a morning swim and drink. They slurp up the water in their trunks like a straw. They curl the straw into their mouths and dump what looks like gallons of water, even though in reality half of it falls to the ground. After their morning thirst is quenched, they start across the river. We, in our little boat, are only yards from them. As they get to the adjacent island to the buffalo, they start to wallow in the mud. They take the straw (their trunk) again and sling the mud all over them - back, sides, even under their bellies. Some of them lie down in huge mud holes and then have a hard time extracting their giant bodies out of the holes. All you can hear is the sucking of mud and splashing of water from these gentle giants. What a fabulous morning this has been, and it's only 11:00

On the way home, Stanley happens to have some fish on a stick and calls his friend the fish eagle, who swoops down, too happy for an easy meal, and just a few feet from the boat to grab it in its talons. We arrive home at 3:15, in time for me to get a quick swim and then another boat ride with Stanley. I am surprising Blaine with a champagne sundowner cruise. Stanley takes us to a spot where the elephants are grazing and we are literally only twelve feet away from a very huge elephant. His legs are down in the water so all you see is his enormous head, tusks, and upper part of his body. If he stretched out his trunk he could easily join us for cocktails with a sip of our champagne.

As we cruise down the river sipping champagne, we are entertained by fisherman gliding by in fishing mokoros. Baboons on the bank, frolicking, looking at us looking at them. More elephant come

An elephant joins us for cocktails.

down to the river for their evening cocktails. Crocodile and monitor lizards slither in the water after basking in the hot sun all day. We go through a hippo minefield. They are everywhere. We haven't hit one yet, but the odds are seriously in favor of us doing so. Back at the lodge in time for champagne cocktails and a last supper with our new friends.

It is really hot at night. There is a very pokey fan in the room, but no cross ventilation. Some air comes through the windows on the balcony, but because of bats and baboons, you can't leave the door open at all. You really don't even need a sweater at night, but early morning a sweatshirt feels good until the sun gets up a bit. I think what's amazing me the most about being in Africa at this time of year is just how dry and bare everything is. There was good rainfall last summer - so this is not because of drought, but just from the animals eating any brown grass that's left and the natural look of winter.

September 16
Chobe Game Lodge, Chobe / Pleasantly Hot Day and Night

Blaine and I are taking our final boat ride with Stanley this morning. Get on the boat at 6:15. The sun is not yet up. The fish eagle are sitting by the river. A few birds are scavenging for fish and insects. The sun breaks through the horizon and we begin another euphoric day. We have only seen clouds two days in three weeks. Full moon, stars, planets, and constellations. Good people, interesting conversations, spectacular animal and bird viewing, great fishing, informative nature walks, scenic flights over interesting diverse terrain, smells both sweet and potent, sights that superlatives can't describe, scrumptious food cooked in the native African tradition. Africa brings out the best in me, because I am always happy. I love the early morning knock, game drives and sundowners. There is nothing I don't love about my days in Africa. Nothing I would change.

We all (7) leave for Victoria Falls at 9:30. Easy customs at the Zimbabwe border, and arrive with no hassle at 11:30, in time for some serious shopping and lunch. Find Finn Allen's shop just as we had left it 2 years ago, and he was standing behind the counter. The same women were selling their crocheted toys and tablecloths. I bought a cow horn bracelet ($3) and Blaine found an African head carved of dark serpentine stone. Finn tells us to keep our eye out for gold serpentine (it has gold lines that look like stripes through stone) or verdite (it is becoming very rare). Try to find verdite that doesn't have iron deposits in it. We leave our friends listening to the sounds of reggae Caribbean African band playing on the patio of the Victoria Falls Hotel under a beautiful flowering tree.

Zimbabwe

Air Zimbabwe takes us to Kariba where we are picked up by John, pilot, and a single engine plane flying us over the Matusadona range and along the Zambezi river at sunset. We will be staying at Chikwenya. Absolutely charming, no other words to describe this place. Only twelve guests can stay, but only four are here when we arrive. Out thatched Cottage #1, completely open in the front, looks out on the Zambezi River and the mountains of Zambia. The cottage is made around large shade trees, with the trunks of several supporting the walls. It gives you a very rustic, out in the bush feeling. Elephant and Cape buffalo are sauntering in front of our cottage, grazing on the acacia applering tree. Dinner is out in the open and cocktails are around the fire. You never see any of the staff, even though there are nine, you have to fix your own drink or have a ranger do it. You cannot leave your cottage after dark without an armed ranger to escort you to dinner. The sounds in the middle of the night are thrilling. Hyena, owl, baboons all raising a ruckus.

Awaken to the drum at 5:30. After coffee, Ian, supreme birder, and I take off for a morning walk. He carries a gun (rifle) and a knife. We take off over the sand river and immediately come upon two grazing buffalo. After giving them a wide berth, we get into the shade of an acacia wood and come upon three elephant. They are not fifty yards away, eating the acacia applering, and are so well camouflaged and so quiet we barely knew they were there. As we walked by them I felt we were making more noise than they. We sit for awhile and I eat my biscuit and drink some water. We see many uncommon and colorful birds including the slate blue widow finch, Livingston's flycatcher, red billed helmet shrike. Continuing on our trek, Ian gets a very strong scent of leopard marking. He feels it is very close, and we detour around the odor. We see the enormous strangler fig tree with roots hanging down from branches, trying to reach the earth, the tsetse fly plant, and a thorn torch tree (which the natives use to extract the oil for cooking and to rub on the skins). Ian tells me if you take the torch branch and put it in water, it sterilizes the water from Bilharzia. We walk further and see the baboons looking very "people-like" dining out on the sausage tree fruit. Ian has used this plant to cure his topical sun skin cancer. He cuts it like a cucumber and rubs it on his skin. After about a month, his cancer disappeared. We head back to the camp for breakfast and can't get there from here. We are somehow totally surrounded by elephant. We decide to brave it, even though it means going between the herd, and we walk up the middle of the sand river until we can cut back in for home. Breakfast at 9:30 tastes great.

Blaine has a great morning, also, on his game drive. A mating pair of lions kept them all riveted, with lots of picture taking, and then, not far from that, was a very nice, relaxed leopard that they followed for about fifteen minutes.

Blaine and I go to a hide at 11:00, where we sit in great comfort on lawn chairs, with a cooler and bird and animal books, and look at elephant eating all around us. The dexterity that is achieved with the end of the trunk is fascinating to watch. The elephant somehow goes right to the applering like a magnet, and sucks it into her mouth. Some of these cows are tuskless - if a bull elephant is born it will have tusks, if a cow is born to a tuskless mother she will also have no tusks. There are about 58,000 muscles in an elephant trunk - about the same as our entire body. The various ways and methods of using this trunk never ceases to amaze me.

Lunch comes all too quickly, after which I fell into a very deep afternoon siesta. On the afternoon game drive, we saw a leopard and two mature saddle billed stork. Cocktails proved interesting. Veronica Stuchbury - who manages Chikwenya, BTP, and I were talking around the campfire when we heard this frightful cry out of the dark. Two or three more screams - the sound is closer. The noise is deafening. It is three hyena not twenty feet from us, about to come into camp. Veronica shines a flashlight at them and they scatter. Dinner and bed and the wonderful sounds of the night.

September 18
Chikwenya / Hot, dry, warm breeze

Ian and I again take our early morning stroll, but this time we can't even get out of camp for the elephant. Finally we circumnavigate and see some lovely kudu, a bushbuck jumps out of our path. The baboons are all congregated on the ground eating sausages and applerings, not far from them are single elephants, and small herds of three or four. I'm getting quite blazé about all this.

Ian describes what's happening inside a termite mound. It is a totally airconditioned hill, the air circulating around the sides and down the middle. The queen lives on the ground floor. She is fed and cleaned by others, her waste is removed. She cannot move because her body is fat with eggs. She's about the size of a slug. The other termites are the size of ants. They get the mound just the right temperature for fungus to grow, which is what they eat, keeping the mound at exactly 37° C. They all have their individual jobs - getting food, building the mound, feeding the queen, and some are just born to acquire wings and fly away and start new colonies. These termintes have no pigment, and only do their work at night, in the dark.

After another hardy breakfast, Blaine and I went out to a hide on the water. For two hours elephant come down to drink. Some were 100 yards away - others further. Huge families of elephant, teenage bulls wrestling with their trunks, one was pushed down in the mud. One young elephant laid down in the muddy water and a very young, no more than one year, tried climbing on top of him. They get themselves completely soaked, splashing each other. They try to shoo the cattle egret and sacred ibis away with their trunks. At one point, the young elephant walking way ahead of its forever eating mother, mistakes the path to our hide as the one to the water. She takes two steps down the path, and into our hide, and not ten feet from us, flares

1994

Termite Mound found on my early morning walk.

What a surprise visit!

her ears and lifts her trunk and scampers away, realizing her mistake. There are crocs sunning themselves along the water plants, and hippo snorting just out in front of us in the river.

Our afternoon cruise down the Zambezi was glorious. Got within inches of white fronted bee eaters and the carmine bee eater of the world all breed in the Zambezi river valley. There must be over three hundred nesting here in front of Chikwenya, on the banks of the river. Veronica, and her late husband Jeff, invented this raft we're on: three canoes held together in parallel fashion by welded metal angle irons on which were bolted eight plastic body shaped chairs in rows, which made this unusual craft a very stable place for game viewing. The ranger sat higher up on a platform with a similar seat and, with his feet, steered the boat that has a small outboard engine. All I could think of were the dhows of Lamu steering their Lanteen sails from a rope attached to their big toe. We circumnavigated a few hippos and crocs, and come back in time for dinner after having our sundowners anchored in the middle of the river, watching the sun sinking in the sky.

September 19
Chikwenya / hot and dry

In our water hide after breakfast, we see very little - the elephants sniff the bank, a few take some gulps of water, but the whole herd is watering themselves somewhere else today. While waiting for lunch, Agnes, the resident elephant of Chikwenya, and her two babies, walk into the kitchen and then across camp. After lunch, and many goodbyes, we are flown to Bumi Hills airstrip by Linda, our gorgeous pilot. It is horrendously rough as we are flying in the heat of the day across the Matusadona range with up/down drafts which really grab our single engine plane like a vacuum playing tug of war. There are peaks and valleys, and at times we are mighty close to those peaks. After forty minutes, arrive at Bumi Hills - no one here to greet us. Linda finds two people in a truck a ½ mile away. She assures us upon returning that the two people tell her that someone should pick us up at 4:30. She takes off and leaves us sitting on our duffles in the middle of a rocky, red dirt air strip with lion and leopard lurking surely not far away. I'm glad I always travel these days with my canteen of water. It is over 100° in the sun - but slightly cooler in the shade of a tree. Which we find. Hallelujah! 4:30 on the dot, Steve arrives to take us five minutes by road to a very fast outboard motor which launches us to Musango.

September 19
Musango / hot 100° +

Musango is an island in Lake Kariba - the thatched cottages are quite luxurious. Two spacious twin beds, a dressing room with a place to hang clothes as well as shelves. A rock walled bathroom made with the red rocks found in the hills, with shower open to the skies, but all enclosed as part of the cottage. There are six thatched cottages. A pool is almost finished. A veranda with two huge wicker chairs looks out on Lake Kariba and the sunrise. A birdbath made of washed stones is always filled and attracts many birds to within six feet of where I'm sitting. Steve and Titch got the last concession from the government to build Musango which they literally have done with their own hands. Steve is a top notch birder, showing us no less than twelve different species between the car pick up and the boat launch.

The lake is eerily quiet of people and as calm as glass. There are hundreds of dead standing mopani trees in the lake which were on land before they were flooded to make the lake in 1960. When the dam was made, the local Tonga tribe were upset and said their spiritual god, Naminyani, would come and haunt the dam builders. He was god of the sea and shaped like a serpent. Two times, in 1956 and 1958, there were monumental floods which completely wiped out the beginning construction of the dam. The Tonga people kept saying it is our god doing this, but eventually the dam was completed. Kariba is a word taken from Tonga, meaning mousetrap, as there was a huge rock jutting out where they put the dam, which trapped fish when it was still part of the wide Zambezi River. There are virtually no large mammals around Musango. The occasional elephant or buffalo are seen on neighboring lands, impala and waterbuck are numerous. The bird life is grand. Tons of new birds for me. I can't wait to mark Blaine's Neuman's.

The schedule of Musango is pretty laid back. Up at 5:30 - hot coffee on our veranda - binoc. in hand - it's dark - but lots of bird calls. The sun creeps over the lake at about 6:00. Spectacular! Mosey up to the lodge about 6:15 for a few biscuits and we're off on the boat, canoeing on the quiet backwaters of the lake. There are all sorts of dead trees in the lake which house not only birds' nests, but birds drying their feathers, and good launching points for malachite kingfishers, as well as fish eagles. A cane turtle dove has mistakenly made her nest in the stump of a dead tree in the lake - she's well camouflaged as she sits on her nest of one egg. The green backed heron has a very flimsy nest of a few grass hairs supporting her three fairly good sized eggs. It is inconceivable that they won't all topple into the lake with the first light wind. A wired tailed swallow has a cup like nest of stucco under a rock that juts out into the lake. Her three chicks are open mouthed, awaiting their next meal.

The hippo and croc are very quiet this early in the morning. The sun is just high enough to wear sunglasses when we disembark from the canoes. Steve, our trusty ranger, rifle in hand, leads us across the hills. We do sight elephant - two babies lying flat down asleep - but it is basically a nature walk - learning about termites and mopani worms, the horn bill's nests, which seal the female inside where her molted feathers make a nest and she stays until her first born chick pecks its way out of the nest. We check out lots of tracks, some of which I am beginning to know.

It's rest time after we get back to breakfast until lunch. I make Steve take me to the middle of Lake Kariba, away from the crocs, for a swim. Even at this distance they won't let me stay in more than five minutes. It's still scorchingly hot at 4:00, but nothing like what happens here in October - March. The rainy season, about the end of November, is the best viewing time for birds, but would be hell as far as living conditions. A very comfortable afternoon sunset cruise ends the day at Musango. The sunset through the dead mopani trees gives an eerily quiet, majestic but somewhat morbid, daunting respect for nature and life. An old bull elephant clumsily walks to the shore of the lake and inhales a trunk full of water. His body is caked with red mud, which takes on a rust colored patina in the sunset. He is about sixty-five, and on his last molars. You can see by his chewing that they are worn almost down to nothing.

On the last day at Musango we go into the fishing village three kilometers away, called Msaba Fishing Camp. James drives us in an old pickup, with Blaine and Pencil riding in back. Some of the names of the local Africans are Hubcap, Manure, and these are actually on their birth certificates. There are about eight hundred people in Msaba, and it is all set in clumps of huts (like neighborhoods.) The thatched rondavels are adobe red, deep burn red. Pencil takes us to the chairman, who has been elected unanimously by the people to run the village. His name is Taylor Mwamba and well respected even though he looks to be between 55 and 65, a lot younger than some of the old men we see. The village is on a peninsula of the lake with the most gorgeous view. There are dried tigerfish and long nets drying in the sun.

We are taken to the middle of the village. Someone brings me a chair to sit on and a bench for Blaine and James. At first, just a handful of people come, some with reed grass mats, some picnic baskets, a bowl, a walking stick. Little by little we are attracting the chil-

1994

Lake Kariba — this elephant isn't used to people on his lake.

dren, then more men come with more baskets, a few wood carvings, a wooden head rest. We wait. Patience is key in this village. At times we sit for two or three minutes when nothing happens. Pencil tells me more baskets are coming. Now we have about 75 or 100 people, it's really hard to tell, men, women, and children all around us. I think only two men had on shoes. None of the children and none of the women did. They really have very few clothes on and they look very dirty. Some speak a word or two of English, but we mainly deal with James, Pencil, and Taylor. After much hoopla, we buy two old stools (the worn thrones of chiefs), a reed music maker, a broom that is made of grass only found in the woods, a carved baboon smoking a pipe. I gave the chairman my black canvas water shoes, and I have taken some soap and kleenex for gifts. They have never seen anything like this and have no idea what to do with either thing. Blaine gives the chairman $10 U.S. and everyone is happy. They are full of laughter and jokes when I want my picture taken with them. They all pose, wanting to be in it. Blaine is offered an old straw hat which he comically puts on his head and all the children giggle. (Soccer is played with plastic bag wrapped in string).

We stop at the Bumi Hills Museum on the way to the airport. It is absolutely in the middle of nowhere, and is also a craft center where locals have brought hundreds of baskets, carvings, serpentine stone sculptures to sell. Musango has been a very relaxing experience and totally different. No game drives, but lots of bird life and water experience.

September 20
Harare / Glorious 80's

The Meikles Hotel is undergoing some major construction. It is noisy, beginning at 6:00 a.m. We are back in civilization with a vengence. A & K didn't meet our plane in Harare, but we're getting to be such old hands. Blaine got a cart for our luggage, and we took the local bus to a downtown bus terminal where the bus driver went next door to the Meikles and hailed a porter for our luggage while we minded his bus. We could never have handled this with such ease and good humor a month ago.

September 21
Harare / 80's, sun, glorious

Our final day in Harare and Africa. We are picked up by Daphne, an owner of a travel agency whom we met at Musango to go to the Mbare market. No words can describe it. Its warehouse contains within it hundreds of rows of vendors selling baskets, serpentine sculptures, walking sticks, wood carvings, spices, snuff, some of the ebony carving items from Malawi. The baskets are woven around Bulewayo, the serpentine sculpture is carved around Harare. The men and women vendors are very low key and polite. They say good morning, how are you - but by and large leave you alone to look at their goods. There

Susan and new friends holding her new bartered for possessions

were very few people buying. I saw two other white people and maybe twenty blacks in the whole warehouse. You see so many of the same things - the carvings are done by hand, the baskets are woven and yet in this quantity it's hard to get excited about any of them. A lot like Kenya and Tanzania. I'll kick myself when I get home for not buying lots more.

The stone factory is just around the corner from Mbare, and Daphne takes us there also. She has brought her chauffeur along to mind the car while we are in the markets. She said her car might not have hubcaps when she returned. There are huge rocks, about two hundred pounds, sitting in mounds uncarved. Each stone carver had his own carving chisels and were tapping away at the large lump of rock. Harare is famous for its serpentine stone. The golden serpentine is very rare and hard to find. Verdite is also getting difficult to find. When the carvers have the huge blob of rock it looks like something we'd get out of a big field stone quarry at home, but the wetting and polishing of the finished product produces a brilliant patina that is lovely. I bought a small sculpture at the factory made of golden serpentine and then met the sculptor. He was one of the oldest men in the factory and had no legs, but did brilliant work with his hands. He had his head covered with a hat made of the cord of a baobab tree. What a sight - if only I had my camera. I paid $7 U.S. for my lovely carving of which Myles Kudzunga got $5.00.

The trees are full of spring in Harare. The flowers are in profusion along the streets. The jacaranda a vibrant purple next to the shocking red of the flame trees. The bougainvillea hug the walls of the private houses, giving them warmth in their bright colors of deep pinks, reds, and oranges. There are about ten million people in Zimbabwe, in which a little over one million live around Harare. The streets are bustling with people. Women in bright blouses and Kanga skirts walk with babies papoosed on their backs. There are many high rise buildings with very definite Chinese influence in architecture.

The Zimbabwe dollar is very devalued right now. I had lunch before we left in the hotel cafeteria. There were three head waiters. One of them took a tray for me and asked which selection I wanted - tuna, chicken salad, curried lamb, or pot roast - about six different choices. He then sat me down and one of six waiters brought me a ginger ale. My head waiter then brought my tray with a chicken salad nicely presented on a bed of lettuce with hard boiled eggs and tomatoes sliced around the chicken, and a hot roll freshly baked.

I had no Zim. $, so we went to reception to trade in the U.S. $ to pay for lunch. The whole bill was $2.80. I couldn't believe it! The present exchange rate is 6.5 Zimb. $ to 1 U.S. South Africa is 2 Rand for 1 U.S. The Botswana Pula is also about 6.5 to 1 U.S.

One of the best expressions all over South Africa is "see you right now" -- which translates into "see you later."

Leave Johannesburg on S.A. Airways - 8:00 p.m., of course right on the dot. The plane is only half full, and Blaine and I sit separately so I can have three seats together to get my beauty rest. The plane, a 747-400, is huge. It has a GPS monitoring our flight on screen for us. We now have been gone ten minutes and we've gone 55 miles at a speed of 512 MPH at an altitude of 19,000 feet. It has a little airplane and map and the plane moves on the map as we progress west. The outside air temperature is 4°F. We are headed 323 degrees west.

Flying over Johannesburg townships you see only the lights from the street lamps outlining the shantys.

- 1995 -

Uganda, Tanzania & Kenya

January 18

Left Pond House in Chadds Ford at 4:45 a.m. - our plane (British Air) at 6:45 a.m. - Backed away from jetport at 7:20 a.m. (on time), then stopped. Broken spring on de-icer valve for 4th engine. New valve flown down from NYC. Finally depart 12:10 - almost 5 hours late. Arrived Heathrow 4 hours late, missed BA flight at 10 a.m. to Nairobi! Considerable difficulty in getting tickets on Air Kenya at 8 p.m. - But finally did, after 3-4 hours in Sheraton Skyline, back at Heathrow at 5 p.m. Major 3 hour hassle with BA to get bags on Kenyan Air, but succeeded just one minute before plane departed. So arrived at 8 a.m. in Nairobi - with all bags. Secured a day room at the Norfolk for 3 hours, a little lunch, and a much needed nap. Our plane to Entebbe, Uganda was packed - mainly by Egypt's soccer team - Hilarious confusion before we left - Kenyan Air couldn't decide which of the two planes was going to Entebbe, with the result that Mombassa luggage was erroneously put on Entebbe plane, had to be unloaded, passengers milling on the tarmac. Finally arrived in Entebbe 41 hours after we had left Chadds Ford, and spent a very pleasant night at the Victoria Hotel. People at Victoria are exceptionally nice.

Samuel (a native Ugandan, and Geoffrey Kent's personal driver loaned to us for this exploratory venture arranged by Abercrombie & Kent) picks us up at 7:30 a.m. sharp, after a splendid breakfast. The drive was unbelievable. Very good vehicle - large, comfortable (seats 8) diesel Toyota Land Cruiser, with extra cushions, 2 hatches, spare petrol cans, etc. Sam is an excellent, fast driver! For first several hours (until almost 4 p.m.) - the road was tarmac, constructed by the Chinese - we "flew" (120KLH) until we encountered many miles of huge potholes created by emergency U.N. relief trucks en route to Rwanda. We passed a number of U.N. food convoys bound for Rwanda to help with the recent (and continuing) disaster. (We did not know then, the "disaster" became the horrific genocide of thousands of Rwandan Tutsis.) We went through village after village, people milling in the streets - walking or on bicycles - selling meat hanging out doors, large fish from Lake Victoria, - no personal cars - numerous "taxis" which are mini buses, with a few large buses. Had lunch at Lakeview Hotel at Mbaraia - only other people there were 20-40 Canadian soldiers with U.N. insignia, en route to Mombasa with their vehicles for sea transport home, and their return home from 6 months service in Kigali and elsewhere in Rwanda. Tourists frightened away by its fearful dictator (Idi Amin) had not been coming to Uganda for several years. We were among the very first to venture back, so we were not surprised to see no other tourists.

Lakeview was filled with Marabou storks lazily soaring from hotel rooftop to lawn. Only had a coke and cup of soup because we were in a big hurry to reach Buhoma, our campsite in the Impenetrable Forest. Drove madly for 3 hours (120 KLH through villages with thousands of people in the streets) and stopped off at Whitehorse Inn for snack (chicken sandwich and coke). Still no tourists to be seen anywhere. The Whitehorse Inn in Kabala was at the end of the tarmac. Road then became dirt track, 9 feet in width mostly, with rain rivulets, holes, you name it. Still Samuel went hell bent for leather; for 4 more hours! Scenery became mountains, green terraced fields, beautiful. Sometimes Uganda is called little Switzerland because of the topography only - not the slightest resemblance otherwise. Many consider Uganda the prettiest and most green country in Africa. Stopped to photograph cows with very large horns (4'-5') but chased away by a

1995

herdsman. We gave him sweet bananas we had bought from a farmer at the Equator. Bananas everywhere literally! Sweet bananas are very short (4"-5") and very sweet. Also stopped to take photos of crowned cranes bunched in a meadow in the mountains. Perhaps 100 in the flock! We marveled at their beauty and their courting antics - had never seen more than a pair at one time in our prior African trips. Stopped by soldiers with lethal looking automatic weapons - searched car - searched us - finally they let us pass - scary!

We have finally reached our destination after our 12-hour drive.

BLAINE'S NOTES ON TREKKING UGANDA GORILLAS

Was growing dark when we finally arrived at the Impenetrable Forest and Camp Buhoma - beautiful Camp Buhoma! They had delayed the normal 7:00 p.m. dinner. Our trip, going full out the entire time, and making only quick stops, took 12 exhausting, fascinating, interesting hours!! A whale of an experience! Twice we stopped only for snacks, once for petrol! They hand pumped the fuel from otherwise modern looking pumps with innards showing. The bathroom at the petrol place was a real experience! We also stopped once to look at handmade drums, once to buy sweet bananas and look at 3 legged stools. Never saw any other tourists.

Dr. Liz Macfie, Director of the International Gorilla Conservation Program, a well-known ambassador of the African Wildlife Foundation, and head of the gorilla program in Uganda, joined us for dinner, with her friend, Phil, a Britisher, also working here with CARE, gorilla tourism, etc. Liked Liz right off - We pumped her with questions about the gorillas in Uganda versus those we had seen in Rwanda five years before. She was in Karisoki in Rwanda, for 3 years the chief vet for the gorilla program. Very experienced, very knowledgeable, very personable and likeable. Susan was bone tired (with a touch of Meniere's) so excused herself after a great fish dinner. Blaine, Liz, and Phil stayed on for several beers more over wonderful Ugandan coffee.

Up for our first gorilla trek a bit too early. First at 1:30 a.m., and again at 4 a.m., and BTP misreading his clock, actually got up at 5:40 instead of 6:40. Susan really miffed, so Blaine went back to bed. Like getting up for duck shooting. Couldn't wait. Night was quite cold - needed 2 heavy blankets. Finally got up for 7 a.m. Breakfast, and registration.

We headed off around 8 a.m. - led by William, who gave us a nice introductory speech (although embarrassed that Liz the Director was listening), and 3 trackers, our porters (Ephram and Stanley), Liz, a young couple from Australia, and Bob Wolf, a crusty old bastard also staying at Buhoma (we were the only 3 tourists). Liz had gone to great trouble to switch our reservations to the second gorilla group, called "Katengere", because we were exhausted from our 68 hour ordeal getting there, and the second gorilla group had been located much closer for several preceding days, having been found by the trackers the day before shortly after 9 a.m. Liz was trying to make our trek shorter and less difficult.

1995

The start of a trek through the Impenetrable Forest

The trackers went ahead - the rest of us in single file, climbing first through a tea plantation, but quickly into the Impenetrable Forest. Everyone had a staff, heavy rugged footwear, and hearty trousers. Everyone carried a rain suit, but did not wear it because rain did not appear likely. Susan and I wore a long-sleeved cotton shirt (no hat). I sweated mine up pretty good in only 45 minutes. At first, we were just on a small path created by smugglers from Zaire, but then veered off that and straight up the mountain. The incline was unbelievably steep. I tried not to huff right at first, but that was hopeless. Quickly, I was puffing so hard I could not get anywhere near enough oxygen (even though we were only at 6,000 - 7,000 feet). The line would stop. Even the young couple couldn't get their breath. Then we would go another ten to fifteen feet. Stop, gasp for air, 10 more feet or 20 more feet, or just 5 more feet, depending on the vegetation, rocks, slipperiness, height of successive steps needed, etc., then stop and heave some more. I did not think I was going to make it, but finally reached the top of the mountain, which is where we expected to find the gorillas.

Liz joked, "Wouldn't it be just like the gorillas to make me look foolish in switching you to this group for them to go on down the other side of the mountain we have just climbed?" And guess what, that is just what happened. So then we began our descent of the far side of the mountain. The puffing was less severe, but going down is far more treacherous - very rough on knees, and hurts the ends of your toes. We went the whole damned way down - to a bog at the bottom we had to cross with considerable difficulty. We were kidding Liz pretty hard by now, although I couldn't decide whether to just quit (how in the hell would I ever get back?) or cry. Damned if we didn't start climbing the second mountain through the thickest, steepest going unimaginable! Nobody thought we would stop, and the trackers would fan out while we heaved and gasped and tried to stop our abused limbs from trembling.

Blaine and Liz with two trekkers

Almost to the top of the second mountain, the trackers came back to tell us that the gorillas were about 150 yards ahead. The porters were required to stop, take our staffs, and give us our binoculars and cameras they had been carrying for us and wait for our return. We forgot our weariness, and proceeded eagerly and quietly on the trackers' heels until they stopped, and there was Mr. Silverback himself, all 400 plus pounds of him sitting in the extremely dense vegetation in Buddha fashion staring directly at us, perhaps 30-35' away! We huddled in cluster around the trackers and started taking photos as fast as the shutters could click. Usually the silverback fakes a charge when

1995

Mr. Silverback guarding his family

humans first appear (at least this was true in Rwanda) but this fellow just sat there. A juvenile was frolicking a bit to his left, but we had a poor view of him because the vegetation was so thick. The silverback sat munching a stalk for possibly two minutes (time in the presence of a 400 pound gorilla is difficult to judge), and instead of charging, he leapt to all fours and was 15'-20' up a sizeable tree in a flash, scaring everyone half to death. He hung one-armed from a 4 or 5" limb for just a second or two, when the limb snapped in a loud crack and Mr. Silverback came tumbling in a gigantic crash!

Everyone was startled and frightened, not knowing what was going to happen next. But Silverback composed himself, scrambled a bit on all fours, and started again on his munchies. Everyone wanted to exclaim and point and talk about this explosive episode we had just witnessed, but bulging eyes and facial expressions had to suffice, for fear if we made a noise Silverback might charge or else lead his group away. So silently we watched in awe of undoubtedly the most impressive wild creature in all of Africa -- all the more fascinating because in the animal order they rank closer to man than any other beings (ahead of orangutans, who are second and chimpanzees, who are third). They are at once fearsome and appealing. They could literally break you in one mighty swipe, yet one comes to think of them, as they are aptly known, as "gentle giants". You know you wouldn't dare risk it if the opportunity arose, but their manner and expressions arouse a temptation to try to give them a pat and befriend them.

This group was not habituated to the presence of humans until February of 1994, and has only 6 members - the big silverback, 3 black backs (as younger males are called), and only one female who has a baby in tow. The total mountain gorilla population in Uganda, according to the best count available, numbers only 280 creatures, and only one other group from that population has been habituated to date. The rest of the world's scarily small population is found in the nearby Virunga volcanoes where Rwanda and Zaire join, and they number perhaps about 300. Until the recent war between the Hutus and Tutsis, most research work with the world's dwindling popula-

Young gorilla in wonderment

tion of mountain gorillas was carried out in Rwanda, but the war and Tutsi genocide has stopped all research and tourist activity there for now. Some gorilla viewing continues in Zaire, but the practices and methods there raise many questions and concerns with knowledgeable researchers. Uganda is the new place, and they are doing it in the way it ought to be done. When it comes to mountain gorillas, Bwindi (the Impenetrable Forest) in Uganda is the class act.

Wise rules for the protection of the gorillas and their continued "wildness" first developed in Rwanda and followed now in Uganda limit tourist contact to one hour. Believe me, that hour flies by in a wink. The guide quietly whispers: "It's time to go", and everyone is sad to leave our new, very special friends.

For some reason, returning was easier than going. Same inclines and descents -- only in reverse. Same huffing, puffing, and wheezing -- but with a hint of a smirk. I had just about quit three different times going, but by golly, I made it. I climbed those damned mountains and I succeeded in seeing gorillas. Too old, too fat, too out of shape! Anything less than a ceremony in the Rose Garden and a report of my glorious achievement by Peter Jennings on the evening TV would be a disappointment. All I did was prove that just about anybody can go see the mountain gorillas. You don't have to be young, run 3 miles a day, work out on the Stairmaster, or even walk regularly. If you want enough to do it, and if you are willing to proceed a bit, stop a bit - proceed a bit, it is a piece of cake. At least in hindsight! And what it will do for you will be unmeasurably unforgettable.

From Blaine's Notes:

Sadly, one year after our experience at beautiful Camp Buhoma (almost to the day), Buhoma was attacked by rebel militants, burned to the ground, and several of the wonderful native staff who attended us were murdered. Tourism was not yet safe.

January 24

Up before sunrise with tea and coffee brought to our tent by Peter, our tent boy. He brings hot water for shaving and a shower. It is 6:30 a.m. and cold. We sleep under 2 blankets at night. I can't believe we're going to do this again. Blaine and I are a little stiff in the legs, but not as bad as we had thought. We meet at the park center again and start off with Caleb as our guide and Thorn joins us. The climb is torture. It is so steep, Caleb has to pull me up as each step you take is about 1 ½ feet above the last step. The ground has a lot of decomposed leaf matter which makes it soft but unpredictable. At times, you don't know if you are going to step on a rock or in a hole. There are no stinging nettles, so you can reach out and grab vines and tree trunks to help pull you up. The path we are taking is very narrow, as it was made by the gorillas yesterday and only wide enough to put one foot in front of the other. On either side it is dense with vegetation. There are at times loose nuts and fruits on the ground that the monkeys and gorillas have dropped from the high trees. Caleb points out the different leaves and bark that the monkeys and gorillas eat, as well as the butterflies, beetles, and spiders (large groups of seemingly floating clawless spiders, a little like daddy long legs, but swarms of fifty all together).

The walk is a little steeper than yesterday, but we come upon the gorillas in 1 ½ hours. It is the first habituated group and quite large, with one silverback, four females, and six babies. We see one baby just five months old being rocked and held by its loving three hundred pound mother. Her head is buried some of the time in a pile of ants, and when she sits up, you can see a muzzle of yummy brown ants. The silverback is very vocal and beats his chest a few times. We see some babies swinging on a vine and others eating leaves. This group is quite gentle and peaceful with their family, it's hard to believe this group has only been habituated since 1992. Which was the first time they ever encountered humans who were nice to them, not out to poach a hand or a baby for a zoo. After filming and viewing for an hour, we went to a shady spot and stopped for a picnic lunch.

Taking a break for a picnic lunch

The rest of the trip back to camp was steep, but downhill and not quite so tough, especially knowing we have met the challenge of the impenetrable forest and succeeded. After a much needed Coke back at camp, Sam, Susan, and I take a great bird walk along the river trail. The river is really clear, and looks as if it would be a perfect spot to catch trout. We see many exciting birds, including the black collared apalis and the long crested eagle. After a delicious dinner prepared by Chef Richard, which was tilapia as well as chocolate souffle, Blaine and I sit around the campfire looking up at zillions of stars and see a perfect V in the sky, made from God, letting the world know we accomplished a great feat, and are victorious! Bed feels oh so good, read my Wilbur Smith book by flashlight. There is no electricity in Buhoma, dinner is by the light of a kerosene lamp, which we also have in our tent.

January 25
Ishasha National Park
Very pleasant a.m., hot (85°-90°) in p.m.

Wake up pitchy dark, 6:00 a.m. to go to Ishasha National Park today. It is not very far, but the road is dirt and full of holes. The first animal we see is a Kob. The male has horns, not the females. They are stockier than impala, but very similar in size and coloration. Lots of savannah. We open the hatches and stick our heads out the top. Swallows follow our land cruiser like gulls behind a boat, or the barn swallows behind my Kubota when I cut the grass. As we drive along we roust out many flies and insects which become a happy meal ticket for the birds. The panorama is breathtaking as we look at Topi, Kob, Cape buffalo, and many birds. We are the only vehicle in this enormous park. The only people with thousands of animals. We come across a very relaxed herd of elephants who seem more curious about us than we are of them. There is a matriarch, a young bull, two very small babies, one of whom nurses as we sit and watch them. There is a mudhole and they wallow and spray themselves with the muddy water. We have a picnic lunch sitting on the hatch of the cruiser watching hippo, Egyptian geese, and white pelican. Head back for Buhoma at about 2:00 p.m. I forgot to mention, early on in the park we had a flat tire and had to jack up the car, get the spare, and repair. Not surprising, considering the rough roads we've been on.

Leave Buhoma Gorilla Camp at 7:30 in the morning for our trip to Mweya Safari Lodge. We will take the short-cut road, which is a bit dicey, but the alternative is to go all the way back to Mbarara, which would be another ten hour drive. This drive is only about 120 K's, but the road has been really damaged by recent rains, and the deep gouges in the muddy road are at times 4' deep. The scenery is breathtaking. As we are leaving Buhoma early we see very few people walking in the road. There are people carrying their water cans, women with buckets of clothes on their heads. Their little mud houses hidden away behind ever present banana trees. As the day goes on, we see more men with baskets on their backs wave and smile as we pass. The women and men look clean and neat, with white pressed shirts for men and bright kangas that the women drape over their heads to keep the ever present dust out of their hair.

After three hours of seeing no cars, we break down on the side of one of these steep, rough, inclines. Sam syphons out some of the dirty bad gas (diesel) he thinks is causing the problem. We lose about ½ an hour, but thank God we are on our way again! We finally arrive at Mweya at 2:30, in time for a lovely lunch of fried tilapia, caught just outside the lodge on Lake Edward. Mweya is situated in Queen Elizabeth National Park, between Lake Edward and the Mweya Safari Lodge on the Kazinga Channel. It is high up on a hill looking down at the hippos, elephants, fish eagles, and Malachite kingfishers. At 5:00 p.m. we took the *African Queen* looking boat slowly around the channel looking at the various birds and hippo life. One hippo delivered

A sunset cruise on the **African Queen**

Two-Day Old Baby Hippo

a baby in the water, as they usually do, who was only two days old. The variety of bird life is the best I have seen anywhere. The boat is extremely comfortable and viewing is excellent.

Our beds feel very comfortable, and sleeping comes easily at 9:30. Awaken fairly late as we have a relaxed day game viewing and driving to the crater area of the park. We drive along a plateau looking down 300 feet both left and right at the crater lakes which are bereft of animal life. An occasional buffalo or kob is around, but all and all very quiet. Drive to a lovely crater lake (salt) and sit above it having a luxurious picnic lunch on a blanket overlooking the hills and the reflection of the hills in the lake. This Uganda is truly God's country. So diverse, and yet so full of the wonders of nature. From tall rocky mountains to deep clear crater lakes and from banana and tea plantations to savannah and acacia and euphorbia candelabrum. From the impenetrable Bwindi Forest, full of kapok, lianas, and tree ferns to the deep green low level altitude forest of Chamburu. All beautiful and God's gift to these kind and gentle people.

1995

JANUARY 27
70'S, HUMID

Awaken way before light to drive to Chamburu Gorge for our chimpanzee trek. Arrive at light, and leave for the gorge, after a very informative lecture from our guide. Blaine and I were accompanyied by our driver, Sammy, our guide, and our tracker (with AK47) to our launch point. We hear the chimps screaming across the river. We climb down a fairly steep precipice, poking our staffs in the mud for support and balance. The forest is lush and green, filled with the most exotic sounds, and truly the vision that movies are made of. You can hear the hornbills and colobus monkeys calling, many doves cooing, and the raucous chimps bashing. Within one hour we come to the tree where the chimps are eating seeds. There is a family of six, with an extremely large silverback (our guide says he weighs about 50-60 kg or 150 lbs). His name is Charlie, and then two females, two juveniles, and one young male named Brutus. They are almost directly above us, and at one point one of them pees just 5 feet in front of me.

In the gorge looking for chimpanzees

They are very human like in the way they use their arms and legs. They are quite high in the trees, and our guide says they are very agile and never fall (as do gorillas). This is the prettiest place we have seen so far in Uganda. The gorge is just breathtaking with the sound of the river, the rustling of the leaves, the sweet fragrance of the saba Florida flower, which the chimps have spread like a blanket on the floor of the forest. There are only 29 chimps in this part of the forest, there are hundreds in the Kabale forest, but none habituated. These 29 will soon be extinct if they don't keep their existing forest. They are running out of habitat and therefore a food supply. They will have to inbreed if their forest becomes smaller and therefore die for lack of new blood. We see a very social family of colobus high up in a tree. Five of them are sitting in the top. One newborn baby, whom the mother shows off to the other monkeys, is all white, with a skinny, long white tail, and a black face.

Our afternoon game drive turns out to be a real surprise. We take the "royal circuit" route of the park, and come upon a herd of elephant crossing the path in front and behind us. One elephant has a broken ear and it dangles forward. They are not shy at all, and we spend a lot of time sharing the afternoon with them. Our drive is very pleasant, looking at lots of birds and just enjoying nature. At about 6:00 p.m. we settle down for our sundowners, and just where we are parked, a herd of elephants come across the "road," and we see that it is the same herd that we saw earlier with the elephant with the broken

"Broken Ear"

ear. They have gone across country, eating as they walk, and we have gone by road (almost 1 ½ hours) and see the same group!

I have made some ice from the little ice tray in the fridge in our room, so our sundowners are especially delicious as it is the first ice we have had since arriving in Uganda. It is our last fun day in Uganda, as tomorrow we must start our long drive back to Entebbe. We have learned a lot about the people. We have eaten Matoke and goat's meat, tilapia and cassava. We have driven on the worst roads conceivable, and have seen some of the most awesome scenery and diverse topography. Even though we've spent literally hours on the road, we've crossed the entire country from east to west and as far south as it goes until you are in Rwanda, and we have been on the Zaire border a number of times, and I don't feel we've wasted a single minute. God has not made a mean Ugandan. They are beautiful people with clean white teeth and short cut hair who care a lot about their appearance and have a love of their country.

January 28
HOT - HUMID

Leave Mweya sadly at 8:45, and after photographing many local sites: the butcher in Benyeni, the fruit markets, the small mud huts, the village women in their bright kangas, all the children waving; we arrive at Lake Mburu National Park in time for a picnic lunch down by the lake. A man comes in his dugout canoe for some firewood he has stacked near where we sit. He will carry it back in his canoe to the fishing village to smoke the fish they catch in the lake. The fishing village is very primitive, with Marabou stork scavenging around the huts, and the men drunk, as it is Saturday. A few younger men are repairing and making fish nets, and some are stringing some bait fish on a stick to hang in the sun to dry.

Mburu is disappointing as far as game viewing is concerned.

Zilched. There are some flowering acacias. But it is neither pretty nor interesting. On our drive back to Mbarara to the Lake View Hotel. Sam, a Kikuyu, tells us some of his tribal traditions. A wife costs 10 cows, and each cow is worth $100. If the man is very rich, he may buy more than one wife. The first wife is the most respected, and the one the other wives must obey. Everyone lives like one big happy family. If the man of the family dies and has lots of wives, the boy child of the first wife can marry the youngest wife, and therefore he is able to have children with her. He told us how the Kikuyu are stocky, and have a receding hairline, where as the Masai have long skinny legs and sharp features. The Luo are the tallest and broadest of all the tribes. The Kikuyu is the biggest tribe in East Africa (Kenya and Tanzania), numbering 14 million. There are about 16 million people in Uganda, and the Bujanda tribe is the biggest, with about 7 million people, and the Ankole (where we have been) is the next biggest tribe. The people of Uganda like Muzeveni (the president) very much, as he has brought stability in the country which was completely decimated until nine years ago. Uganda was a disaster during the Idi Amin era, then came

Blaine and Susan by car with their trusty driver, Sam

1995

Obote, then came the Tanzanian government, pillaging, and raping the women all over the countryside. The Ankole women were treated very poorly. Musevini has given the people respect again and hope for a better future. In the entire country there are only about eleven places to stay because they have not catered to tourists until recently.

January 29

Between Entebbe and Buhoma, which is a 12-hour drive, there are only two places to stop. MBarara and the Lake View is the first stop, and then the White House Inn in Kahali about three hours later. There is literally nothing, not a place to stop in between! If you have to go to the bathroom, you do it in the bushes along the side of the road, but throw a rock to scare the python away. The place is still very wild and primitive. Where they've never heard of ice and you brush your teeth with bottled water. Some places have just gotten electricity, but they make toast over an open fire and the staple is chicken, tilapia, and Nile Special beer. The vegetables are fresh and delicious, as well as

A roadside hotel

the fruit, which adds up to a pretty wholesome diet.

We have a pleasant drive to Kampala, our last day of taking in all the great sights along the road. Pied kingfishers, black kites, and long crested eagles all vie for the electricity lines.

Go to the Sheraton Hotel for lunch in Kampala, a quick trip to the local botanical garden in Entebbe, and then a 5:00 p.m. flight to Nairobi. Everything works like a Swiss watch, and we arrive at the Norfolk with time to spare for for cocktails and dinner.

January 30
dry 70°-80°

Our day is at leisure, and we are taking advantage of that by going to the giraffe center first thing. Mimosa, Betty June's sister and Buttercup's daughter, is awaiting my arrival and has her tongue all ready for yummy pellets. She is a lovely Rothschild and likes me so much, she gives me a big kiss with her long 18" tongue. There are seven Rothschilds at the manor, and even a Daisy II. These are all translocated giraffe - their markings are different as their spots look like butterfly wings.

After a bit more shopping in Karen, including Sue Wood's bead factory, which is now called Kizuri (there are now 110 women in the factory, up from the 10 of 1987). We spend the rest of the day at the Norfolk, and a few hours at the pool. Dinner with Debbie Sneltson of AWF, she's fun, a great mountain hiker, bright, English, and has lived in Nairobi since 1979.

Tanzania
January 31
Mahale - Katavi / crisp morning

Picked up by Roland Purcel at the Wilson Airport to fly in his single engine Cessna to Mahale in Tanzania. Fly over Lake Ndutu, the

1995

Serengeti, Gelai Mountain. Everything looks dark and brown and dry. Stop at Tabore in Tanzania for a customs check and a picnic lunch of cheese and bread and paté sitting on a stump next to the BP gas fill up. Arrive at Mahale grass airstrip at the base of the mountain. Porters come from nowhere, as do lots of little children. What fun to video the children with my camera, and let them see themselves in motion. None has seen themselves before, they have no idea what they look

First time these children had ever seen themselves

like, and so wowed by the video they don't want me to leave. Get in a leaky 40' boat (Zoe) to transport us the next hour to Mahale. We left at 11:00 a.m., arrive Mahale at 6:00 p.m. It is set in a cove, facing west on Lake Tanganyika. You see the verdant hills rising above the camp. There is a bar-dining-library tent, white, very Arabian looking, with an Oriental rug on the dining room floor, and huge cushions in the bar area. We have the use of two tents, since we are the only ones here, and use the other tent for our duffles and dressing room. Drinks are around a huge campfire, with wonderful roasted nuts and Finlandia

Luxurious tent at Mahale on Lake Tanganyika

with ice. This is perhaps the most luxurious campsite we have ever been to.

February 1
Humid - Feels Like Rain

Awaken at a very respectable 7:30 a.m. with tea and coffee at our tent. We are off on a chimp safari by 9:00 a.m. They are really far away today, so we take a skiff, pick up a tracker on our boat, and then go north to try and find them. The weather is sultry, and our clothes are drenched the first ten minutes of our climb. It is very steep entering the jungle from the lake. There is a main group of 85 chimps, but during the day they break off into groups of 6, 10, or 15. We hear them after about one hour of crossing very steep terrain. Our tracker/guide has been slashing away with his machete through the flora to make a path for us. They are on the move, and now we have to retrace our steps. We zig zag across the mountains for three hours. Each time they have changed directions and we have to back pedal. Finally at 12:30, our guide makes a loud yelp, which sounds like a chimp. Another guide, up on the mountain, returns his call, and we follow that method of tracking until we come upon them. There are three of them sitting in a wild nutmeg tree, eating without a care in the world. There are two males and one female, and at one point the female backs right into the male for a bit of nucky-nucky. Their mouths are stained red with the juice of the nutmeg. They seem totally at ease in our presence.

The Japanese have researched this group of 85 for twenty years, and the chimps are tracked everyday. The researchers have learned

Mahale Chimp Eating Nutmeg in a Tree

that they eat a certain plant called aspilia and veronia when they have diarrhea or an upset stomach. These plants, in fact, have a lot of antibiotic in them. We can't believe our luck after watching these three for about ½ an hour. The alpha male and his entourage walks up the path where we are standing. He is a big silver-back, and has a group of probably 12-15 chimps with him. They decide to sit and rest right where we are. One chimp lies down by the path, another leans against a tree and yawns, a couple start to groom each other, and another one picks at his feet. A couple of them just stare at us, as if we are the ones on display. We have a very entertaining show for almost 1 ½ hours, and then trekked down the mountain at a fairly good pace for our boat trip home.

After a delicious lunch of salads, fresh vegetable, cheese, and paté, I take a swim for about one hour. The water in the lake is too rough to snorkel, but I do it anyway as it makes the swimming easier. Mahale is a cove, about ¼ of a mile long, yellow baboons play on the beach, and the pied wagtail is ever present at the tent or on the bow of the boats. The sand is course, but not hard on the toes, and I have seen only two shells, a large mussel that is pearly shiny white and a snail shell that resembles the kind you get with escargots. There are lots of rocks, quartz, and the water shimmers with the specks of mica. Tea at 5:30 p.m. proceeds our evening fishing and sundowner trip. We go south on the Zoe, and start to troll after passing our cove. Within minutes we are into all kinds of fish. They range from about 15"-25". The largest one, and the best eating, is the koohee, which has a bright yellow belly and turquoise splotched sides with wide black stripes. BTP caught two of these, which we will have for lunch tomorrow. We caught seven different varieties of fish, all good eating, all very pretty, and all, like the koohee, just found in Lake Tanganyika. This has to go down as one of the exceptional days of our lives.

February 2
sunny, 90°

Awaken to glorious sunshine and a calm lake. Take our boat trip again to find the chimps. Hike up the same steep path as yesterday, but hope to be on them a lot sooner. The sunlight is playing marvelous tricks of color on the forest leaves, turning the jungle into various

1995

shades of burnished greens. Warmth gives me a sense of physical well being and optimism. Being here in this most remote part of Tanzania, I feel as one with nature. We could very easily be back in the time of Stanley and Livingston, nothing here is even slightly changed. We are one hour by plane from the large town of Kigoma, and a twelve hour boat ride. There are a few small fishing villages between here and the nearest serious village, but no white face is anywhere near here. We have been on the lake for two days now, and have seen only the occasional mokoro with one fisherman pulling a hand line with tin foil on the end of a hook to attract the fish. The forest is dense with kapok, fig, palm oil, flame, and battress trees, Battress being the ones that the chimps bang on the side as an alert that danger is near.

After a great deal of climbing and listening to the chimp chatter, we come upon them in the same wild nutmeg tree of yesterday. There

Wash Day in Mahale

are only three chimps in the tree, as most of the fruit was eaten yesterday, so we wander on after a few minutes. On a new path, winding our way around the jungle, we hear a lot of hooting and follow that to a beautiful river stream and waterfall. The chimps are walking from rock to rock drinking a little as they go on talking to each other. This is a scene out of shangri-la. The sound of the rushing water, the chimps hooting, the lush green vines and verdant trees, the smell of wild spices, fruits, and flowers, the sun filtering through the leaves giving a warm glow on the shiny rocks. What an experience.

FEBRUARY 2
MAHALE - SUNNY, 90° SNORKEL AND SWIM

The snorkeling isn't all that it's cracked up to be, in that the rocks are all sort of gray brown, and there are some fish around them, but it is still something fun to do. I spy an eel, about 8" long, black, going into a rock, and since I have my trusty underwater camera, I decide to take a picture of these creatures when I spy a very fat (about 3 " in diameter) very slithery water cobra.

Roland told me they are shy, so I'm not too worried and try to get a picture of it. I hope it turns out! As I'm snorkeling and swimming the length of the cove, I look up and see the baboons coming down to drink. I think I'll fool them and play submarine until I get close enough to take their picture. No shot. Next time I look, they've all scattered. So much for my stealth! There are lots of pretty fish - none looking remotely familiar.

Our sundowners are again by boat. We go north tonight and don't have much luck fishing, but stop in a cove and have drinks on the rocks, watching the sun setting over Zaire. Lake Tanganyika is the second deepest lake in the world, is one mile deep in two different places, and is five hundred miles long. It is bigger than Lake Victoria. It has some rivers feeding into it, but only one flushes out (River Lakuga, and the town on the lake from which the river flows is Kalemie Zaire) which is directly across from Mahale Camp in Zaire.

There is no industry polluting the lake, and only a couple of steamers going from Bujumboro Port in Burundi, down south to a village in Zambia, called Mpulungu, which is where Lanzua Falls is. The lake is 35-40 miles wide, and we can easily see Zaire across from us. Tonight, the lake is so clear because it is calm, and we can see the bottom as we troll along, probably twenty feet down. This place in Tanzania is uniquely beautiful, in that the lush mountain side falls directly into the lake. A new moon is coming up in the sky as we approach camp, and we see a million stars. There is a roaring campfire burning and kerosene lanterns light our way back to Mahale Cove.

It is almost 8:30 when we get back and sit down to a delicious beef stew dinner with a glass of South African red wine. Roland is an intriguing person, and at 35, is wise beyond his years. He came to Nairobi as a Sotheby's auctioneer, just out of Edinburgh University, and knowing nothing about art or auctioneering. He was young and brash, and learned a lot about people, flying airplanes, and Africa. After Diane Fosse died, and there was no one in Rwanda to run the gorilla camp, he did that for six months (mainly because he could speak French and repair cars, not for his knowledge of gorillas). He can really speak on a lot of different subjects, but doesn't pontificate or bore. He leases the land here at Mahale from the park service, and has had a wonderful rapport with the Japanese researchers as well as the local people. Mahale is only open from December through February, and then again from May or June to October, and has been open for five years or so. Katavi is his brainchild too, so I can't wait to see what that's about.

February 3
Mahale / Windy, Mostly Sunny, Hot and Humid

Had a soothing and cooling rain shower last night, the sound on the top of the tent and then the waves beating the shore was a great sound to sleep by.

We have only to go to the research station to see the chimps today. Virtually around the corner by boat. They are raising a ruckus, and the alpha male bangs his head on the research center metal frame to draw attention to his importance. With that, the beta male becomes very docile and subservient. This is the same group of chimps we saw yesterday, even though they are about two hours from yesterday's habitat. Other groups are around also, but we focus on the alpha male group as it is the most vocal. We follow them through lots of dense vegetation. This is actually a secondary forest, having been inhabited by a village until about twenty years ago. There is a lot for the chimps to eat as the people had planted mangoes, lemon, nutmeg, and other fruit bearing trees. It is also beautiful as the canopy is lower, and there is more open space for the sunlight to filter in. We sit for a long time looking at a strange little male chimp named Hambi. He's unusual, as his face is still white (pale beige pink) and he is about eight years old. He looks us straight in the eye as he sits in the crotch of a tree, in-

It's grooming time for these chimps.

specting his toes and scratching himself. He is the first chimp we see to actually use a small stick to reach into an ant hole and bring out the ants on the stick to eat. An amazing tool for a very bright chimp. We hear a young, four or five year old, throwing a temper tantrum, which is what they do when they are being weaned. He is screaming his head off, sounding very much like Lawton or Katharine (my grandchildren) wanting his or her way. We slash and cut our way through a lot of 20' high vegetation as we are hearing them eating the shoots of this plant, but even though they are only three or four feet from us, we can't see them through the dense growth.

I opt to walk back to camp with Roland, while Blaine boats it with Hamici and our teacher guide. The walk is beautiful, and we see lots of green scarab beetles, a lot of swallowtail, and turquoise and black butterflies eating on some squashed yellow swallowtails. There are two red tail monkeys howling in a tree. They have white spots on their noses and white chin whiskers with long red tails they wrap around tree limbs. We see a whole family of red colobus jump some 30' from one tree to another in a free fall acrobatic wonder. One of them misses the branch he tries for and falls 50'. The babies are more cautious and go for the closest branch to the neighboring tree. I have just learned from Roland that these monkeys can be carnivorous, and do need meat on occasion in their diet.

A quick swim before lunch cools me off, and the afternoon is spent leisurely writing in my diary or reading Peter Mayle's "Toujours Provence" on the sandy beach in a lawn chair under the shade of a large umbrella. I can see the vulturine fish eagle, a species between a vulture and a fish eagle, soaring above me out on the lake looking for fish. I must have taken ten dips in the lake, and also used the biodegradable shampoo and soap to wash in the lake. Altogether, a most enjoyable afternoon. Our sundowner safari takes us back out on the Zöe for another fishing trip. We haven't gone fifteen minutes

The Red "Snake Boat" Zöe

when Hamici, Roland's Tongwe helper yells, "Snake!" He is slithering under the floorboards where the water leaks in from the bow of the boat. Roland is most cautious as these snakes are very poisonous and fast. We lift up the floorboards to try to contain him in one place. Then we dock the boat in a cove, and Roland and Hamici leave us (with the cooler) and try to flush him out. Of course, we are left in the small cove with a crocodile, but he seems to be off eating something else right now. Blaine and I find a very comfy log to watch the sunset and have icy cold vodka and tonics in silver goblets! Presently the two snake trappers return (unsuccessfully) and we start out fishing. Before many minutes we are in some frothing perch. I catch about a 2 ½ to 3 pound one, Blaine follows on my heels and a whole pod of perch go after Blaine's hooked perch in a feeding frenzy. What fun! Back at camp leaves us exhausted, ready for another delicious dinner (leg of lamb) and bed.

February 4
Katavi

Leave Mahale via Roland's single engine Cessna on our way to

1995

Katavi National Park. Have a pleasant peaceful morning saying our goodbyes to the staff of six. They are of the Tongwe Tribe, and exceedingly handsome, gentle people. Being from a fishing village, they are naturally very quiet, sensitive, and kind. They smile readily, and nothing is too much trouble for them, from carrying heavy buckets of shower water to refilling our glasses with ice. Blaine and I have used one tent as a dressing room and another for sleeping, so we gather all of our scattered belongings.

Our Zöe boat ride is really rough (they never did find the snake). The swells knock us around and up and down for the one hour ride to our grass airstip. Roland is an excellent pilot, and manages to skirt a lot of the very severe cumulus clouds all around us. We follow the lake quite a ways south, and the scenery is breathtaking. The mountains going all the way down to Lake Tanganyika, only interrupted a couple of times by secluded sandy beaches. There are a number of cascading waterfalls, and the mountainside is lush and verdant and you just know it's teeming with wildlife and birds. Roland says there are warthogs, bush pigs, lots of monkeys, lions, and any number of unusual birds.

Roland's Cessna as we arrive in Katavi

Arrive at Katavi after only a one hour flight. Coming into the park is a thrill. We fly only a few hundred feet off the ground and see herds of elephant, Cape buffalo, and hippo grazing in the swamp. Everything is popping with new growth and life. The grass strip isn't 100 yards from the camp. We get off the plane and walk to our tent. If we thought Mahale was remote, it doesn't touch Katavi. We are the only people in the park. There are no roads except the one Roland has made to his camp. The hippo are literally feet from our tent, wallowing in the swamp by day, and munching away at our tent flaps at night. The next morning we see tracks right in front of our tent that the tracker says are leopard tracks.

Our sundowner trip is hard to recapture in words. We start out in an open land cruiser, BTP and I sit up very high, and Roland and a park ranger with an AK47 sit up front. We go cross country, naturally, and see wonderful zebra, giraffes, and impala, all who seem to be startled to see us. We wend our way by a very nice herd of elephant, very small ivory tusks, some tuskless. We drive by some Layard black headed weavers, all busy making and building their hanging nests. There are enormous swamp holes, and aardvark holes, and we are in a constant state of shake, rattle, and roll. We end up by the Kavu River, where the hippos and crocodiles play. They are snorting and coughing and yawning and belching, and basically being rather obstreperous, and quite enjoyable to observe.

After we had our fill of hippos and drinks, we head back for a candle-lit dinner to the sounds of hippos and hyenas, and the ever present woodland kingfisher. It's been an incredible day of boating, flying, and driving; all three being great sightseeing opportunities. We go to our spacious tent, that even has a little dressing area in the back, for a very comfortable night's sleep. The temperature is perfect, just a sheet to start, but then pull up the heavy blanket half way through the night. The shower and toilet area is uniquely covered with palm fronds, and is only a short twenty steps from the tent. However, hearing such close munching noises from the hippo and yelps from hyenas, we don't seem to need the facilities at night quite as often as at the Norfolk. Moreover, the fronds overhanging the toilet and shower are populated with hundreds of bats, who somehow glow in the dark.

1995

February 5

Katavi / Tented Camp in Katavi National Park
Clear, cool, about 65° - 70° in a.m.

I video the sunrise as it just comes up a bit after 7:00 a.m.

Our morning safari will be a walk after we cross the Kavu River by inflatable boat. This is a little dicey as Julius, Blaine, Roland, Prosper (our park ranger), and I are all fitting in this ever so small zodiac, and there are hippo all around. We have a hard time even getting away from the bank, as it is weighed down so much, and then on the other side (where we paddle very fast), we can't get past the reeds, so Roland and Julius get out and push in the waist deep water. When Julius paddles back by himself, we have to yell at him as he is heading right for a hippo, so he paddles back fairly fast.

Our walk is through all sorts of swamps and acacias, woods, and savannahs. It is very isolated, wild territory. We see impala, zebra, many birds, Cape buffalo, and two black mambas that scared the hell out of us. Blaine is walking with Prosper, who is carrying an AK47. Prosper is so scared by seeing the mamba that he jumps back and trips over Blaine and steps on his toes, getting them both off balance, but successfully scares the mambas away. It is hot, but at times we walk under great umbrella acacias and get cool. At other times, we're in grass as high as an elephant's eye, and we are wet with the morning dew. There is a kaleidoscope of color from the bright reds of the Red Bishop to the iridescent blue of the woodland kingfisher and the psychedelic green of the beautiful sunbird. Africa brings out only superlatives when you talk about the senses. Everything is magnified tenfold: in color, sight, smells, and sounds that are never ending. Night and day frogs and hippos, hyenas, and fish eagles, and locust strum to a steady beat.

We are to rendezvous with the land rover at about 11:00. It starts to rain. We are on the bank of the Kavu. There are very ambitious malachite kingfishers diving, finding a little soupçon, and sitting on a branch on the river to devour it - hippo are cavorting and snorting, but no vehicle on the other side of the river in sight. Finally, about ½ hour after enjoying this little interlude of birds and beasts, we hear the vehicle approaching. We have to cross the river again, but somehow between the time we were first in the rubber inflatable and now, the front half has deflated. Blaine and I gingerly get in, sitting on the wet floor of the half inflated zodiac. Roland paddles like a hippo is charging, in fact - several were, not to mention the hungry looking crocodiles that were watching. We do reach the far bank in record time, and then Roland returns for Julius and Prosper. Everyone finally makes it safely to shore, if not a little damper, at least in one piece.

Then we're off on a picnic. All six of us, Julius, Nelson, Prosper, BTP, me, and Roland, the half inflated inflatable, all the picnic food, and the cooler, all in our land rover. We bounce around the swamp for about twenty minutes, avoiding the great deep water holes, and come to a lovely acacia glade for our picnic. From out of the land rover comes a huge tarp for a tent, chairs, a table, tablecloth, linen napkins, icy beer, paté, cheese, bread, salads, oranges, silver glasses, a washstand, water, and soap! Unbelievable!! Relax and birdwatch for a couple of hours, and slowly wend our way back to camp. All six of us jostling around, hitting major aardvark holes, bush pig holes,

In Roland's Land Rover heading to a picnic spot with our half-deflated inflatable.

swamp water laden holes. The grass is just at eye level, with Roland driving so he has no clue what or when he is going to hit one of these things. Julius stands up and tries to direct, but often it is impossible. Arrive back at camp close to 5:00, and decide to have sundowners at 6:30, which gives us just enough time for showers and a hair wash. John brings some wonderful hot water and lowers the shower bucket to fill. It feels luxurious to stand under the bucket and pull the chain and start the flow of water. - a great relaxing treat after a fairly grubby day in the bush. Sundowners takes us to another beautiful part of Kavu River, watching the bird life and hippo. After sharing many stories and experiences over cocktails, meals, and game drives, we feel Roland has been a truly exceptional guide and friend. Dinner is relaxed with a nice South African red wine and pork spare ribs (we had rabbit last night).

FEBRUARY 6
KATAVI / COOL A.M., WARM HUMID BUT PLEASANT P.M.

Took a morning game drive to the other end of the park. Lots of tsetse flies and very bumpy conditions. Of course there is no one else in the park, but not many animals either. The camp register indicated we were only the 27th and 28th visitors ever. If we could stop and look at the birds, I think we would see a lot, but the flies are just impossible. There are a number of giraffe, zebra, eland, impalas, warthog, but no elephants to be seen. Back to camp for lunch, naps, packing, birding, and writing.

At 5:00, Roland, Prosper (with AK47), and I head out by foot along the river. It is so wonderfully quiet when walking, we can really get up on the animals. Our first encounter was a great herd of giraffe. It is incredible how insignificant one feels next to a 20' tall moving object. We can hear their thundering hooves as they finally see us and tear away. We walk by two Cape buffalo who are keeping cool in the water. They didn't see us at all, but after we walked by, three francolin were spooked

Hippos wallowing in the Kavu River

and started screaming, and that alerted the buffalo and they galloped off at a very fast clip. We saw a baby jacana, just learning to fly, and mottled brown in color, but with the long jacana legs. And the most exciting thing of all were two smooching hippos. Two hippos were gently coming out of the water, and with wide open mouths touching, sort of nibbling on each other's very pink mouths. Then they would very slowly descend into the river again. We watched this behavior for about ten minutes, and they did it over and over again. Every three or four seconds they'd come up, kiss very lovingly and tenderly, and then flop back down in the river. A most intriguing experience to watch.

We probably walked two or three miles, sometimes in grass over my head, at times through acacia woods, at times along the bank of the river. Blaine joined us by car at about 6:45 with cool drinks, which we enjoyed as the sun set, and the fish eagles worked the river, and the pied kingfishers and great white egret all vied for fish. Our dinner of fried frog legs and wild kojoni was an interesting mix, washed down with what is left of the red wine. Katavi camp closes tomorrow when we leave, until May, so we are eating whatever is left in the larder box. After some final tales around the campfire and some star gazing, we say goodnight and settle in for a good snooze. We are awakened at God knows what hour to the most extraordinary sounds. Definitely munching and grunting of hippo. But Blaine looks out the tent window next to his bed and sees something brown (we think waterbuck), and then Prosper tells us in the morning that leopard tracks are clearly visible also. Blaine goes out of the tent at 6:30 to brush his teeth (just as it is getting light) and is surrounded by the unusual, translucent African pink bats.

February 7
Flying from Tanzania to Kenya

Leave Katavi via APESH Cessna for Tabora and customs check and then go to Nairobi. Run into a horrific thunderstorm after leaving Tabora. I am totally sweaty palms and clutching my seat belt as we descend 1200' in seconds to get out of the turbulent skies. Huge cumulus clouds all around us make our Cessna look like a kite tilting and swerving. Rain pelting the windshield, dark gray all around us. We finally get under the clouds instead of in them, and then try to avoid what rain is falling all around us. We fly over Lake Natron and Ndutu. We fly over the cliffs where the Rupert's and copper faced vultures nest. We fly over the rift valley, and the heat is building up outside, and it's getting really bumpy now. I am once again clinging to my seatbelt for dear life. We again are jostled about as if we were a toy at the whim of the winds, and I really cannot get out of this plane fast enough. Finally we land at Wilson at about 1:00, five hours in that little plane, as comfortable as it may be, is just a little too long for me. Blaine says that it was the scariest plane trip he has ever experienced.

I need to walk around and get back in touch with civilization, so I walk to town from the Norfolk Hotel. Shop at all sorts of little hole in the wall curio shops along the way to the African Heritage Shop (where I bought a pillow case cover for $45!!) Prices have changed a lot, as well as the shop keepers, who are all Indian and don't like to barter or discount. Bought two wood carvings (they say are Machonde) for $20. Back at the Norfolk after my nice walk, I never felt hassled or worried in the least walking downtown. Dinner at the Lord Delamere Terrace dining room - terrific!

Kenya
February 8
Ol Donya Waus, Chyulu Hills, Kenya

Took the scenic drive out of Nairobi, leaving at 9:00 from the Norfolk and heading towards Langatta, towards Kajeda, and then a back road through Masai country for 100K. Our driver, who has worked for A&K in Nairobi for 29 years has never driven this way before. It is a dirt road where vehicles fear to tread. We are often stopped by herds of cattle crossing, tended by long, straight, and tall Masai, in their splendid red kikois flowing in the breeze. The ground is dry and dusty. I don't know how much grass is left for the cattle to eat. They are bunched up at times at watering wells, where the cattle and Masai drink and cool off together. We pass a well where three men, tall and naked, are washing. The Masai all have their earlobes wrapped around their ears, or dangling with many beads. The men and women both wear beaded bracelets and necklaces. They both often have shaved heads, so you can't tell if they are man or woman.

Arrive after 5 bumpy, dusty hours. Ol Donya Waus is set in the Chyulu Hills (waus means spotted in Swahili - spotted mountain.) The ranch is 300,000 acres, and is both plains and acacia woodland. Our cottage sits up on a high ridge overlooking the acacias, plains, and 80 miles away is Mt. Kilimanjaro. Our cottage has a huge king size bed, lots of closet and shelf space, flush toilets, and a large heated shower. The only sounds are the birds, the crickets, and the occasional howl from a monkey. The lunch is elaborate, consisting of paté, cheese, salads, icy cold Castle beer. The weather is fairly sultry at 3:00 p.m. and cloud covered in places, we can't see Killy today. Our afternoon game drive takes us on one of the hills overlooking 360° of plains game, and four quietly stalking lion. It is great fun watching them slowly follow a herd of wildebeest. We think a kill may be imminent, but then the lazy lion lose interest and flop down in the maize colored grass, an exact camouflage color for a lion.

FEBRUARY 9
OLD DONYA WAUS

We awaken to a glorious day and go out on horseback at 8:00 across the yellow plains, encountering only a few Grant's gazelle along the way. Crossing from the tawny plains up into the acacia woodland, we see giraffe wrapping their nimble tongues ever so gently around the small acacia leaves. We go through a grove of whistling thorn acacia, with ants living in their little brown cocoons, chasing all the predators away with their smelly, stinky aroma - a very symbiotic relationship. Our sundowners take us up to what has been renamed Church Hill - where Richard Bonhomme (owner) will marry in April. On our way back to camp, almost ran down the four lions we saw yesterday. Three young males just getting their manes and a female - their sister.

FEBRUARY 10
AMBOSELI NATIONAL PARK

We had a huge and long light and sound show last night, lasting all through the night, and dumping a great deal of water on the ground. The birds are out in abundance this morning, all chirping loudly with happiness at wet, cool leaves and flowers. We leave at 8:00 for Amboseli. Jackson, a tall, long legged Masai is driving us. The dirt roads, already in such bad shape, have even deeper holes and runoff ruts than usual. It takes about one hour to get from camp to the main road, then left on the main road, which is really bad, almost untraversable - to the turnoff for Amboseli, which is 32K on another frightful, hole infested road. We are here to have lunch with Cynthia Moss, and see her well researched elephants.

We drive to the bush and, as she said, later in the day the elephant move to the swamp. We see a very undisturbed group of about 18, 4 suckling babies, lots of juveniles, no tuskless, but none with very impressive ivory. They are great fun to watch from our open hatched land rover. The babies are especially amusing as they learn to use their trunks to pick up sticks and gather bunches

Cynthia Moss and her friend, Martin Katito

of leaves. One little one gets stuck in a bush and charges out only to be in a tangle of vines, and has to retreat back into the bush again. Over and over he charges out on his fat stumpy legs, only to be thwarted by the persistent vines. His mother seems to be totally oblivious to his plight as she munches away and makes him fend for himself. Of course, he succeeds in the end, and the two walk off in search of more to eat.

Cynthia is not at all what we expected. Middle aged, American, a jolly loud voice, a quick laugh, and only about 5'4" in height - which was surprising as her fame has made her, in our eyes, larger than life. She lives in an isolated enclave near a public campsite and close to Amboseli Lodge. But totally private and hidden by palm trees. She lives in a tent with no toilet facilities even attached. The dining tent is just a regular tent which could hold six people, maybe. Martin (the

1995

A herd of Cynthia's Amboseli elephants

A young elephant resting in a felled tree

man doing the wildlife documentary films) has a tent, as does Peter, the cook. I did see a shower boma with a bucket above, this must be for everyone.

We have lunch on the new verandah, which Cynthia has never seen as she has just come back from Nairobi. She is sure the elephants will be rubbing their backs on the posts and demolishing the structure within the week. Such is life in the bush! Martin is just finishing up his second series on Echo, the elephant who had a new baby (Ebony) in May, 1994. Ebony was poked in the eye shortly after birth by a thorn from an acacia, and is partially blind in that eye. Martin and Cynthia followed Echo for 18 days and nights so they could catch the birth of Echo's baby on camera. It happened at dusk on May 5th, and we shall see it all in technicolor sometime next year. Martin has just come back from the badlands, filming prairie dogs, and before that in Sumatra studying orangutans (where one nearly killed him by pushing a very large tree over, meaning to kill Martin. He moved just in time, but his $75,000 camera was smashed to smithereens). Cynthia talked a lot about the three bull elephants shot (legally from a vehicle) by hunters just across the Tanzanian border. The ivory was the biggest left in this part of Africa, weight 90, 96, 80 pounds, and the bulls were in their prime. So sad and unwarranted.

We left Cynthia and Martin Katito (who is Cynthia's assistant) all laughing hysterically as I gave my Bass walking shoes to Cynthia, that she coveted. We have the same size foot, so I left them with her and certainly know they will be worn in far more exciting places than if I were to keep them.

Stopped at Jackson's Masai village on the way back (it's only 34K's from Ol Donya Waus). We met all of his family. The children (about 14 of them) all came up to Jackson and bent their head for him to touch (like in the King and I). The women all wore colorful red kangas, and had beaded necklaces and earrings. The flies were worse than

1995

I have ever seen anywhere, or have ever imagined. The faces of the children were covered with literally 50 or 60, maybe 150, 160. They were in their noses, mouths, and especially their eyes. Half the people were blind, but they all smiled gayly as we took their pictures. The manyatas were simple dung huts, only four or five feet tall. Jackson, who is about 6"3', towers over these little houses. He is 29 years old and has one wife and two children. He feels he is very poor, as he only has 50 cattle. He says you are only rich if you have 1,000 cattle. He says the young warriors of his village still go out to live off the land for three years, from ages 15 to 18. I think that as civilization creeps ever so slowly into these people's lives, it will be impossible for them to go back to living in the squalor of the mud huts and the nomadic existence of the Masai as they now live.

FEBRUARY 11

OL DONYA WAUS, STILL HOT AND HUMID

Jackson's Dung Hut

Took a bird walk with Jackson this morning as Blaine decided he really just wanted to hang out and read. Birding with Jackson is interesting. He walks his long gait like a giraffe, and carries a spear, and only sees animals, which is fine with me as long as he sees the lion before it sees us. Giraffe, Grant's gazelle, impala all around. I spot a few new birds and share my binoculars with Jackson so he can learn too. I sit for a long while on a log, just looking at the sights, enjoying the scenery of acacia, dung from the impala, dead bones, dung beetles, butterflies, the ever present sounds of the doves.

Some very attractive English people are here now, Charles and Tessa Rogers-Coltman, Sam and Jane Whitbread, and Sir Charles Morrison. They are all friends of the Queen and her family - think Prince Charles has behaved abominably, and that Prince William will be king, and the Queen will keep her monarchy until William is old enough to take over. Our meals are very interesting, as all these very upper crust English are both amusing and informative, and they all have a great sense of humor. Jane, Charles, and I bird walk in the afternoon. We have a huge downpour, and sleep to another night of sound and light entertainment.

FEBRUARY 12
OL DONYA WAUS

Again a wonderful and clear bright day. Sir Charles and I take a bird walk, and meet Blaine and the rest, who have ridden horses for a bush breakfast. It tastes wonderful having eggs, fried tomatoes, sausage, toast, coffee, and juice after a great walk. We leave for Nairobi at around 11:00. We go via Mombasa Road, but it still took us five hours. It is amazing to see giraffe, Grant's gazelle, and European stork out in the fields along the road just 30K's from Nairobi.

Catch an 11:00 p.m. British Airways flight for London, and then on to Philadelphia, arriving the afternoon of Feb. 14, Valentine's Day!

- 1996 -

ARGENTINA & CHILE

JANUARY 21

Left Pond House, Sunday, January 21, 1996 for a 2:30 flight to Miami on US Air. Arrive Miami on time - went to the airport restaurant after retrieving our seven checked bags (1 gun case with Blaine's 2 shot guns, fishing rods, reels, flies, clothes) and had a delicious stone crab dinner.

Our plane for Buenos Aires leaves at 8:45 in the evening, we are on Aerolineas, and have two business class seats in the third row of a 747. We are seated right under the pilots in the nose of the plane. Except for a few bumps, the eight hour trip was uneventful. We arrive at 7:45 in the morning, which is 5:45 EST, and we are picked up by

Llao Llao - an old resort in Nahuel Huapi National Park

The Andes Mountains and snow-capped peak of Tronador

Denise Stella, who is with Frontiers Nature Style. She and Fernando, the driver, take us in a van about forty minutes away to downtown Buenos Aires and the Alvear Palace Hotel. Dinner at Las Nazarenes was great grilled food. Blaine and I take a long walk from our hotel, which is in the Recoleta district, to downtown and Florida Street, which is the downtown pedestrian shopping area.

January 23

Llao Llau, Chile

Fly to Llao Llao morning of January 23rd. It is pronounced zhau zhau. It takes us about 1 ½ hours to get to Llao Llao, driving by some fantastic scenery, including Lake Nahuel Huapi.

Llao Llao means dulce dulce, or sweet sweet, and is literally a nut that forms a mantra around a coihue tree, which are abundant around Llao Llao. We took a long, three hour walk through the Nahuel Huapi National Park. Saw a few birds, lots of interesting trees, including a grove of brrayaa trees. The Lodge at Llao Llao is made of pine and cypress trees, and the front hall is 500 feet long with stores (chocolate shop, dry goods store, and sports store) on either side of the entrance. The great room is huge, with mammoth chandeliers made with racks of deer antlers, and a winter garden room, which is a long porch with 30 foot high glass windows so you can look out over the lake and the Andes Mountains. One of the largest snow capped peaks you see is Tronador, an extinct volcano with a peak full of snow.

Swam in the indoor pool, not very clean, but perfect temperature. Blaine had a massage, he said his masseuse almost broke his neck cracking it. I played with three other people what they call paddle, which is played on a hard court about half the size of a tennis court.

There are two places to eat at Llao Llao - Les Cesare, which is a more formal served dinner, and the huge regular dining room which is buffet style. The less formal big room has a much better view and the food is equally as good.

We are picked up after two days of R&R and cross the border back into Argentina. Nicholas, our driver, who is a local from St. Martin, drives us 3/12 hours to San Martin, where we stop for lunch. It is a cute little ski town of 15,000 people, and reminds me of a small Jackson Hole or Aspen. After a quick lunch, we drive another 2 hours to get to Quemquemtreu. There has been an enormous fire in the Nahual Huapi forest and the smoke is unreal. Just driving down the road for about five miles the visibility is zero. The air is soot, and smells very smokey. It is lightly raining and the wind shield turns black with soot. Everything around us is a brown cloud of smoke. It is as if we are in the middle of a fire. You can't see the road at all. We go no more than 10mph, hoping someone doesn't careen into the back of us.

The fishing lodge at Quenon is charming. We are here with only one other angler, an Englishman named Graham Bourne. We can't wait to get out to the stream and fish for about 45 minutes on the beautiful Collon Cura. Dinner isn't until 10 p.m.

Next morning our guide, Adam Cohen, thinks it may rain, so we opt for fishing the Chimehuin, which is scenic and lazy wading. The first fish Blaine caught was a perch weighing about 8 pounds. Blaine and I both catch a fair number of rainbows, but all under 1 pound range. The wind is fierce. We are fly fishing in a gale, but it is sunny and not too hot. I am wearing my heavy neoprene waders and they are just right with so much heavy wind. The water isn't very warm. I am also wearing light weight long underwear, a long sleeved shirt, and a windbreaker jacket. We fished dry, and Adam has a fly he's tied that we use called Turk's Tarantula. It looks like a Madame X but is all gray. It can both dry fly and swim under water and also hop when on retrieve.

Blaine and Susan enjoying a picnic lunch

We don't eat until 3 p.m. We've been so busy fishing we can't even think of food. But when we do eat, it is delicious. We have quiche and breaded veal, apples, and delicious pickled eggplant, cheese, hard salami, fresh bread, and banana bread for dessert.

Our second day fishing takes us floating on the Collon Cura. We fish a sinking tip 6 weight on a 9 foot rod. Using the green flash wooly bugger seems to be the hottest fly. The sun is pretty bright, and the brown trout fairly leap out of the water for the fly. The wind is fierce, another gale. Adam is rowing a zodiac with heavy wood oars, and even though we are floating downstream, the wind is hitting us in the face and making for horrendously difficult fishing. We get out and wade quite a bit. I caught a really nice brown trout that leapt out of the water and grabbed my green flashing wooly bugger. It was almost 20 inches and very fat. We are catching rainbows mostly, about 14-20 inches, and a few browns. Lunch is picnic style under the shade of a willow.

Blaine Fishing the Collon Cura

Our third day of fishing we float the upper reaches of the Collon Cura. The day is splendid with no wind. The first two days were just unbearable with gale force winds, sometimes 40 mph, but today is crisp, sunny, and calm.

1996

I wade just in shorts and my wading shoes. I have fleece socks and my little booties. We catch tons of fish on the green flashing wooly bugger. Toward the end of the day, Blaine puts on a brown wooly and slaughters them, catching 3 of the biggest fish we've caught all day. At times, Blaine and I have both had fish on at the same time. I had 15 stikes in 15 casts, bringing in about 8. Blaine had 2 hat tricks, and also a ton of fish. All are between 1 and 2 ½ pounds.

We get back from fishing for tonight's assado, which is an outdoor barbeque. We are having fresh beef from the ranch, and lettuce from the garden. Also, something called Empanadas, which are fried fritters with bananas, onion, and beef inside. Our room is the best in the lodge. It is downstairs with a king sized bed and a nice bathroom, and fireplace, which is lit every night when we return.

Jim Sharp, owner of Quemquemtreu is here and couldn't be nicer. Paula is the manager of our lodge, in charge of getting lunches organized for fishing, and Martin, her husband, manages the ranch. It is mostly a cattle ranch, with 5,000 head, and the chief polo practicing place in the Argentine. There are two games while we are here on Saturday and Sunday. The day we leave, Jim gives us a two hour tour of the operation. From the hydro-electric generator plant, to the polo ponies and two playing fields, to the airstrip and the garden, the tack rooms, the main house, the guest cottage, and cattle grazing. All most interesting.

Adam drives us in the vehicle we have using for these three days to San Huberto. Gorge Trucco, whom we met on the Ponoi River in Russia, runs his fishing operation and hires five guides on a permanent four month basis. We have met them all, and truly think Adam is the best. Your guide starts with you at the beginning of your fishing trip and remains with you all week. It took us about two hours to drive from Quemquemtreu to San Huberto. The only small village we went through was Junin de los Andes.

1996

San Huberto is a charming place; a big white stucco structure that houses the dining room, bar upstairs, and eight bedrooms all in a most beautiful setting. We are in #2, which is the worst one at the place. It is the first one in a row of eight, and on the road side right next to the driveway, so there is no privacy at all and no view. The bathroom is the pits. The entire room is about five feet long and three feet wide. The shower has a curtain, and shares the space with part of the standing area where you go to the john or wash your hands. We take a short afternoon nap after a very large lunch, and start fishing about 5:45. We fished the beat past the lodge, across the bridge. We fish the lower river on the down side of the bridge and there are lots of very small fish. We must have caught 20 fish, but none were over 12". We are fishing an Adams parachute with a flash back green nymph dropper. The fish seem to be taking the dry fly, so we take off the nymph, also change to a size 12 caddis & royal dumpy.

The next day we go to Tres Picos in the little canyon of the majestic Malleo, an extremely hot beat. Some mother of all mother fish hang out in some of these pools. This beat has a fantastic view of Mt. Lanin (which is a glacier). We hook into quite a few 10" fish, I have a sizeable rainbow, about 16". There are also some lovely browns. Blaine hooks one of the huge lunkers. It jumps four or five times and spits out the hook, but he can see it is at least 22-24". I hooked one, but I pulled too hard, and he broke my leader. Fished until 3:00, when we returned to camp for a picnic lunch.

In the early evening we went to the wire fences beat. Again we bring up lots of small browns and rainbows. One very large fish is sitting in a pool and I flick my fly at it from 7:30-9:30. Put on Adams irresistible, elk hare emergers, CDC emergers, caddis all in the 16-20 range. He wanted none of it. He kept rising to eat, but not at my fly, a very smart fish.

During the early part of the morning when fish are rising, we fish dry, until about 2:00, when they slow down. Then we put on ei-

Fishing in the Malleo with Mount Lanin in our sight

ther a nymph with an indicator or a dry with a nymph dropper. Even though the morning air is cool, by 10:00 we fish in shirt sleeves and light weight waders with long underwear, the water is really cold. The rocks on the little canyon stretch off the malleo are huge basket balls and very slippery. I have on cleats, which help, a wading staff is handy, but Blaine and I think they're too much trouble. If Adam didn't help us in the heavy currents it would be really tough without a staff. I fell all the way down and got a river full in my wader, but the air is so warm it doesn't matter. There are lots of willows lining the banks, but you can wade out far enough so they aren't a problem.

Breakfast at San Huberto consists of individual tables. Blaine, Adam, and I sit at a table by ourselves. Breakfast is from 8-10 a.m., lunch is a picnic on the stream, and dinner is again about 10:00 p.m. At Quem, you eat at the lodge. It only holds 8 people, and you sit in a charming dining area at one big table. There is always a roaring fire when we have dinner, and again when we quickly change out of our waders, go to the bar, which is in another building, have a drink, and then to the main lodge for dinner. If we come back, I think we would try to get Blackie (an Argentine) to guide us. He is very knowledgeable about birds. He's about 35 and seems like a very keen and serious guide. Adam is OK, but only 23, and so technical that he only wants you to fish minute flies and doesn't care much about quantity, but wants you to fish for one fish a day. Bring a 4x or 5x leader for these fish and a 5 weight line is better on the Malleo than a 6x which I'm using.

Interesting coincidence meeting Bob White and his wife, Lisa, who spent their summers at Tik Chik in Alaska, and knows John Cella. He would be a super guide.

Leave San Herberto on January 31st to a glorious sunny day, fly to Buenos Aires, again at Alvear Palace, room 709 - Jr. Suite - nice room.

February 1

Blaine leaves for Cordoba at 6:30. I walk from Ave Sante Fe to Florida Street and browse all the shops.

February 2

Leave on a 6:50 flight for Iguazu. Jose Luis meets me and we go to the International Hotel to drop off my bag and let me change to a sleeveless shirt and sneakers. It is only 85 degrees here now. Last week it was 120 degrees. It feels like 120° today with the humidity. The falls are absolutely awesome. We walk across the top of them on the Argentine side, and then get in a truck that holds 20 people, but there are only 8 of us, and we drive throught the jungle for about 25 minutes. There have been some very heavy rains this last week, so the road is squishy mud. The silt from the ground going over the Cataracts are Albemarle red - so too is the river. Last week there was just a trickle down the cataracts - today it is a roaring powerful forceful falls. Last week you could swim in many parts of the river, which have natural swimming pools. Today it is a raging water torrent with no islands on which to walk and no natural pool, all is raging river. A man is filming for a movie in BA. He is a stunt man in "The Mission" and he is climbing up a rope at one of the major cataracts with tumultuous torrents of water falling down around him.

Iguazu Falls, the color of Albemarle County, Virginia

After lunch - at a dreadful place that can feed 2,000 people an hour (luckily we ate late and the only people here) is a huge warehouse of a building. We go to the Brazilian side of the falls which is equally as impressive. The bridges that are made to go over the falls, around them, and really into them are extraordinary. People are wearing bathing suits because you get so wet.

Das Cataratas Hotel is old charm personified, a lovely old pink stucco building. It is built the old Spanish way. My room is on the first floor, looking out at lovely trees and grass. The windows vibrate amazingly with the force from the falls, so there is a spike you wedge in between the two sills to keep the vibration down.

1996

I took a nice long swim in the pool after returning from our trek through the river. It is a very large pool and very clean. There were only a handful of adults (no children) around, which was delightful. Had a delicious barbeque out by the pool, listening to the tunes of folklore music.

Got up at 6:30 a.m. on February 3rd, so José and I can go birding before we leave for Posadas. It is just sprinkling a little and not as warm as yesterday. Jose is just as good at spotting and naming birds as Dave Richards. He also knows every tree and flower. His whole name is José Luis Acosta, Chingold 17 PTO Iguazu 3370 Argentina. We drive back to the Argentine side and take the bridge across to Devil's Throat (where they filmed the Mission). We see kingfishers, cardinals, seedeaters, finches, and many other birds just standing on this bridge. Devil's Throat is awesome and gives you a feeling of vertigo as the bridge is right on top of the raging water. When enough heat builds up with the waterfall, a huge spray of mist comes shooting out of the canyon like a geyser, and while on the bridge, you get soaked.

José, my guide at Iguazu Falls - rushing, raging water

1996

There are clumps of grasses growing right out in the raging water, and small trees growing out of the rocks.

We see an enormous rodent called a capybara, which is the largest rodent in the world. We are on a zodiac boat going to the falls, and spy the mother rat protecting her babies in some grass. She looked like a large bear with tusks.

On the Brazilian side, we see hundreds of coatimundis absolutely everywhere. They are in the racoon family, and have a very long striped tail, and long snout like a possum. They are very tame, and stand for photos constantly.

After seeing Devil's Throat, we start on our 300K safari to Posadas. Stop at Wanda and look at the gem mine (boring) which takes about 10 minutes. They speak no English so José translates. Our road is only two lanes and there are many lumber trucks that make driving up hills very slow going. Sometimes we go as slowly as 5 KPH, and when we're free of the lumber trucks we make it up to 100K's. The scenery is very lush green, mostly pine forest, tea plantations, and orange groves. The road we are on by-passes all of the towns, so we go into Monte Carlo just to see what a typical small Argentine town looks like. This is on the Parana River, and is known as a fishing village. It is German and Lutheran and very clean and seemingly prosperous. It is Saturday, so not many people are out, and the stores are all closed. Another clean little German town is Gardin America, which specializes in exotic plants and trees. At 5:30 we arrive at San Ignacio, where the missionary ru-

Feeding a coatimundi

ins are. They date back to the late 1500's, and José gives me a quick history lesson about this part of Argentina, which is in the province of Misiones. I watched the movie, The Mission, when I returned to the U.S., and it depicted this missionary and this part of Argentina perfectly. We then travel on south, about 50K, to Posados, which is a thriving metropolis of about 30,000 people. We arrive about 7:45 after about an 8 hour van ride. I would not repeat this, as there is very little to see along the way, and the scenery is pretty, but much the same throughout. I was hoping for some quaint little town with local crafts to buy along the way, but there is none of that at all. Posada is definitely lacking in any charm, and the Hotel Posadas (which I assume is their best) is 3rd rate. Walked 1 ½ blocks down the road to a restaurant for dinner, as they serve none at the hotel. The Quernencia Restaurant has waiters that look like they belong as "21 Club", but in fact the restaurant is not great and no charm. They specialize in Parilla (the local barbeque), but I think a pizza at the local pizza parlor (of which there are many) would have been just as good.

Picked up at 9:00 a.m. for a 10:10 flight to BA, no hitches as I am taking only a carry on bag, and arrived at BA at 11:30. Was met by Denise Stella, who then transports me to the Alvear. Denise and I go to the San Telmo flea market, as it is Sunday, where everyone in BA goes. The place is full of junk of all kinds, lots of silver and brass among other trinkets of necklaces, jewelry, and chandeliers. This is the oldest section of BA, and was settled in the 1700's. The San Telmo Church has a lot of mosaic tiles and two steeples, which are very impressive. The old houses, which now house some of the antique dealers, are very charming, with two and three courtyards leading back from massive doors at the entrance. The ceilings are 20 feet high, and are brick, with wooden beams attached to the brick, and huge trees growing in the courtyards. Tango dancing is going on in many parts of the square, as well as folklore music, and the area is fairly jumping with activity. There are sidewalk cafes everywhere to sit and watch the crazy people go to and fro. Didn't buy anything, as the prices are normal by U.S. standards, but no bargain. When returning to the room, I decided I needed some exercise, so went to the health club for a swim. Got to the 2nd floor, people with walkie talkies everywhere. They won't let me into the club, as they say a celebrity is in there and didn't want anyone else. The manager came up to placate me, I tell him I won't gawk or ask for autographs, so I am allowed to enter the portal of the celebs. It is Antonio Banderas and Melanie Griffith, who confided in me in the small dunking pool that she had just found out that she was pregnant. They were recently married, and here along with her two kids. The management was so embarrassed by this turn of events that they sent me beautiful flowers and a bottle of Meemous extra Brut and a platter of hors d'oeuvres, which I enjoyed all by myself.

Tango Dancers in San Telmo flea market

Next day I go to the public pool in the Palermo section of the city, next to the domestic airport. I get there at about 11:00, when it opens. It costs $15, and I have taken my own towel.

I get a lounge chair and a beach umbrella and settle down for the day. Luckily it's Monday, so few people are here. It is windy, but hot and sunny. No one speaks even the slightest word of English, two French women are in front of me, but the rest are the young 20-40 year olds from BA.

Go to the cemetery in the Recoleta after returning to the hotel.

1996

This is the second most famous cemetery in the world, after Genoa, Italy. The mausoleums are enormous, and either touching or side by side, only inches apart. It is a little city unto itself, and many famous Argentines are buried here. It was the first cemetery in BA, about three hundred years ago, and at that time all denominations were buried here. It is so popular that some of the mausoleums have changed families two or three times. They remove the old bodies to a new cemetery, and a new family fills the crypt. This has happened because it is very expensive to keep the mausoleums up and renovated. Eva Duarte (Peron) is buried here with her brother, some family, and also a few close friends. Juan Peron is buried in a totally different cemetery.

The Pilar Church, next door to the cemetery, is Spanish style, beautiful white stucco on the outside with lovely statues and paintings inside. Definitely worth a visit.

Blaine arrives at around 7:30, but has had La Touriste for a few days, so we order room service and go to bed early. He had a great time dove shooting in Cordoba, even though the weather was lousy. The first afternoon he shot fifty birds, and then in the hundreds the

Blaine at a dove shoot in Cordoba, Argentina

next three days. They really had to go search out the birds because it's been raining so much. The dove have fled to different fields. He stayed at the Bremer Hotel, which he likes a lot. Blaine shot by himself for the first couple of days, and then some very attractive English 40 year olds came, who spent all fall doing nothing by shooting in England, and who Blaine said were charming and fun to be with.

February 6

Left for Chile on a 6:30 plane early next morning and we arrive in Santiago with forty minutes to retrieve seven bags from the baggage claim.

Through customs, and go to our Lodeca connection for Puerta Montt, which leaves from a different airport, about a ten minute walk with all our bags on two carts (12 bags and fly rods), and run for the plane, which we make with three minutes to spare. In fact, they said they held the plane for us!

Arrive in Puerta Montt and it's raining. Rent a car, and get lost trying to get out of town. We end up at the dump. It takes us about half an hour, no one speaks a word of English. We are exhausted, and getting a bit slap happy and giddy at this point. It really was pretty hilarious. An hour later we find Puerto Vares and the Colones del Sar Hotel (which is only about twenty minutes from Puerta Montt). Room 208 is a suite, and has a great view of Lake Llanquihue and Osorno Mountain. Go to the local craft market across the street. There are sweaters, hats, scarves, socks all knitted with beautiful Chilean wool, but we don't buy anything.

Next day we leave for Castro, driving south on Ruta 5. About one hour south is Parque, where you catch the ferry. The trouble is there is a two hour wait, even though there are three ferries running. Every vehicle, from trucks, lumber trucks, tourist buses, and cars must cross by these ferries. Blaine and I are well entertained by the filthy children who think nothing of throwing all their trash out their cars, or taking a piss in the bushes in front of everyone. There are vendors walking up and down the street selling empanadas with cheese or meat, fresh roasted nuts, cold cokes, fresh raspberries, and apple pies. We have a couple of empanadas, which are flaky hot dough and delicious melted cheese.

Finally on the ferry, with God knows how many busses and trucks, arrive thirty minutes later in Chacao. The drive from there, on a very good paved road, is about 120K, but takes us about three hours. It is not a very scenic road, right in the middle of the island of Chiloe. There has been so much burning, the smell is in the air. This used to be a lush rain forest, but now it is useless fields with some cows. We are here in the middle of summer, and there's nothing nice about it. Castro itself is a cute little seaside town on a hill. There are lots of Mapuche (Indian/White mix). We are staying at Hosteria Castro in room 201. There is a view of the water, but they do not use the view very well. This is definitely the best room in the hotel, two twin beds but no sitting room. The hotel is on a steep hill. The food at the Hosteria is excellent. We arrange for a boat ride to take us to some of

Quaint, seaside town in Chile

the other islands. Our guide is Javiera, and speaks excellent English. She teaches at the local private school, which has opened due to the salmon farm proliferation. There are hundreds of them, and the farms hold thousands of salmon. The boat we are on is a slow putt-putt fishing boat. There is little bird activity, and except for the salmon farms, no fish activity. We putt along to Chonchi, and then around a few more islands which are sparsely populated. Nothing is so staggeringly beautiful that you want to write a book about it. Blaine and I are wearing lots of clothes even though this is mid-summer and there is no wind. The sun is out and the water is calm. I have on a shirt, sweater, and windbreaker, and Blaine is wearing a long sleeve undershirt, shirt, fleece sweater, and windbreaker.

Go to a great place for lunch after we get back to the dock. Not an English speaking person either as a patron or a waitress. The place is on stilts, right on the water, with a great view, and we have a waterside table. The menu is in Spanish, and even with my Spanish dictionary can't find any of these Chilean words. Blaine orders "the special,"

One of many salmon farms

We are entertained by local villagers.

which is something like large raw eyeballs in a clamshell, which tastes so bad I can't believe he's not going to keel over and die. The mounds of seafood on the plate is mind boggling. Huge lumps of clams, mussels, sausages, all lumped together, it actually tastes more appetizing than it sounds. There are strolling musicians who come, pass the hat, then leave. One group, of about 12, sing, dance, and get the whole audience involved. Walked through the market. Tons of sweaters. I found a beautiful salad bowl for $15, made out of Rauli wood, local Chile which is a hard wood. The Chilean peso is about 40 to $1. Prices of the sweaters are about $20, but hard to pack.

We finally got smart at dinner and ordered choritos, which are small locally farmed mussels, which are steamed and great. Also, the grilled salmon is delicious, but you never get a fresh green veggie, only french fries or mashed potatoes. This is one of the great potato capitals of the world.

I talked Blaine into taking the scenic route back to Chacao and Puerto Vares. We take Ruta 5 until the sign to Quemchi, and then take the scenic route from Onece. First of all, we can't get out of Quemchi. It is a sea port of about two blocks, but there are no signs for the scenic route. I finally get directions (in Spanish of course, no one has heard of English here), and we get going on the scenic route which takes us through lots of green rolling cow pastures, but no water vistas, which looks like it should be on the map. To compound problems, the road is so rocky and hilly, our little car can barely make it up a hill, and we have to drive in second gear most of the time (shades of Costa Rica). Even more familiar, we get a flat tire, and this is a road absolutely no one goes on. We look in the trunk for the tire and jack, but can find little to help us. Our guardian angel must be looking after us, as a car load of eleven Chileans in wedding attire drive by and stops to help. They lift the car up on the side and change the tire within a few minutes (what good fortune). To shorten the story, we finally get back to Chacao on the ferry (having a few more delectable empanadas con queso) and arrive in Puerto Varas in time for dinner, which we have at IBIS restaurant, very good.

Our scenic route and no cars

1996

Help was a very welcome sight!

Off to Petrohue in the morning, the word means place (hue in Mapuche) of the petros (which are the little biting flies all around the place), and the place we are staying is called El Tundo del Salto, run by Jan Williams-Caldwell and her husband, David. David mines copper in northern Chile, but is here for a few days and takes us out fishing. The farm is very small, only taking six people. We have the best room, overlooking Osorno Volcano. We fish wooly bugger black with a flash of green, size 4,6. Olive green is OK also. There are a number of fish in the Petro here, but there has been a terrible drought, and they are really hard to catch. The water is really low, the sun is high in the sky. The water is warm and the fish are hiding.

Boat the next day with John Naisbitt. He's floated the Petro many times, but not since November, and has no idea what flies or where the fish might take them. He is just as nice as can be, about 45 years old, and he handles the boat great. They are old wooden McKenzies, with high sides, and I fish from the bow and Blaine form the stern.

There is a nice stretch of shady river about ten minutes after starting down river. It is a 12 foot high bank, fairly rocky, and then there's a ledge that drops off after a few feet. You fish the wooly bugger to the bank, let it float until the swing, or J, straightens out, and then strip in about 1 ½ feet at a time, imitating the pancora crab, which is abundant around the banks. Their color is blackish green until they molt, which is about to happen, at which point they turn orangey pink. We catch a number of nice size trout, about 12-15", on this ledge, but one or two very nice lunkers break off of the fly. This is the highlight of our morning. Meet the other boat from the lodge, which has Ellen and Dick Rogers from Dallas, and their guide Doug; whom we join for lunch.

This fishing on the Petrohue is really tough going. In order to make the best of the hot sunny days, we get up at 7:00 a.m. for breakfast, and out by 8:15. Because the fishing is so slow, we must make a million casts a day. On the Quemquemtreu we'd have pockets of really hot fishing, and then we'd take a break and enjoy the birds, but here

Fishing the Petro at the foot of Mt. Petrohue
old wood McKenzie boat and staggering scenery

1996

you're afraid of missing the one pocket that might be holding all the fish. Luckily there is little wind, and the scenery of the mountains is a beauteous sight to behold. By 11:00 it has gotten warm enough to take off my sweaters and light waders, and fish in my shorts. Which compounds the problem as the water is quite warm. They say 59 degrees, but it's more like 65. I discover also, that the fish really like the beady eyed wooly bugger better than just the plain one, and they also like a green fly wrapped in gold. (I'll have to look for it at Orvis). They seem really picky when they do take. The trouble with slow fishing is you get lax, and start looking around after the hundredth cast, and that's when the big lunker strikes, and either breaks the fly off and part of your leader, or it just comes out of his mouth because you're too slow to set it properly. In other words, there are a hell of a lot of frustrations with slow fishing.

The schedule is grueling as we boat for 13 hours and some 18 miles of river, and then go back to the lodge for 9:30 cocktails and 10:00 dinner, which is three or four courses. By 11:30 I'm frantic to leave the table and get to bed.

Just so I don't forget, the big fly with two spots of orange on either side is called TABANO, not the fishing kind but the live fly, and come out to haunt you around December 15-20, and doesn't stop until around February 1st. We had a couple of them around us. The biggest irritant to me was their constant loud buzzing noise all around you. They'd buzz around your glasses, your ears, your hands, which is very distracting. One bit Blaine (of course) and he said it really itched badly, but normally they are just a nuissance.

At about 7:30 p.m., the last day of fishing, a classic thing happened. Blaine was fishing on one side of the river, and a farmer and his wife and child came to the river from their house in the hills to fish the other side. This farmer and his wife live off the land, and maybe cross the river once a month to get provisions. We're talking ex-

Chile's beautiful streams but not easy fishing

tremely primitive conditions. His fishing rod consists of a coffee can wrapped with fishing string, with one hook on the end of the line. He uses a heavy nail as a sinker, and he'd twirl his line like a bolo, using his coffee can as a real. Blaine looks on with envy as he catches a fish within thirty seconds, and it's not just a puny one either.

He rebaits his coffee can line (probably with a worm) and reels it out again to catch his second fish before you can catch your breath, and his wife is also catching fish with ease. That puts Blaine in a very competitive spirit, and he also starts catching fish. So you have the Orvis Power Matrix $2,000 man and the old primitive farmer doing equally well catching trout. The difference being that the old farmer takes his out of the water and bangs it on the head with a rock.

The day we leave I go to the falls, which is only ¼ mile down the road from El Fundo. They are really awesome, even though they are in the middle of a very serious drought. There is one flume that drops a couple of hundred feet, and you can hear the force of the water at Jan's house.

1996

We drive to Puerta Montt early afternoon for a 3:00 p.m. flight. It is 1 ½ hours late. Spend the night in Santiago at the Hilton, probably the finest hotel as far as amenities are concerned. Lovely area for afternoon tea and morning breakfast. Huge pool, but unfortunately this is where the Americans who have been on cruises come. We go to a marvelous restaurant about ten minutes from the hotel called Aqui es Coco. No Americans, and no one speaks English, but very local foods, and wines, and delicious fish.

Next day we have a very concise and well orchestrated tour of Santiago by our nice guide who had picked us up at the airport yesterday.

We first stopped at a lapis jewelry store and bought some lovely earrings and necklaces. Then off to downtown Santiago and a tour of the streets where the government buildings and law schools are. The temperature is warm, probably about 90 degrees, but no humidity, and the city people wear light looking summer clothes.

We drive to the local race track, not five minutes from downtown, racing today (Wednesday) and Saturdays. Lots of horses out exercising. Then off to the suburbs going past Bella Vista area where my nephew Louis Bickford and Ana lived. A very Bohemian area in midtown Santiago. Lots of lapis factories on either side of the main street. The suburbs are fascinating. Many very ritzy houses cut out of dry scrub land. There are now green trees, grass, and bushes lining the lovely oases. Each one has a large wall surrounding it, either of stucco or plants, very Spanish in style.

Our last jaunt is over to Los Domingos, an enormous shopping area of local arts and crafts. You can find live macaws and parrots, chickens and doves, silver and gold, sweaters and carvings, jewelry and furniture. You name it - they got it.

Back at the hotel, a quick swim in the very large pool (with very cold water) and then to the airport for our 7:00 p.m. flight to BA.

Arrive at BA airport at 8:30. We are met again by Denise, who has

1996

Blaine's guns. We then catch the 11:00 flight for Miami on Aerolineas Argentinas. Business class is very comfortable. The plane is half full in our class, only Blaine and I have two seats each to ourselves.

We have a five hour wait in Miami, having arrived at 5:30. Blaine and I retrieve our bags from Aerolineas and get them over to US Air flight, and then go to the Miami airport hotel for a long breakfast and an even longer read of the U.S. newspapers. We look forward to getting back to Chadds Ford this afternoon, and Home Sweet Home!

– 1997 –

Russia, Ponoi River, St. Petersburg

September 16

Left JFK at 6:00 p.m. on FinnAir flight #4 - nonstop to Helsinki. Business class very comfortable. Arrived Helsinki 9:00 a.m. about one hour behind schedule. Met at airport - we landed and were on our way with bags in 10 minutes. Staying at Hotel Strand (Intercontinental) room 718-20. View of water on three sides, balcony, living room, nice bedroom.

After napping, walked around town. Just a few blocks from the oldest Lutheran Church in Scandinavia which is large, white, three gold domes, and sits high on a hill so we can even see it from our hotel room. It is on Senate Square, which is made of cobblestones, and has a statue of Emperor Alexander II in the middle of the square. Lots of good shopping in this area. Had dinner at Havis Amanda, known for its seafood. Walked home, about 10-15 minute walk. Helsinki streets safe at night.

September 18

Went on a city bus tour. It took two hours, and picked us up at our hotel. Very worthwhile to get a handle on surroundings. Went to the rock church, Sebelius Monument, Finlandia Hall (where the events and concerts are performed), Embassy Row, and the docks where they build large cruise ships (the "Elation" is now being built for Carnival Cruise). Tour ended at Stockman's, the biggest department store in Finland. We had lunch at Fazers, a famous cafeteria that has delicious shrimp salad, fabulous bakery goods, and homemade ice cream.

The weather is cold (about 50°) and damp. It rains on and off all day. Somehow we still have been able to do a lot of walking. There are 5 marks to $1. Everyone is bilingual in Finland. 96% have Finnish as a first language, 4% have Swedish. The young are all learning English in school.

The Swedes controlled Finland until the 1860's, then the Russians until the 1917 revolution when it became independent. It now has a parliament, and has a president. Finlandia Hall is where the Vietnam Treaty was signed. Eric Sarinen's father lived in Finland, and was the architect for the train station (lots of arches). He was the architect not just of the arch in St. Louis, but also the St. Louis Airport. He moved his family to the U.S. in 1920.

SEPTEMBER 19

Blaine and I took the hydrofoil to Tallin, Estonia. The boat trip takes one hour and thirty minutes (at 34 knots). Coming back, we learned to sit aft to avoid the bone-jarring produced by the six foot seas in the bow section.

Tallin looks like a medieval town, with stone turrets and slits in the wall for cannons to peek through. The old cobblestone streets are very narrow. There are no cars in what they refer to as Old Town. Lots of tourist stalls selling woolen sweaters, socks, mittens, and hats. The little shops accept American dollars, but none of the cafés or restaurants do. We charged one lunch to BTP's Visa, and it was $3.00.

I found an antique shop down on an old cobblestone road, the only store that sold lacquered Russian boxes. I found one with bears on it, hand painted, signed, and the name of the village where it was made. She also had wonderful icons, but it's hard to discern the quality of them.

Back to Helsinki on the 4:00 p.m. boat arriving in Helsinki 1 1/2 hours later. Before leaving Tallin we went to Alex Nevsky Russian

Orthodox Cathedral which was very impressive. It was our first experience seeing a Russian Orthodox church.

September 20

We awakened early for our two hour FinnAir turbo prop ride from Helsinki to Murmansk, carrying a group of eager, mostly British, and almost exclusively salmon fisherman. Murmansk is not an attractive entry into Russia, with wrecked airplanes and rusted hulls of dozens of helicopters littering a most unwelcoming airfield, featuring an ugly, in need of repairs, barracks type airport. Its interior was worse, and getting through customs was fearfully difficult; especially since every passenger had long flyrods and gear to be inspected by a single, very unfriendly soldier. Despite everything bad, the general morale of our new fishing friends remained surprisingly high - everyone anxious and excited for what is reputed to be the best salmon fishing in the world. This difficult relay of travel was all well worth it, however, and it was finally followed by our two hour helicopter ride over tundra, arriving at our destination: Ryabaga Camp on the Ponoi River at 3:00 p.m. It's been a long day.

Weather FREEZING! Sunny, but 40 degrees. Fish the home pool before our 8:00 dinner, no luck. The order of guide and beat rotation decided by drawing lots after dinner.

We are so tired. Tent #3 is warm and toasty, with super small wood burning stove, two beds with heavy duty sleeping bags, four shelves for each of us, and two sets of pegs. Plenty of room. Sink with water in a metal can. You pump like getting soap from a dispenser, and water comes out. It is 22 degrees in the tent when we wake up in the morning!

September 21

Fish upper Tomba. Slow. Use #2 Mickey Finn and shrimp fly. Ev-

Helicopter ride gives you a good view of the terrain.

eryone using very large flies. I had one grilse. Blaine had no salmon, but lots of grayling and sea trout. Went with Don, young guide, first year, from British Columbia. Excellent guide and nice guy. Take one small, six-person helicopter to this beat, only 5 minute ride.

SEPTEMBER 22

Misha. One of three or four Russian guides, spoke limited English. Fished the Pornache beat. Slow. Blaine had 2 salmon. All bright fish. I had one. Weight range from 6 pounds to 10 pounds. Caught on Mickey Finn #2. Lots of grayling and sea trout. Fished with single handed fly rod.

SEPTEMBER 23

Dema - another Russian guide from St. Petersburg. Owns a hardware store in fall and winter. Fished Hourglass. Slow. Blaine caught 3 salmon, one was 12 pounds, all bright. I had one about 6 pounds, all

1997

caught on Mickey Finn. Tried shrimp and blue charm, no luck. Very pretty beat, weather about the same temperature, 40-44 degrees., but no wind, so feels OK. Some sea trout.

Everyday I wear: 1. Long underwear, 2. Turtleneck silk long underwear, 3. Lightweight cashmere sweater, 4. Lightweight fleece pullover, 5. Neoprenes, 6. Rainsuit windstopper or a Simms windstopper, fleece, and then rainsuit if windy and rainy, 7. Leg warmers over bottom long underwear, 8. Thermal socks, 9. Fleece socks, wool hat with earflaps.

September 24

Our fishing guide today is Robert Ramsey - probably the top guide. From Georgia, U.S. Was Blaine's guide throughout Argentina last March.

Took helicopter down to Lower Tomba. We had also taken it to Upper Tomba on the 21st. Glorious sunny day, not a cloud in the sky. In the 20's when we leave at 8:45, and the helicopter has frost on the window panes and the rotors, so the pilot takes about 10 minutes to get things defrosted. We fly at 200 feet, paralleling the river, over tundra, where we saw two moose walking, then lands on the river bank on a gravel bar. The fall colors of the white birch are a golden yellow, and there is a beautiful ground cover that has rusty red leaves, and a bright red holly berry looking fruit.

The day was extremely slow. I never had a fish touch my line until

Awaiting our helicopter for the seven minute flight back to camp.

4:00 p.m. That's 7 hours of fishing, with an hour off for lunch, without even a nibble, and casting almost once every minute. The nicest part of the day was stopping for a picnic lunch next to a cascading waterfall. We sat on some nice smooth rocks and had soup, ham, and cheese, carrot salad, apples, and cookies. The sun was radiating heat off the rocks, and it was just delightful. In the afternoon, Blaine went through a nice beat of water, catching a grayling, native brown trout, sea trout, and hooking a salmon, but it got off. Meanwhile, I am still without a sign of salar, or any other pesca. At 4:00 - 4:30, Robert Ramsey, our guide, finally feels sorry for me. He puts on a skate fly, a bomber, and I catch a ton of sizeable sea trout. Exciting way to fish!

SEPTEMBER 25

Sergei - another Russian guide. Woke up to rainy drizzle, but a little warmer, about 35 degrees. Fishing Golden Beach, which is the closest beat to the camp, down river. The Pornache is the closest beat, upriver, and the home pool is in between these two. I have a #2 shrimp on, catch lots of nice grayling, probably 1-2 pounds. Even though it is rainy most of the day, it is not as cold as you would think, and our windstopper jackets are life savers.

Blaine catches a very old salmon after lunch. He caught it on a Rusty Rat, which Sergei had said, "Nyet," shaking his head. Lunch is in a tent by the river. Sergei, from Murmansk, is the fish biologist, kills the grayling and sea trout we catch, we assume to check for disease. But he speaks no English, so we can't be sure. He puts the old, skinny salmon back in the river, the very fish that looks like it is extremely sick. Sauna in the afternoon when we return, feels great. I wish I had a back brace, because I am getting a stitch just under my right shoulder blade.

Blaine and I have been on no beats that are very productive. It is a very slow week, (turned out to be the slowest of the year), but there are a few 7 and 10 fresh fish beats a day. Some beats, fished by very

1997

Soggy and cold after nine hours of fishing

experienced anglers, are getting skunked completely as we are. I am definitely casting better every day. The 13', two handed rod has simplified casts. Jorge Trucco, acclaimed as one of the finest anglers in the world, has been about even with us. I think it would help if I had a sinking tip, or even a sinking line, but we don't - so too bad.

September 26

Max - another Russian guide, but very enthusiastic. This morning we take the helicopter up to Kolmac, the furthest upriver beat. It borders the public fishing of the Ponoi. It is rainy, foggy, and cold!!

The helicopter takes about 8 minutes, flying at 200 feet above the ground. Our first run takes us almost to the border, about a 10-15 minute trip. I sit on a cushion on the bottom of the boat, facing backward to lessen the cold air. This is our last day, and I'm crossing my fingers for a salmon.

Max is from St. Petersburg, but speaks very good English, and is about 20 years old. He ties flies for the Ponoi camp, and when he returns to St. Petersburg, he ties flies for a fish store. So he knows what's up. He gives me his sinking line, and we go to some deep water. The

1997

After many casts, finally a very fresh salmon.

Taking a short fishing break to enjoy the colorful fall foliage

first cast, the line falls off the rod, Uh! Oh! The second cast, I have a nice salmon hen, about 10 pounds. Hallelujah! Blaine has a sink tip, so isn't as lucky. We are using the Gary Dog fly, about #2. I have two more salmon before lunch, and Blaine also has two. What a hot day!

The fish are so fresh they still have sea lice on them, which fall off usually within 24 hours. They have come from the Barrents Sea, to Kolmac, which is 70 miles, so they have been really steaming up the river!

After lunch, Blaine hooks into a couple more salmon, and then about 5:00, I land two more very nice 10 pounders, and lose one more. My last cast, at 6:00, was a 10 pound salmon that took about 15 minutes to land. I caught all the afternoon salmon on a long tail shrimp #2. At the end of the drift I play the strip about 5" at a time, tempting the fish with some movement - it works! Ten salmon in one day. This is more like it. Dinner of smoked salmon. Some vodkas add a perfect ending to a great day.

Hooray!
Bringing back dinner for some delicious sushi salmon!

Ponoi River Camp

Beats starting up river: Kolmac, Alexevski, Pornache, Home Pool, Golden Beach, Falls Creek, Clough Creek, Upper Tomba, Lower Tomba. There can be six climate changes within the 8 beats. The Ponoi has about 45 miles of river. We had a warm afternoon on the Kolmac, it was cold and rainy on Falls Creek. We had a warm day with some sun on the Pornache, Upper Tomba saw heavy rain from after lunch all afternoon. The bugs don't get bothersome until the last week in June

1997

Sixteen tents nestled into the fall leaf colors on the Ponoi River

- first week in July, and bugs leave by September 1st. Of course all of this is subject to change with the weather.

This year the leaves were just turning golden yellow and orange. Last year, at this time, we were told there were barely any leaves left on the trees. This year was extremely hot, but not many bugs, therefore the prolonged summer and leaf colors. There are 16 tents, but can take 20 guests.

We are beginning to see a real change in temperature now that it is the end of September. This week on the Ponoi is the last one for guests until June of 1998. The guides will now close down the Ryabaga Camp, and a nice couple will move into the sauna, keep the fire going all winter, and live here for 6 months. The man will hunt all winter for rabbits, wolves, reindeer, bear, or any other four legged creature that would make a good meal. His wife will cook up all the vegetables they have kept fresh over the summer. It will be dark for the next 6 months.

The helicopter trip back to Murmansk was 2 hours and 15 minutes, non-stop. Transporting 24 of us, sitting on boards in single rows along each side, with duffels and rods and gear stacked so high in the center, one row of passengers could not see across the aisle. We delayed leaving Ponoi until 9:30, due to fog in Murmansk. As it turned out, it was foggy for the whole trip.

I should have gone to the bathroom before we left!! After 1 hour and 45 minutes I was desperate. There were 24 of us sardined into the helicopter, with duffles piled in the center about four feet higher than we were. We sit on hard benches on either side of the helicopter. There are porthole windows to look out, but we fly in fog the whole time, so not much of a view. We finally land, and there is a bus to take us to the terminal. I tell BTP I can't make it, throw my pocket book and brown bag on the bus, and go behind an old wrecked helicopter to take a pee. The last words I say to BTP is, "don't let the bus leave without me!" As I emerge from behind the chopper, I see the bus making its way down the tarmac towards the terminal. We are in a God forsaken area of the terminal. Deserted, I have no identification. We're in Russia for God's sake, and I'm left to find my way to the terminal. A hippy in a beat up truck comes by and offers me a ride. He speaks no English, and puts his radio on full blast. We go through a guard, who lowers a rope to let us through. This may be the end of me, and I'll live in Murmansk forever! Sasha, the driver (and my new friend), takes me right to the terminal, and I arrive shortly after the bus. Apparently Blaine, when asked by John Evans, "Aren't you missing your wife?" Says, "Oh, she'll find her way here, no problem." As it turns out, he was right.

September 28
St. Petersburg, Russia

We leave Helsinki, 6:30, via Finnish train, "Sebelius," to St. Petersburg, arriving five hours later. Natasha, our guide, picks us up for a tour of the Russian Museum. Chronologically we start at 11th Century icons (painted in egg tempera) and go through each century until Kandinsky and abstract experimentation. There is so much to see and learn I wish we had an extra day here. St. Michael's Palace is incorporated into the museum, and two rooms are left as in his day in the 1800's. The ceilings of this museum are 20 feet high, with beautiful Parque floors and birch wood doors.

Petersberg - The Baroque Palace of Peter the Great

After the Russian Museum, we go to Spilt Blood of Our Saviour Church. It just opened in August after many years of renovation, within walking distance of our hotel, Grand Europe. Spilt Blood got its name from Alex the First, who was assassinated at the spot where the church is. It is #1 unbelievably beautiful Russian Orthodox Cathedral. There are icons on every pillar. The iconastasis, or alter, is gold and very ornate.

Hotel - our room, #135, is called a Belle Chambre, 15 foot high ceilings, enormous oil paintings, oriental rugs, French rococo furniture, huge bathroom.

Jorge Trucco (our friend from Argentina) came also to St. Pete from our fishing trip, and joins us for dinner at the Charter House Restaurant. It is across the river from the Winter Palace, in a very old section of St. Pete. It is a very Russian restaurant with international cuisine, not many tourists, and the waitresses don't speak English.

SEPTEMBER 29

Natasha picked us up at 9:30 to go to a Russian Orthodox day service, one of the few churches that were left open during the communist regime. Everyone goes and kisses his (her) favorite icon, gives the sign of the cross, lights a candle, says a prayer, choir singing chants, priests saying sermons, other priests chanting, another priest going around icons waving incense. Smells wonderful. The Russian Orthodox Church has an altar, only priests are allowed at the altar, this area is called the iconastasis.

We went to St. Isaacs next. This is now a museum. St. Isaacs was the patron saint of Peter the Great and family. It is the third largest church after St. Peter's in Rome and St. Paul's in England. It took 40 years to complete. The architect was Montferand from France. There are 122 granite columns on the outside. It took 10 years just to lay the foundation on marshy soil, so the builders put wood pilings down first, and then laid the foundation over that. The church was finished in 1858, and the four gold domes, and the big center gold dome, have never needed renovating because they mixed mercury and gold and melted it on brass to create this gold look which remains in mint condition, even today.

Building Peter's fountains was a monumental undertaking.

Next we went to Peter and Paul Fortress - prison - church where Peter the Great is buried. This fortress is built on the island that Peter the Great built to defend Russia from the Swedes in 1700. The war lasted for 21 years, and Russia was then declared independent from Swedish rule. The fortress is fairly dilapidated, but two interesting points. First, Peter and Paul Church, where Peter the Great is buried, is also the burial site for Catherine the Great and Catherine II, Elizabeth, Paul, and Peter III. The church is very small, relatively speaking, and has all the tombs of the nobility placed around the room. The second point of interest is the prison, where they put the political prisoners until the 1930's. These were solitary cells, and had only a high window, and a hole for the latrine. The bed is cast iron, and the table as well, and they are nailed to the wall. Before electricity, they had one candle behind heavy glass, so the prisoners couldn't take the oil and burn themselves.

We can't believe our luck!! Swan Lake is the ballet that we see this evening. One of the private classical ballet schools is performing. The ballet is within walking distance of the hotel at one of the oldest theatres, Alexandrinsky Palace. We sit in the tzar's box. Jorge Trucco, our Argentine friend from Patagonia, joins us for dinner after the theatre in the caviar room at the hotel.

September 30

Natasha and Sergei, our driver in stretch Mercedes limo, pick us up for an early admission to the Hermitage Museum. It officially opens at 10:30, but Dr. Malanina (the curator) meets us at 10:00 at a private entrance, and takes us on a private tour (thanks to Blaine's longtime association with Winterthur, whose director was a school friend of Dr. Malanina). We see the highlights from the the Jordan Staircase, the Malachite Room, many of the private chambers of Peter the Great, Leonardo da Vinci (2 paintings, the only 2). Fralippo Lip-

1997

Sergei obeyed his own rules of the road.

pi (2 paintings, the only 2) Rembrandt - The Genre Flemish School, the classic Greek statues. The most amazing thing is the opulence of the rooms. The floors are sometimes 14 different woods, starburst designs, or herringbone design. All different. The walls have tapestries, chandeliers made of amethyst or sapphire and crystal. Some chandeliers hold over 400 candles. Some were made of paper maché, and weighed a mere 150 pounds. Most chandeliers were lowered by pulleys in order to put in the candles.

From the Hermitage we go to the Yusopov's Mansion, very elegant, with a beautiful staircase. The problem with the palaces and mansions is that they aren't heated, so you're freezing when you go through the rooms. A lot of the places aren't completely refurbished, so you go through some rooms with bare walls, no furnishings, and in need of lights and paint. The highlights of the Yusopov's mansion is the basement, where Paul Yusopov asked Rasputin for dinner, and then poisoned him. He put arsenic in his wine and cakes, but Rasputin lived. Then Paul shot him, and left him for dead. The arsenic hadn't worked, nor had the shot. He crawled out of the basement, and then was shot again by one of the plotters. Rasputin was thrown in the Neva River, where his body was found two days later. He was cremated, and his ashes thrown in the wind over St. Petersburg.

We grab a quick lunch at a place close by, and also just down the street from the Grand Hotel Europe, called Fast Food Cafeteria. Sub sandwiches, very quick and good.

Go to the Ethnology Museum for a quick tour of the different groups in Russia. There are over 130 languages and cultures. Siberia takes over 70% of the land, and is still part of the country of Russia.

We drive about 1 hour outside of the city to go to the circus. It is a very amateur performance and encircles the audience. We are sitting on either side of old babushkas who are clapping and laughing. About 70% of the audience is adult. Mostly old women. You have to wear your hat, gloves, and overcoat during the performances. It is so cold that you can see your breath. They have family acts, the horse acrobatics are 15 year old girls, boys, men. There is one act with 4 or 5 year old girls, 12 or 13 year old girls, young boys all doing somersaults, etc. tumbling. We grab a taxi to Adamant Restaurant after the circus and meet Jorge Trucco. Not a great restaurant, average, and the cigarette smell is pervasive.

OCTOBER 1

Today we find ourselves at Petershof - Peter's very Baroque Palace. Peter I installed 144 fountains, all created by natural springs above, that flows water down to the fountains, then takes the water through trenches down to the Gulf of Finland, which flows into the Baltic Sea. There are holding ponds up by the natural springs to regulate the water. This was all invented and installed between 1716 and 1723, when Peter lived in his summer palace. He had about 265 acres, which have wonderful views of the Gulf. There is a small hermitage right on the water, where he stayed when he wanted to get away from the crowds of the summer palace. Peter had to take all the clay soil away from Petershof, and import potting soil for his trees and gardens. A monumental undertaking, because St. Petersburg is so marshy, it is hard to build without shoring up the land first. Each tree and plant was brought in to Petershof. We were delighted to be given a few acorns which had fallen from an oak tree onto the ground which we will take home, plant, and hope for some Russian oak trees.

There are 5 million people in St. Petersburg. Most people, probably 85% of the people, live in apartments. The highest apartment building in the city is five stories, and in the outlying areas, ten stories. Usually a young couple will live with a grandmother (who babysits) or parents. Men and women both work (women can take a leave for 1 ½ years after childbirth). Retirement for women is 55 and for men, 60. There are kinderkare places to take children starting at 3 years, but sometimes there is only 1 supervisor for 16 young children.

The lines for buses, streetcars, and metros are long, and the buses etc. packed. I took the metro, and there must have been 100,000 people in the station with me. The traffic in the city is choked on every corner. There are one way streets, and streets that are blocked off due to reconstruction. At one point, Sergei (our driver) drove down a one way street, the wrong way, and then went up the sidewalk with our stretch mercedes, and narrowly missed a crew where they were digging. There are no left hand turns on many streets, so Sergei just makes U-turns in the middle of the block.

It is late fall here, and very cold. People are wearing boots, heavy coats and scarves. It gets dark starting in November at about 4:00 p.m. and doesn't get light (totally) until noon, so there are about four hours of light.

We tried to send flowers to Dr. Melanani at the Hermitage, to thank her for being so nice to us. The people of St. Petersburg do not have any delivery service for anything. You must pay with rubles at all state stores, a few will take some credit cards. No one speaks English, all the signs everywhere, including the museum, are only in Russian. Contrast this with St. Petersburg's greatest asset, its museums and churches; which are opulent, gold, marble, semi-precious stones, grand. Even the theatres are old palaces. The layout of the city, along the Neva, is spectacular. Rows of five story houses or palaces, all attached, some green some yellow, red pink, blue. The architects were known for certain color schemes. Rossi's was yellow and white, so most buildings with columns, and yellow and white, were designed by Rossi. Restrelli and Cameron also had their styles: Restrelli - Baroque; Cameron - Rococo with English dominance. The architects would not only design the outside, but would design the interiors down to the parquet floors and crystal chandeliers.

OCTOBER 2

Valentina Bykanova is our guide this morning. We leave at 9:00, to another cold, about 40 degrees, and overcast day. We work our way out of the city, which is always an ordeal. We are driving to Pavlovsk, the summer palace of Paul, Catherine the Great's son. She had the palace built on about 600 acres close to Pushkin, the town of her summer palace. She didn't like her son at all, so didn't want him underfoot, but worried about a conspiracy if he was too far away. His palace is very modest, as palaces go, only 55 rooms, and is the first and only one completely refurbished. There are pictures of the demolition of the palace by the Germans during WWII. It is amazing that they were able to put back together such a ruination. Our guide, Valentina, is a fountain of knowledge.

Paul was not very popular, and as it turns out, only reigned for about five years. He was autocratic, and very bright, but he didn't handle the people very well. He married Maria, from Germany, and had eight children. She was a very intelligent woman, who read extensively, was interested in botany, and was a superlative wood carver (we saw samples of bowls she had made).

We went from Pavlosk to Pushkin, where we saw Catherine's summer palace and gardens. This place is vast. It is blue and white, and Baroque and opulent. It was built by Peter the Great for his wife's summer estate, but was used more by Elizabeth, Peter's daughter, and Catherine the Great, her daughter-in-law.

Only a small portion of these rooms are refurbished. There is one long corridor that is the length of the palace, and has Baroque gilded doors, which are over 25' high, and very impressive looking, where you are able to view the entire length of the corridor. The parquet floors, again, are uniquely designed. The rooms were designed by Restrelli and Cameron, giving the Baroque feeling as well as the English and French. The throne room is the most impressive, with a painted ceiling and gold sconces lining the mirrors around the room. The room is about the size of a football field, and the views overlooking the ponds and woods are magnificent.

We are so lucky, as there are very few tourists. We have had Pavlovsk's Palace totally to ourselves, as well as the summer palace, because school groups, and other tourists who are here, seem to be in other rooms from the ones we are viewing. We had the entire gold throne room to ourselves. From the palace, we retrace our steps and go to a quaint restaurant on the way back to Pavlovsk, called Povorye. It is an authentic Russian traditional cuisine, and we are entertained at lunch with Russian folk music.

We will soon be on our way back to Helsinki. The contrast between Helsinki and St. Petersburg is vast. Bureaucracy takes forever in Russia, they look at every single paper 100 times. In Finland, you are rushed through customs, you get your bags through in five minutes. The cabs are dirty and old in Russia. In Helsinki, they are Mercedes and Volvos, and cleaned and vacuumed every day. Not a gum wrapper on one floor. The pollution in the streets of St. Petersburg, with fumes of cigarette smoke, is overwhelming. Pot holes in the street are everywhere. Sergei showed us one that had an entire Volkswagon Beetle sunk in it (Sergei just grinned).

October 3

Awaken to a beautiful, crisp fall day. I have my Russian mink hat, so I'm nice and toasty as I walk down to do some last minute shopping. I'm trying to find some cute souvenirs for the grand children, but slim pickings as summer is over. I did find two darling dolls dressed in local Roviemi reindeer outfits for Katherine and Annabelle..

Our plane leaves this afternoon from Helsinki, so we leave the hotel at 2:00 p.m. for a 4:50 flight. The flight home is delightful. Eight hours later we arrive in New York City at 3:50, one hour before we left!

Blaine and I have been talking all the way home about when we will return to Russia. This was all a new part of the world for us, and one which we are going to know very well, as we will be returning for many years to come.

– 1998 –

Russia, Ponoi River, Moscow

June 10

Helsinki Flight #4 left at 6:00 p.m. Arrive 9:00 a.m. in Helsinki. It is warm. Sun and rain, 65°. On June 12th it is Helsinki's 448th birthday. The city is full of magicians, singers, open air markets selling everything from fresh flowers to Lapland reindeer skins, wooden baskets to knitted socks and sweaters, fur hats, fresh fish, and beautiful fresh vegetables.

Dinner at Havis Amanda both June 11th and 12th. We are staying at the Strand Hotel, in the Panorama Suite. Boats are constantly going up and down the canal, we walk everywhere from the Grand Strand into town. The World Dog Show is in Helsinki. There are 17,000 dogs. We went and it was an absolute bedlam of dogs. Huge convention hall, hotel, and streets full of dogs, dogs everywhere.

June 13
Ryabaga Camp, Ponoi River

Left Grand Intercontinental Hotel at the crack of dawn. Of course, it's light all night, so there is no crack of dawn. We are back this summer to fish the Ponoi River again, hoping for better conditions than last September when we were here. The fishing group looks and seems most interesting. 10 out of 20 guests are repeats from the same week last year. Helicopter ride a bit unnerving, as it was very rainy and foggy in Murmansk, so they hustled us out in a hurry. The non-stop, 1 hour and 35 minute trip took 2 hours and 10 minutes because it was so foggy, the pilot had to follow the river the last 45 minutes, and when the fog bank was too thick, had to clmb 400 feet and then come down to 250 feet when he thought he could follow the river again. Camp is just the same. We have cabin 11. The temperature is really warm, and I take a long walk after we arrive. Had to go to the bathroom at midnight, it was ...

Summer solstice allows for daylight for 24-hours

June 14

... just as light as at noon, without the sun. The sun actually sets at 11:30 p.m. and rises again at 2:00 a.m. At about 5:30 a.m. I got up, because the sun was so bright in the tent, and it was so warm I couldn't sleep. Took a long walk up the hill before breakfast, which was at 8:00 a.m. - pancakes, bacon, scrambled eggs, lots of cereal, fruit, juice, and coffee.

Fished the Alexevski beat with Dema. Have a long tailed shrimp (invented by Alistair MacClean and called an Alise shrimp) about #2, and catch a 2 pound brown trout. Blaine catches a very large salmon on a tube (Mickey Finn) - so after another few casts I switched to a tube that looks close to a Mickey Finn, but didn't have the eyes, and started catching lots of salmon. I had 7 salmon - one 11 or 12 pounds - all on one same tube with a double #2 hook. Blaine had 3 salmon - 2 on the Mickey Finn - one 12 pounds, and lots of strikes that got away. It is 80° and sunny, but very windy, with huge gusts every few minutes that almost knock you down. There is no helicopter riding because the river is so high that here is no beach on which to land, so we took the boat. Alex beat is one down from Kolmac, which is the top beat on the river.

June 15

Steve is our guide who is from Tierra del Fuego, Argentina. We fish only the lower half of Hallway. It's Steve's first time at the Ryabaga Camp, his wife Patricia (Pata) is the woman manager. Steve knows little about Salmon fishing, he knows nothing of this beat, but we manage to catch 10 salmon. It is very hot, almost 90°, which is hard to fathom as we are about forty kilometers north of the Arctic Circle. Hallway has a few good fishing pools, we seem to repeat going up and down the same stretch all day.

Fishing a Mickey Finn, Willie Gunn tube. The water is very high in the river, with few places to wade. My Thomas and Thomas 14', 9 weight rod is a dream. The Loomis reel is working very well, but the drag keeps slipping.

June 16

Tom, our guide for today, is from British Columbia. We fish Golden Beach, beautiful beat, many stretches of great pools. Tom has been here for 5 years, so knows which flies to use on which flats. There is terrific wind, making fishing really difficult. Blaine is fishing out of his mind! Has some fish as large as 28-30" in the morning, and in the afternoon has a really big monster.

He is fishing Willie Gunn, dark tube Thunder and Lightning. The water temperature is about 50°, lots of wind. We catch 15 fish, amazing in the wind, and no wading, just boat fishing. I catch the last fish at 6:00 p.m. Quitting time, and we bring it in for the dinner table. There is a nesting pair of gyre falcons, with a nest in the cliffs, and three fuzzy babies.

Fog and bleak .. dampen our spirits

June 17

Misha is our Russian guide. Helicopter down to Tomba on a bleak, fog ridden day. Follow the river all the way, as fog covers the ground, and we can barely see the river. We are wearing: 1. Long underwear, 2. Cashmere sweater, 3. Lightweight fleece pullover, 4. Gray capeline windbreaker, 5. Green Patagonia rain coat. It spatters mist all day. We catch 9 fish, which is good, as Tomba has fished pretty slowly. Fish with a shrimp, Willie Gunn tube and Thunder and Lightning tube.

At night we have been eating with the other fishermen. Tables of 6, and changing tables every night. The most affable, gregarious person is Peter Kaine, from Toronto. Also interesting, Grant Parr, heart surgeon. Paul Dresher from England and Charles ?? English. Most everyone fishes the home pool, both before breakfast and after dinner. Most everyone here can spey cast, and all but a few of us wade the river everyday.

I have to walk to the loo every night at 3 or 4 in the morning, because it is dead light out, and I fear going behind our tent, which most of the men do. There is one other woman, JoAnn Clough, her husband, Robert, is a heart surgeon from Bangor, Maine; and was here in 1991 when there were only 4 guests. He said they thought nothing of catching over 100 fish a day, and they were here in June, same week as we are here.

June 18

Fish Hourglass. Ian Nealle is our guide. From Scotland. He is desperate to teach us spey casting, so we try, but have been fishing with sinking tips, and that is really difficult spey casting. The weather is fairly nice, about 60°. We sit out at lunch on the rocks, and have a lovely picnic. The fishing is very slow, as the water is very fast. It has risen one foot since yesterday. We had enormous rain last night. The fish are facing out at the river, so the only way they can see the fly is if we wade.

We have seen a lot of wildlife - unlike when we were here in September. European terns (which should be Arctic terns, as our camp is north of the Arctic Circle), bald eagles, mergansers, herds of reindeer, the cuckoo bird, and wading birds.

Blaine and I have a really hard time casting. We catch 8 fish, but with enormous difficulty. This has been our toughest day of fishing, all my bones are sore, and I can't wait to hop in the sauna. I have been going to the sauna every night after fishing, and it has saved my back. My rhomboid and upper trapezoids are really sore, and I warm the muscles in the sauna so they feel great! Then I can enjoy the fishing in the morning!

The weather changes so fast, today we started out with long underwear and a turtleneck shirt, by 3:30 it was so cold, I was wearing my capeline gray windbreaker and rain jacket. We finished Hourglass with tubes, Wooly Gun, they are the easiest to spey cast on a sinking tip.

Dinner is four courses: 1.. soup, 2. Salad, 3. Main course, 4. Dessert. On three nights we had salmon as a first course. The kitchen is great, but the food is excessive. Dinners: 1. Reindeer, 2. Lamb curry, 3. Cornish hens, 4. Baked salmon, 5. Strip steaks.

June 19

Marius is our guide and also the manager of Ponoi River Camp. We fish the second half of Hallway, which is called Kolamai Creek. I am really surprised, Marius is a wonderful guide. He knows the river, and the flies, and where the fish are. He takes Blaine to the shore to wade, and lets me fish from the boat. He takes the sinking tips off our lines, and we fish floating lines. He teaches me how to spey cast, where I can really get some line out. He says the more line out, the easier it will be, and he is right.I am fishing with an Alise shrimp, a #2. Blaine started with a Willie Gunn, lost it, and broke his sink tip, and switched to a special shrimp tied by Max. Blaine and I are having a great day fishing. I hooked a 15 pound cock salmon, that gave me a huge tug for about 10 minutes. I landed him after a tremendous fight. Another large salmon jumped 3 or 4 times before I landed him. We had about 6 fish over 12 pounds, 3 over 9 or 10, and 7 about 5 or 6 pounds. Landed 16 fish all on floating line with Alise shrimp #2. After oohing and aahing at our fish for a minute - they are tagged or looked at by our guide for any off signs of disease and then released.

The weather is really cold, it was 29° when we got up, and hasn't warmed up much. The day begins by lighting our wood stove to warm up the tent. It has sleeted for about 4 hours, and is misty most of the day. We join Jack and Peter (from Sweden) for lunch in the tent out on

1998

the river. The wood burning stove feels great, we are really wet. I am even fishing in neoprene gloves. My Nova Scotia red fishing hat keeps my ears warm and dry.

Dinner is a festive celebration. We sit with Charles, Paul, Peter Kaine, and Hadley Ford; all great fun. Lots of vodka before dinner, the red (wente) cabernet and cancannon (white) Chardonnay with dinner. Speeches and farewells said by all.

Lunch in the tent helps warm up our cold bones

June 20
Moscow

Arise at 6:30 a.m., 7:00 breakfast. Helicopter at 8:00, but Marius tells us at breakfast the helicopter is delayed. I take a 2 mile walk up to the foothills. Take a nap. Take a shower, watch a video. Lunch at 12:15. Marius tells us the helicopter is just leaving Murmansk at 12:36.

We have missed all connections. Arrive Murmansk, helicopter flight very easy, and it only takes 1 hour and 40 minutes. They put all of us on an Aeroflot plane to Moscow (which the Russians have re-

Our delayed helicopter allowed for a spontaneous trip for Moscow.

quired to sit on the ground for hours waiting for us) . No other plane will leave Murmansk til Monday (2 days from now).

Well this is an interesting way to get to Moscow! The Aeroflot plane is full of locals. The plane is old and dilapidated (and smells!!). There is a big schnauzer dog in the seat in front of me, sitting on the seat, no cage. Many more dogs from the World Dog Show in Helsinki are on our flight, and sitting in seats. When we land, the seats all collapse forward, and the dogs and their owners walk on top of the line of collapsed seats to disembark the plane. We are led to the Novatel Hotel near the airport. All 20 of us!

June 21

Sunday, today is the longest day of the year. We've decided to stay in Moscow for 24 hours, so we take a taxi in the morning(cost $50!) to the Olympic Penta Hotel Metropol (only room left was $1500). The Kampeski and Aerostar were all full.

As we drive in to town, we observe a horrible catastrophe. As we slept soundly at the hotel, a hurricane or tornado demolished all of Moscow. We apparently were the last plane to land before the storm hit. The ride from the Novetal into town is about 40 minutes, billboards were blown down, trees cracked in two and uprooted, roofs were damaged. There are many parks, Gorky Park being one in between the Avenues. All the trees in these parks are cracked and down. Every tree along the street of the Kremlin, by the Moskva River, are completely uprooted, and have fallen like dominoes. The devastation is more amazing every street, every corner, every alley we see. We get a tourist bus to take us on an English speaking guided tour, but they have closed Red Square because of all the damage. There is no place for the bus to take us, most places have suffered so badly it will be weeks before they open again. Even GUMS is closed.

We return to the hotel a little disappointed that our only day in Moscow is a failure. The hotel has supplied us with caviar and a bottle of Stoly, lots of fruit and breads, so we have a very pleasant cocktail hour. We have three rooms (rooms 1045, 1046, and 1047). Dining area, sitting area, and bedroom, and three bathrooms.

We're off for the Moscow circus at 7:00 p.m. 4th row seats. It is spectacular!! Highwire acts, chimps, clowns, and the highlight; 2 elephants and 5 tigers that put on an act together. The tigers get on the elephant's backs. The elephant crawls underneath the tiger, whose front and back legs are separated by 2 stools placed about 8 feet apart. Presently, a man in uniform comes up to me and says no photos allowed, which is what was being announced in Russian over the loud speaker! Oh my! What a faux pas.

Dinner at Sirena. We are the only Americans. Aquariums are on the walls with exotic fish, very darkly lit restaurant, with lighting from the aquariums. Marvelous fish menu. Very expensive, but excellent. None of the waiters spoke any English, I wanted a glass of ice to add to my vodka on the rocks, and they never did understand me. It looks like most everyone here is Russian mafia, with young tarts dressed to the nines.

Departing was highly frightening! There was no phone to call a taxi. We left, entering total darkness, no streetlights. The few houses had full blinds over the windows. There were no cars, dogs were barking. We walked a considerable distance before finding a street with some lights. We had no idea where we were. We just stood on the street curb until a car finally came by. We wave madly, it stopped, and the man driving it took us back to the city area. He even smiled at the fat, fat tip we gave him. It was a really scary experience.

June 22

Julie, who is arranging our tickets, has us on a 4:25 flight to Helsinki, with a connecting flight to NYC at 5:50. She informs us that the Moscow airport was closed yesterday from 11:00 tp 3:00 p.m. as there was no electricity at the airport. She had to get out 18 different people on 8 different flights, and many of the booked flights were cancelled. Peter Kaine has a two year old horse running in the Queen's Plate in Toronto, he missed that. Grant Parr is meeting his wife on a ship in Budapest, he missed that, etc. Meanwhile, we have the concierge call GUM's and find out if it has opened, and go over at 9:30 (It is open 8:30 a.m. - 8:30 p.m.).

Red Square opens at 10:00, and we pretty much have the place to ourselves. St. Basil's Cathedral opens at 10:15, and for 26 rubles we can go inside. There are some icons and oil painted walls, but not many rooms. There are about 4 rooms, totally open. We are the *only* people in the cathedral. I wander into a Russian Orthodox Church, a choir is chanting, and a priest is chanting, many babushkas are lighting candles and crossing themselves. There are beautiful icons on the iconastasis. Blaine needs to go to the john, so we try to get to the port-o-potties we see on Red Square, but there are police everywhere,and we cannot get to them. We hear a marching band, and with my binoculars I see that it is the army band. A Zil goes right by us (10 feet away), followed by a police car. We ask a policeman if it is Yeltzin, and he nods, yes. Lots of excitement going on, which is in celebration of Hitler starting war with USSR in WWII. Soldiers are marching, all

1998

the armed services are represented, the band is playing, a wreath is presented, and here we are looking at the whole thing. We are the only non-soldiers. How exciting.

As we wander around, we are the only two persons in Red Square. A woman comes up to us and asks if we speak English, and would we like a private guide. She is wonderful, and for $50 takes us on the metro (which is much cleaner and nicer than the NY subways) and to the Kremlin. We are in the Kremlin before any big tour groups arrive. Because it is June 22, and a holiday of sorts (and also because of the awful storm), none of the nationals are allowed in the Kremlin today for fear of mass demonstrations against the government. The miners haven't been paid in months. They are just one of the groups the government wants to keep out. So here we are with a private guide, and the Kremlin (which means fortress and red) to ourselves. It was built to protect the dynasties in the 16th Century. It is surrounded by water, but now the river flows through a tube, and there are trees and grass under the bridge. The Church of the Ascension is where all the monarchs are crowned. The largest bell in the world is in the Kremlin, and the private chapel of the tzars is here. The entire square has 4 churches with gold domes, another square has the yellow building of the duma. Yeltzin's working rooms are here, but our guide told us the roof was torn off during last night's hurricane. There are beautiful trees inside the Kremlin walls. Chestnuts, oaks, birch, apples, and many more. They have already cleared debris from those trees, but none seemed to have sustained the damage as those outside the Kremlin.

All of Russia is measured from a brass medallion in a circle at the Kremlin entrance. This is the center of the country. Kruschev built a huge modern building in the 50's, which today is used for concerts and the the better performances of the Bolshoi. It seats 6,000 people. It is the first building to the right as you enter the Kremlin gates.

During Lenin's time the government people lived inside the walls of the Kremlin, but that was the last time the buildings were used as sleeping quarters. In Red Square we saw Lenin's tomb. Only on Mondays you aren't allowed to go up and look at him, just a minor disappointment after an extraordinary day.

After spending two glorious days in Moscow it is now time to check out of Olympic Penta Hotel Metropol and head back to what we assume will be a functioning airport.

As with so many of our adventure trips, this one did not end as we had planned. A trip to Moscow with no visa, no hotel, and no return flight.It just doesn't get any more exciting than this!!

Sometimes I think we must have a guardian angel on our shoulders, saving us from more than one disaster. But now it is time to return to reality, and to the United States, where being exposed to many 3rd world countries - and Russia counts as one of those - we have to thank our lucky stars that we have such a free and loving country to return to.

When we arrive back at the Moscow airport, two days later, our friends were still there. Some flights had left, but not one of our group had gone into the city of Moscow. The airport was still in the dark, cold, dreary, and crowded with unhappy people. We were a little timid about boasting about our exploits as it would be a little like rubbing salt in the wound, but all the way back to New York City we had time to reflect on our very spontaneous, adventurous trip, and a very perfect ending to Volume One of Nomadic Dreams.

Remember: Let your dreams run wild and be brave enough to follow.

APPENDIX

You may have wondered, as I did, why have 2 volumes of journals that span 30 years? I had no intention of doing this until I finished the first volume and realized if I only had made one book it would be close to 600 pages. There was no way I could lie in bed at night with a whale of a book on my lap, nor could I slip it into a pocketbook for those long waits at the doctor's office, so Nomadic Dreams became Volume One and Volume Two.

As I'm sure you can imagine, re-reading my journals from 1987-2015 gave me great joy, laughter, and amazement. When I timidly walked into Salt Water Media in Berlin, Maryland, to ask if they would undertake this plan of mine, to make the journals into a book, I would not have been surprised if they had shooed me out of the door with a "come back when you have your journals typed and on a computer." I could not have been more shocked when they offered me a seat in the room of their publishing house, and with a smile said they would be happy to put the book together for me!!

There are only four people in the wonderfully friendly Salt Water Media office: Patty, Jeff, Stephanie, and Andrew. They all played important parts in assembling this very complicated assignment of putting together a book of 30 years of memories. Each had a specific job, but they all worked together like a well-oiled machine to render the final product.

Lastly, and with all my heart, I want to thank Blaine for reading through the text with a keen eye. He is an extraordinary writer and kindly did not try to challenge my journalistic style of writing, but he did help enormously in editing and spelling.

I was also reminded in reading over Nomadic Dreams what fun Blaine and I have had traveling together the last 30 plus years. We never wasted a minute, and when we had different interests on our trips we did "our own thing", and then looked forward to the cocktail hour when we could share what we had done. How lucky for me, who has such a wanderlust, to have found a soulmate ready to pack a bag and be gone.

If you liked the first volume of our "treasured moments", you will be excited to now read volume two. It will take you to Timbuktu in Mali, Niassa Reserve in Mozambique, the wild and uninhabited Aleutian Islands in Alaska, and twice more to the calming Galapagos Islands in Ecuador.

www.ingramcontent.com/pod-product-compliance
Lightning Source LLC
Chambersburg PA
CBHW061247230426
43663CB00021B/2935